Camus on Justice

THE BEGINNING AND THE BEYOND OF POLITICS

Series editors: James R. Stoner and David Walsh

The series is in continuity with the grand tradition of political philosophy that was revitalized by the scholars who, after the Second World War, taught us to return to the past as a means of understanding the present. We are convinced that legal and constitutional issues cannot be addressed without acknowledging the metaphysical dimensions that underpin them. Questions of order arise within a cosmos that invites us to wonder about its beginning and its end, while drawing out the consequences for the way we order our lives together. God and man, world and society are the abiding partners within the community of being in which we find ourselves. Without limiting authors to any particular framework we welcome all who wish to investigate politics in the widest possible horizon.

CAMUS
ON JUSTICE

A Metaphysics of Revolt

CRAIG DELANCEY

University of Notre Dame Press
Notre Dame, Indiana

Copyright © 2026 by University of Notre Dame
Notre Dame, Indiana 46556
undpress.nd.edu
All Rights Reserved

Manufactured in the United States of America

Library of Congress Control Number: 2025948058

ISBN: 978-0-268-21077-9 (Hardback)
ISBN: 978-0-268-21079-3 (Paperback)
ISBN: 978-0-268-21081-6 (WebPDF)
ISBN: 978-0-268-21080-9 (Epub3)

GPSR Compliance Inquiries:
Lightning Source France, 1 Av. Johannes Gutenberg, 78310 Maurepas, France
compliance@lightningsource.fr | Phone: +33 1 30 49 23 42

For Lorena and Aletheia

CONTENTS

	Acknowledgments	ix
	Introduction	1
ONE	The Absurd	9
TWO	Suicide and Murder	48
THREE	Metaphysical Revolt	98
FOUR	Historical Revolt	121
FIVE	Just Revolt	138
SIX	*The Fall* and a New Paradox of Liberalism	174
	Notes	201
	Works Cited	215
	Index	221

ACKNOWLEDGMENTS

Thanks to Lorena DeLancey, Aletheia DeLancey, and Joseph Fornieri.

Thanks to three anonymous reviewers for the University of Notre Dame Press. I appreciate their kindness in taking time to offer their very valuable advice.

I am indebted to my students. My thanks to Renson Bruckman, Derek Bullard, Ivan Calero, Ian Campbell, Douglas Carey, Nicholas Cocks, Allison Fausner, Esther Gabriel, Christopher Haddad, Connor Landers, Camillo Licata, Gage McGill, Jack Schirtz, Wesam Shanaa, Robert Sova, Kara Stoffel, Nathaniel Swezey, Taylor Tessier, Kaela Towne, Jesse Welch, Jonah Williams, and Nicholas Williams. Special thanks to Zach Diamond and Katrina Johnson. Thanks to my colleagues for advice: Chetan Cetty, Richard Cocks, David Lambie, James Lee, Jared Peterson, and Lizzy Stewart.

I wrote some of this book while on a semester-long sabbatical from my teaching duties at SUNY Oswego. I also received some support from Oswego's Office of Research and Special Programs. I thank the university and ORSP for their support.

Earlier and substantially different versions of some parts of chapter 1 appeared in the journal *Philosophia* as "Camus's Absurd and the Argument against Suicide" (2021) and in the volume *Coming Back to the Absurd* (2022) as "Explanation and the Unreasonable Silence of the World." A substantially different version of chapter 6 appears in *The Interpretive Imagination: Literature in the Light of Philosophy* (forthcoming).

Introduction

PURPOSE AND JUSTICE

Albert Camus was a thinker obsessed with a monumental question: If the universe is absurd (that is, if it lacks any purpose), and if human history is absurd, then is there such a thing as a good human life and can we create a successful ethical theory? For many centuries, philosophers derived their ethical theories and their accounts of the good life from claims about the purpose of the universe or the purpose of history or the intent of a god. To those philosophers, it may seem that deriving an ethics from an absurd world is to derive something from nothing. And, indeed, Camus described his task in a similar way, as being to "seek out and create, on the basis of negation, the positive values which will permit reconciliation of negative thought with the possibilities of positive action" (2022 [1946], 30).[1] Or, as he describes this task in his Nobel Prize acceptance speech, "this generation, within and around itself, on the basis of its negations alone, has had to restore a little of what makes the dignity of living and dying" (2022 [1957], 228). Here "negation" means the absurd, the painful fact that history and the universe are without purpose.

Some people are rarely troubled by this question. For them, we come into life with things expected of us. Perhaps you are expected to learn, to succeed at school, to become a self-sufficient adult. Achieving those things is hard work. Why make life more difficult by doubting your goals? Why add to your troubles by questioning whether your purposes are justified? If we doubt all our purposes, our life becomes unsettled and our freedom becomes overwhelming. Is this not sufficient reason to avoid this question?

But some people instead find that such a question compels their attention and their concern. They want to know what their place is in the order of things, even if the answer will discomfort them. Albert Camus was such a person, a person troubled by this question, but who also wanted a true answer to it. Throughout his work, he tried to understand the possibilities for human purposes in a history and a universe that are absurd. Camus is a strong and empathetic guide for those who find these questions haunting.

Camus sees this question as essentially related to questions of justice. Our need to understand our purposes is in part expressed by our revolt against a purposeless universe. But our need to foster progress toward a society where human beings can better pursue and satisfy their own purposes is in part realized by our revolt against human injustice. Thus, for Camus, the question "What are our purposes?" is inseparable from the questions "When is revolt justified?" and "How can one revolt in a just way?"

Camus's theory of revolt remains a compelling and challenging way to understand ethics and our moral duties. We can learn about the possibility of moral progress from careful reflection on his theory. Also, Camus was an active and important part of the political debates of his time. His time differed from our own in many ways. But there are also some problems of his time that remain with us and that are perhaps permanent challenges to the modern condition. And (as I argue in chapter 6 of this book) Camus foresaw a problem that, though only nascent in his time, has come to fruition in our own. The interesting parallels and contrasts with his time offer us an opportunity to reflect anew on the political problems we face.

In this book, my themes are the relation between Camus's metaphysical[2] thoughts and his views on revolt and political action. For this reason, the main focus will be *The Rebel* (*L'Homme révolté*). I neglect other of his works, such as *The Stranger* (*L'Étranger*) and most of his plays. I also neglect his extensive discussions of aesthetics. *The Rebel* attempts many tasks, including a critical account of some strains of argument in philosophy over the previous two centuries and a critical evaluation of some revolutionary moments during the same period. But its primary contributions are that it seeks a way for human beings to confront the absurd while still developing and maintaining an ethics, and that it offers a theory of when revolt is justified and how revolt can be ethical.

Camus develops a unique understanding of human aspirations for justice. His view is that human beings do have justified purposes, some of which arise from their human nature, but that these purposes are often uncovered and then realized and defended through revolt. Human beings must revolt against a purposeless universe in order to assert their own purposefulness, and they must revolt against human injustice in order to discover and assert their purposes while striving to create a more just society (that is, a society where some of our purposes are better respected and are more likely to be realized).

This book aims to explore these themes in the work of Camus. This book is not a work of history—not even of the history of philosophy. It does not strive to provide context for Camus's intellectual development, nor to assess his relation to his peers, nor to assess other critical evaluations of Camus except in as much as they reflect on Camus's theories as I understand them. In this book, I treat Camus as a contemporary, with two goals in mind. First, to reconstruct some of Camus's claims and arguments in an effort to sympathetically understand and defend these. It is possible to reconstruct a coherent metaphysical theory as an interpretation of Camus's discussion of the absurd and revolt. Although there is a significant literature on Camus, almost none of it attempts to understand the metaphysical theory of purpose that he strives to develop. Indeed, many scholars would argue that there is no metaphysical theory there to be discussed. In part, this is unsurprising; Camus and the existentialist philosophers who were his contemporaries are primarily concerned with issues of teleology (the study of purpose), but strangely they never explicitly state that they are developing teleological theories. One of my own contentions is that many philosophical problems and debates are concerned with teleology, and because we have not made this explicit, and because we have left teleology largely undeveloped, these problems or debates often end up obscured. I don't defend this contention in this book, but I do apply it. The existentialists were always struggling with questions of purpose, but they always did so in a roundabout way. Drawing this to the fore is very helpful and allows us to clarify many otherwise obscure features of these theories and debates. It can be beneficial to reconstruct aspects of Camus's philosophy, and some of his debates with his contemporaries, explicitly in these terms. Thus I spend some of this book discussing views of Sartre and Beauvoir, but this is not meant to provide context so much as contrast. The three of them often indirectly influenced and responded to each other. It can be very helpful to understand Camus's theories by contrasting them with the contemporary alternatives. My second goal for this book is to show what we can learn from Camus about revolt and injustice.

This book is thus largely concerned with metaphysics. However, because the questions that Camus struggles to ask and to answer are of interest to all of us, I hope the book is accessible to anyone interested in Camus or his themes. To help in this, I tried to define technical terms in philosophy when first using them (sometimes in the text, sometimes in endnotes). It is my hope that this book will be of use not just to philosophers but also to others interested in revolt or interested in the struggle against the absurd.

PHILOSOPHER OR JOURNALIST?

Simone de Beauvoir, who came to profoundly dislike Camus, told one of her biographers, Deidre Bair, that

> Camus had a very simplistic mind, and he took extremely simplistic views in politics, ethics and philosophy. He wrote well, but he was not a profound man. The difference between him and Sartre is that Sartre was a true philosopher and Camus was a pure journalist, a journalist who was also a bit of a writer. When you put his work next to Sartre's, really, you are going to find that he didn't make any impact. Nobody in France reads anything he wrote. (Bair 1990, 290)

Some of this criticism is motivated by Beauvoir's need to assert that Jean-Paul Sartre was an unrivaled intellectual. Some is motivated by her personal dislike of Camus. The claim that Camus was "also a bit of a writer" is petty, and obviously so given how Camus's novels have endured and are enjoyed by a far larger international audience than any novel written by Beauvoir or Sartre. But Beauvoir does raise a question here with which others have struggled: Was Camus a philosopher?[3]

Probably because the measures of progress and for what counts as a method for philosophy are unclear and contentious, philosophers sometimes evaluate a philosopher by appealing both to the authority of pedigree and also to whether the individual engages in contemporary arguments using the most recent terminology. That is, one often establishes whether something is "philosophy" by whether the person doing it has the right degree from the right university, and by whether the work engages with difficult philosophy texts in ways that are approved of by the philosophers doing the evaluating. Fields with more clear measures of progress and more clear methods do not need to indulge in such policing (e.g., G. H. Hardy did not dispose of Srinivasa Ramanujan's letter of mathematical results because the latter was a clerk using unconventional presentations—the results were fruitful and some were true, and that was what mattered). So, to some degree, this policing of borders should be met with skepticism: academics police intellectual borders most aggressively when their methods and results are weak.

Nonetheless, there is some insight in Beauvoir's criticism. Camus was a journalist, a playwright, and a novelist. Camus wrote more words of journalism than philosophy, and more words of fiction and of theater than philosophy. He was educated in philosophy, and wrote a thesis on Augustine, but he lacked the pedigree that either Beauvoir or Sartre had, and he lacked the extensive training that Sartre, Beauvoir, and most academic philosophers have today. And, it must be admitted, Camus's analysis of the work of some other philosophers was sometimes inaccurate; his analysis of their role in the history of ideas sometimes serves more to squeeze them into his narrative than to illuminate their original intent. And, on the few occasions where he attempts metaphysics using the terminology of his peers, the result is (by my estimation) a muddle.[4] It is worth noting that Camus was aware that he was a writer first. In his notebooks, he wrote in

October 1945, "Why am I an artist and not a philosopher? Because I think according to words and not according to ideas" (1978, 113).

I believe it is helpful to think of Camus as an amateur philosopher. I use the word "amateur" here in the older sense, of an outsider, someone who undertakes the task seriously but not from within the usual channels, and also perhaps without respecting the expectations of the professionals.[5] Many substantial intellectual accomplishments, in many different fields, have come from amateurs. In part, the power of the amateur is to ask the questions that the professionals have obscured or neglected—sometimes because the questions are overlooked, but also sometimes because familiarity has made those questions seem blasé. Also, sometimes amateurs ask questions that are old and thought insoluble or too difficult for any direct attack. For example, Camus asks the kind of questions most professional philosophers will avoid simply because the fundamental nature of those problems makes them so difficult: What are our purposes? What should our purposes be? Can we justify our purposes in a purposeless universe? Can we form an ethical theory from very minimal starting assumptions? And so on. Camus attempts to answer such questions essentially starting from scratch. It is a naive approach, but it is the kind of approach where an amateur may contribute overlooked or new insights. Philosophy could stand to improve through more tinkering, more trial and error, and more diverse approaches. Two bicycle mechanics built the first successful airplane; perhaps a journalist might have some insight on questions about purpose and revolt. Thus, I treat Camus as a philosopher in this book, but I recognize that he is not a traditional academic philosopher—and as a result he may be more susceptible to some kinds of error.

In addition to the potential for innovation, there is another benefit of listening to the amateur philosopher. Most intellectuals are herd animals. There is potential benefit in attending to those very few intellectuals who are outsiders. All is a matter of degree here: I am not claiming Camus was not unreflectively swept up in some popular beliefs.[6] But he had an ability to resist, more than his peers, some of the social pressures that surrounded him. He also was a cautious, tentative thinker. In contrast to most other intellectuals of his time, Camus was a voice for moderation, for cautious change, for skepticism about grand political projects. Furthermore, Camus always thought of his works as attempts, as preliminary experiments open to revision; and he did revise his views openly—for example, he revised his views on capital punishment. Such sincerity is rare.

OUTLINE OF THE BOOK

Central to the entire corpus of Camus's work is the concept of the absurd—a term he later replaces with "negation." Chapter 1 directly addresses the question of what "absurd" means for Camus. It means several things, but I show that only one of these meanings is required to explain the central theme of all his work: the teleological absurd. Something is teleologically absurd if it is without a justified and sufficient purpose. This meaning also helps to explain Camus's other, secondary uses of the term.

Chapter 2 illustrates the benefit of having clarified the meaning of "absurd," first by reconstructing Camus's valid argument against suicide in *The Rebel*. Camus reasons that his argument against suicide extends to an argument against murder. I assess this claim. Camus is attempting to build an ethical theory from minimal presuppositions—but this was a task that the French existentialist philosophers also attempted. It is helpful to contrast the effort of Beauvoir, and the failure of Sartre, with Camus's effort. I show that Camus has succeeded in creating a minimum ethical theory.

The next three chapters turn to Camus's theory of revolt. Chapter 3 describes metaphysical revolt. Here we can first introduce Camus's notion of *mesure*, or balance. Camus makes highly plausible claims about how metaphysical revolt without *mesure* can lead to unethical outcomes. I claim he also identifies a new, highly general, paradox of freedom. Chapter 4 describes historical revolt, which is Camus's term for revolt against human injustice. In *The Rebel*, Camus describes historical revolt through a kind of sampling of historical events. In order to evaluate this method, I contrast it with a similar undertaking by Karl Popper in *The Open Society and Its Enemies*. Chapter 5 presents a summary of the various constraints that Camus recognizes as required to maintain *mesure* in revolt, in order to keep it from sliding into cruel revolution. This is an interesting place to consider the criticism of Camus's theory raised by Sartre, Francis Jeanson, and Beauvoir. It is also a place to contrast the implications of their diverse political theories.

In the final chapter, I argue that Camus's last completed novel, *The Fall* (*La Chute*), has been misunderstood. *The Fall* is a prophetic novel, best compared to a work like Dostoevsky's *Demons*. It presents us with a second new paradox of freedom and warns us of a danger that we continue to ignore while, at the time that I am writing, this danger comes to fruition.

ONE

The Absurd

THE AMBIGUOUS ABSURD

Albert Camus is often called "the philosopher of the absurd." Is this a fair description? The answer depends on what we mean by "absurd." Camus himself began to eschew the word in his later work. In an interview in 1951 he said, "This word 'absurd' has had an unhappy history, and I confess that now it rather annoys me" (1970, 356). The term appears more than a hundred times in his early work *The Myth of Sisyphus* (*Le mythe de Sisyphe*), but only sparingly in his last philosophical treatise, *The Rebel* (he uses it, and its cognates, frequently—about twenty-five times—in the short introduction to *The Rebel* because in this introduction he returns to a question of *The Myth of Sisyphus*, but in the rest of the lengthy book he uses the word, by my count, just another dozen times). He seemed to recognize that the term—especially as he used it in *The Myth of Sisyphus*—could invite misinterpretation.

The word does invite a host of diverse interpretations. This is true in everyday use of the term and also in Camus's earliest work. In *The Myth of Sisyphus*, Camus used "absurd" in a number of different senses. Some of these he clearly distinguishes, but unfortunately some of these he does not clearly distinguish. It also seems plausible that some of these senses were a bit confused in his own early thinking. I will argue, however, that only one sense of "absurd" is necessary for the primary insights and arguments that Camus makes—indeed, this one sense of "absurd" will reveal that his reasoning was remarkably consistent across all his work, throughout his lifetime. My task in this chapter is therefore partly revisionary, since other scholars of Camus's work have not made the claim that I will be making. Also, it is fair to say that, at least in his earlier work, it appears that Camus did not resolve some of the important ambiguities of the term "absurd," and that he endorses at various times disparate meanings. I will argue that Camus most makes use of "absurd" in one sense—which I will call the "teleological absurd"—and it is this one sense that is alone required to articulate the strongest and most consistent interpretation of his arguments throughout his writing career, but I will also argue that at least three of his other uses of the term are closely related to the teleological absurd, so that there is a deep coherence even between these different meanings. Other scholars of Camus have described how his various uses of "absurd" can be seen as distinct but consistent with each other (e.g., Carroll 2007). My concern is different: it is to show how clarifying the nature of the absurd, as Camus understands it, reveals a deep coherence in all his work.

THE TELEOLOGICAL ABSURD

A remarkable difference between Camus's early and late work is evident. *The Stranger* portrays a solitary man incapable of sharing the purposes of his peers; *The Plague* (*Le Peste*) is an account of men in solidarity fighting against "creation" as they found it. His play *Caligula* is a dramatization of violent nihilism; *The Just Assassins* (*Les Justes*) is a portrait of extremists who willingly die in absolution for their violence. *The Myth of Sisyphus* offers us a denuded ethics of quantity of experiences over quality of experiences and holds up Don Juan as a tragic model; *The Rebel* implores us to recognize a shared human nature and to use this recognition to guide the development of restrained political institutions that help us to continually and incrementally improve the human lot.

And yet, Camus insisted that there was fundamental continuity in his work and in his concerns. In his 1955 preface to the American edition of *The Myth of Sisyphus*, written well after publication of *The Rebel*, Camus claims that "*The Myth of Sisyphus* marks the beginning of an idea which I was to pursue in *The Rebel*. It attempts to resolve the problem of suicide, as *The Rebel* attempts to resolve that of murder, in both cases without the aid of eternal values which, temporarily perhaps, are absent or distorted in contemporary Europe" (1991a, v). From this perspective, the solutions that he at times entertains have changed, but the central concerns have not. In this chapter and the next, I will show that Camus was correct: there is remarkable continuity in his thought. This continuity rests on his concern with the consequences of the absurd and with the question of how human beings can best organize their lives in light of the absurd. However, Camus's views did change with respect to his answer to this question. His experience in the war led him to revise his thinking, and to revise and refine his argument against suicide. I will also describe this change.

Four uses of the term "absurd" stand out in Camus's early work. First, Camus uses "absurd" to mean without purpose. The stunning first words of *The Myth of Sisyphus* capture the idea: "There is but one truly serious philosophical problem, and that is suicide. Judging whether life is or is not worth living amounts to answering the fundamental question of philosophy" (1991a [1942], 3). He goes on to say, "I therefore conclude that the meaning of life is the most urgent of questions" (4). French, like English, suffers from this same ambiguity where "meaning"—*sens*—can mean both purpose or semantic meaning, and perhaps may have other senses. Here we are talking about purpose; the question of whether one's life is worth living is the question of whether one's life has the right kind of purposes. This will be made clear as we see the kind of work that Camus makes this concept do.

Sometimes the monotony of life makes us question whether we are acting with sufficient purpose: "But one day the 'why' arises and everything begins in that weariness tinged with amazement" (1991a, 13). The "why" is to ask, why am I doing this? What is this activity for? These questions throw one's purposes into doubt. We can call this the "teleological sense" of "absurd"—or "the teleological absurd" in short.

A second use of "absurd" refers to an experience we have in recognition of this absurdity. When one realizes that the cosmos, or history, has no purpose, one feels a kind of *Angst* or anxiety—what Sartre called anguish (*angoisse*). This experience can be profound and change one's life in significant ways. Here, Camus is consistent with existentialists like Heidegger and Sartre, and importantly in *The Myth of Sisyphus* he cites and endorses Heidegger's concept of *Angst*. *Angst* is the experience (the attunement, some philosophers call it—Heidegger's term is *Befindlichkeit*; see Heidegger 1962 [1927], 172 [134]) in which a person "sees" her purposes as contingent, as without any justifying foundation. Camus certainly has significant differences from Sartre and Heidegger, but he also shares some important common beliefs. This would be one of them: there is an experience of the absurd, which some have called *Angst*. This is a feeling that we have when we recognize certain aspects of our existence.[1] For example, speaking of the recognition that one must die, Camus says, "This elementary and definitive aspect of the adventure constitutes the absurd feeling" (1991a, 15). And "From the moment that absurdity is recognized, it becomes a passion, the most harrowing of all" (1991a, 22).[2]

Camus's third use of "absurd" refers to a relation to purposelessness that is significant for human beings. This is a kind of tension that exists between the human being and nature. The human being longs for purpose, wants to understand his own purposes, and wants to find purposes in the natural world. "But what is absurd is the confrontation of this irrational and the wild longing for clarity whose call echoes in the human heart" (1991a, 21). Because it is we who long for purpose, a purposeless world is a disappointment. We want a purposeful life and even a purposeful nature, but nature is without purpose, and (for the early Camus) perhaps even our life is also without sufficient purpose. Avi Sagi has argued that this is the fundamental meaning of "absurd" for Camus, placing it in a history of modern alienation: "the absurd is an experience built on two contradictory elements, one positive and one negative—a negative experience of rift and separation, and a positive experience of yearning for harmony and unity" (2002, 23). David Walsh also has a clear discussion of the role of this concept in Camus's thinking (1990, 59). Interestingly, *The Myth of Sisyphus* is explicitly an attempt to think and write in this tension:

> Reflection on suicide gives me an opportunity to raise the only problem to interest me: is there a logic to the point of death? I cannot know unless I pursue, without reckless passion, in the sole light of evidence, the reasoning of which I am here suggesting the source. This is what I call an absurd reasoning. (1991a, 9)

This absurd tension is also a tension between honesty and longing. If we are honest, we see the universe is without purposes, and we fear that we are ourselves without justified and sufficient purposes. (I will explain what I mean by "justified and sufficient" below. But in brief: a purpose is justified if it withstands questioning, and it is sufficient if it gives reason to continue to live.) But we long for both of those. We even see this tension in historical epochs, Camus argues: philosophical movements arise that, guided primarily by hope, claim the world can be revealed as purposeful; other movements arise to reject such views. "On the plane of history, such a constancy of two attitudes illustrates the essential passion of man torn between his urge toward unity and the clear vision he may have of the walls enclosing him" (1991a, 22). Here, the walls that enclose us are the evidence that, in fact, the universe is not purposeful.

Camus takes as his early project to attempt a balance between these two extremes that arise from this longing and this knowledge. We can give in to "hope" and nostalgia, and take some form of leap of faith. Thus, like Kierkegaard, we might leap to believing in a god who created the universe with a real but hidden purposefulness. Or we might leap into some kind of philosophical theory that, without sufficient reason, argues that the universe or that history has this or that goal. But at the other extreme, we could give in to despair. Our knowledge that the universe is without purpose, and the suspicion (for this early Camus) that perhaps we ourselves are without sufficient purpose, could lead us to suicide or some other act of rejection. We might conclude our lives are without a sufficient purpose and therefore that there is little reason to go on living them.

To give up on the knowledge of the absurd is for Camus a kind of dishonesty. In one part in *The Myth of Sisyphus*, he even calls the use of philosophical theories to evade this tension "philosophical suicide." He wants to try to recognize the absurd without giving in to despair. In a passage that expresses a view that remains essential to his work, he writes, "Living is keeping the absurd alive. . . . One of the only coherent philosophical positions is thus revolt. It is a constant confrontation between man and his own obscurity" (54). Camus will call this "metaphysical revolt" in his later work. It is to assert one's purposes in a purposeless universe. We reject the absurdity of the universe by trying to create and maintain space and conditions in this universe for human purposes to flourish.

In *The Plague*, the protagonist Doctor Rieux illustrates this attitude when he describes his efforts against an outbreak of bubonic plague as "fighting against creation as he found it" (1991b [1947], 127).

In this book I argue that Camus came to believe that we have intrinsic human purposes that are justified and sufficient purposes. This does not mean, however, that the absurd tension disappears. We are always able to ask whether our purposes really are justified. This doubt will always lurk, in the same way that a fallibilist is always open to questioning his fundamental beliefs even though those beliefs may be true. The absurd tension is not dissolved by the observation that we have justified and sufficient purposes and that we are constituted by those purposes. Let us call this view,

Fallibilism about purpose: *It is always possible that one's purposes are neither justified nor sufficient.*[3]

This is an important element of Camus's philosophy. Even if we have an answer to the corrosive "Why?" we may still sometimes find that doubt haunts us.

Camus's fourth use of the term "absurd" is the most problematic. In *The Myth of Sisyphus* he argues also that the universe is absurd in that we cannot understand it. "In this unintelligible and limited universe, man's fate henceforth assumes its meaning" (1991a, 21). Thus, "With the exception of professional rationalists, today people despair of true knowledge" (18). He suggests that earlier philosophies, along with religions, offer a narrative or theory in which the world is intelligible. But it is nostalgia to look back toward this belief in an intelligible universe. This is a view Camus claims is shared by the existentialist and pre-existentialist philosophers (such as Nietzsche); Camus writes that "Whatever may be or have been their ambitions, all started out from that indescribable universe where contradiction, antinomy, anguish, or impotence reigns" (23). In his journals on February 10, 1943, he writes, "The whole problem of the absurd ought to be able to be centered on a critique of the value judgment and the factual judgment" (1978, 57). In *The Myth of Sisyphus*, this view of the absurd culminates in his dismissing the findings of contemporary science as somehow inadequate.

Some philosophers take this fourth sense of the absurd to be Camus's primary meaning for the term. In his review of *The Rebel*, Richard Wollheim claims that for Camus,

> What is *absurd* is man's lot, his situation in the world: the *sentiment de l'absurde* arises in one who takes in the inherent incompatibility, the inevitable incommensurability between what man demands of the world and what the world has to offer.... Where the world fails one is in its unintelligibility, its otherness, its opaqueness to the understanding. (1953, 7)[4]

Similarly, in his interesting study *Albert Camus and the Literature of the Revolt*, John Cruikshank argues forcefully that this is Camus's central intent: "by the absurd Camus generally means the absence of correspondence or congruity between the mind's need for coherence and the incoherence of the world which the mind experiences" (1960, 41). John Foley reasons similarly, arguing that Camus believes that "Human beings are naturally inclined to want and expect the world to be intelligible" but that "the absurd arises because the world is resistant to this kind of intelligibility" (2008, 6). A similar view is found in Scott (1969), who argues that the absurd for Camus means that "the mind's hunger for coherence is countered by irremediable incoherence of existence" (20), and in Willhoite (1968). In an essay that considers *The Stranger*, Sartre wrote, "This will be the source of the feeling of the absurd or, in other words, of our incapability of *thinking* the events of the world with our concepts and words" (2013, 34–35).[5]

Camus definitely does use the term "absurd" in this sense in many passages in *The Myth of Sisyphus*, but when measured against his later arguments and his intent, it is clear that he made little or no further use of this notion. And all of Camus's examples of the absurd show that his primary objection is not really to his lack of knowledge but rather to his sense of place in this world that science reveals. We can begin to see this when we reflect more fully on how Camus describes this sense of the absurd. He writes, "Yet all the knowledge on earth will give me nothing to assure me that this world is mine" (1991a, 19). And "to understand is, above all, to unify" (1991a, 17). Camus uses the word "unify" without explanation, but when we look at his many applications of the term, the sense becomes clear. "Unity" is his term for a purpose or set of purposes that are justified and sufficient and which make it possible for our own individual purposes to be justified and sufficient, if our individual purposes serve those other purposes. This is precisely the role that God played in religion: God's purposes were justified, sufficient, and good. This was given. When our purposes served God's purposes, our purposes were justified, sufficient, and good.

Applied to factual knowledge, the concept would mean that to unify some domain of knowledge is to describe it in such a way that we understand its purposefulness, and how its purposes relate to our own purposes. Then, a unified world would be "mine," because its purposes would shape and reflect my own purposes.

Camus is writing, let us note, during a golden age of physics. During his lifetime alone, our knowledge of the physical world exploded and our ability to grasp nature through reason grew more powerful than ever before. There is something jarring then in any description of nature as beyond reason, made at such a moment. It would be patently false to deny an improvement in our understanding of the world, in terms of causes and physical laws.

It may well be that Camus is unclear on this point in his own mind. In *The Myth of Sisyphus*, he writes sometimes in a way that suggests he has not thought this through fully. Also, his understanding of science is sometimes obviously incorrect. For example, in the journals in August 1942, he wrote, "Science explains what happens and not what *is*. Ex.: why various species of flowers rather than a single one?" (1978 [1942], 27). This is of course false; modern biology does explain why there are various species of flowers and not just one. But, setting aside ambiguities and errors in Camus's thinking on this matter, I would argue there is a clear central issue that coheres with his other concerns. Surely, additional knowledge about causes, or additional mathematical descriptions of physical relations, of a kind that we might call "rational" descriptions of the world, are not going to render, say, a child's death no longer absurd. Thus, what Camus should have said is that we cannot see a purposeful order, a purposeful "rationality," to nature or history. In this sense, then, to describe the world as resisting reason or rationality is consistent with the claim that to say the world is absurd is to say it is without purpose. Nature is teleologically absurd, and therefore rationality and reason find in it no purpose, nor ever will do so.

I would defend this interpretation with another observation. It simply is not plausible that Camus was plagued by skepticism and doubts about knowledge and method. In his fiction and plays, doubt about the facts is never an important plot point. If skepticism and our inability to know about the world were what concerned him, he could have written fiction like that of Kafka, or plays like the absurd dramatists, where the world presents us with inexplicable accusations and events. But Camus always writes realistic fiction where it is the teleological absurdity of the world and history, or the sense of purposelessness of a character, that rises as a theme; never is an inability to know Camus's theme.[6]

In the 1955 preface to the English edition of *The Myth of Sisyphus*, Camus does not mention any inability to understand the world. Rather, he says, "The fundamental subject of *The Myth of Sisyphus* is this: is it legitimate and necessary to wonder whether life has a meaning" (1991a, v). He goes on to argue that "this book declares that even within the limits of nihilism it is possible to find the means to proceed beyond nihilism. In all the books I have written since, I have attempted to pursue this direction" (v). "Nihilism" here means, at least, the conviction that human life is without a justified and sufficient purpose.[7]

In an interview in 1945, Camus protested that his task in *The Myth of Sisyphus* had been to start an exploration; the book was a beginning and not a theory. He said, "Accepting the absurdity of everything around us is one step, a necessary experience; it should not become a dead end. It arouses a revolt that can become fruitful. An analysis of the idea of revolt could help us to discover ideas capable of restoring a relative meaning to existence, although a meaning that would always be in danger" (1970, 346). So he does not see the task as one of doubting our ability to understand, but rather as exploring the implications that follow from accepting teleological absurdity.

However, I believe that there is a deep connection between the teleological absurd and some kinds of epistemic concerns. I turn to this issue in the next section.

THE T-EPISTEMIC ABSURD

The teleological absurd is the primary notion of the absurd in *The Myth of Sisyphus*, and it will allow us to understand Camus's later work in philosophy. However, as we noted, Camus does use the term "absurd" in other ways in *The Myth of Sisyphus*. He refers also to the absurd as the world being resistant to explanation. We can find ourselves "perceiving that the world is 'dense,' sensing to what a degree a stone is foreign and irreducible to us" (1991a, 14). His concern at first seems to be that theories do not satisfy us; they do not explain the world as we would want. "This world I can touch, and I likewise judge that it exists. There ends all my knowledge, and the rest is construction" (19). Furthermore, he suspects that his method of beginning with the absurd and trying to derive its implications seems to trap him in a position of doubting the possibility of knowledge: "The method defined here acknowledges the feeling that all true knowledge is impossible. Solely appearances can be enumerated and the climate make itself felt" (12).

This underlies Camus's critique of Edmund Husserl in *The Myth of Sisyphus*. Camus believes the phenomenological method[8] at first holds out the promise of being an austere realism, where a strict discipline of observation allows us to identify features of our experience. But in the end, Camus laments, Husserl embraces a kind of Platonism. Husserl claims the method can identify essences, which are themselves independent of the phenomena: "When . . . Husserl exclaims: 'If all masses subject to attraction were to disappear, the law of attraction would not be destroyed but would simply remain without any possible application,' I know that I am faced with a metaphysic of consolation" (46). Here "consolation" is what Camus also calls "nostalgia," a longing for a kind of theory (such as a Platonist theory) that we had rightly rejected but that offered us consolations that are not available in the absurd. Chiefly, such a theory holds out the promise of some metaphysical grounds for unity. We long for such a theory, and sometimes give in to the temptation to believe it. That would be to live with "appeal," and Camus likens it to a kind of philosophical suicide.

Camus is willing to extend his critique of "rationalism" to science. Speaking to what is presumably a scientist, he says:

> You describe [this world] to me and you teach me to classify it. You enumerate its laws and in my thirst for knowledge I admit that they are true. You take apart its mechanism and my hope increases. At the final stage you teach me that this wondrous and multi-colored universe can be reduced to the atom and that the atom itself can be reduced to the electron. All this is good and I wait for you to continue.

But you tell me of an invisible planetary system in which electrons gravitate around a nucleus. You explain this world to me with an image. I realize then that you have been reduced to poetry. (1991a, 19–20)

This part of his critique is rather unconvincing, if read literally as an attack on the claim that science produces knowledge. By the time he is writing, it is not the case that the atom was understood to be similar to a little solar system. Rather, he is writing at a time of explosive and continuing progress in the sciences. It is interesting to wonder how familiar Camus was with the natural sciences. He did develop a friendship with Jacques Monod, later to receive the Nobel Prize for his work in biology. It is noteworthy that Camus does not again, after *The Myth of Sisyphus* and after this friendship, attempt to criticize the ability of the sciences to produce reliable knowledge.

At first, it might seem that we can summarize this version of the absurd as the epistemic absurd as

x *is* **epistemically absurd** *if and only if* x *cannot be explained.*

This characterization is preliminary; I shall later argue for a weaker, more narrow interpretation.

I have already argued that the teleological absurd is more fundamental, because it is consistent with the primary concern across all of Camus's work. But in *The Myth of Sisyphus*, Camus does clearly sometimes use the term "absurd" to refer to an epistemic limit or failure of some kind. Furthermore, in the initial portion of the book where he lays the groundwork for the absurd condition, he spends more time discussing this epistemic absurd than he does discussing the teleological absurd.

We must note also that Camus does introduce another notion of the absurd, closely related to the epistemic notion of the absurd but noticeably distinct. This is the absurd as contradictory or paradoxical. "If I accuse an innocent man of a monstrous crime, if I tell a virtuous man that he has coveted his own sister, he will reply that this is absurd. . . . 'It's absurd' means 'It's impossible' but also 'It's contradictory'" (29). Here, Camus appears to remain open to the idea that the world may allow for contradiction or incoherence. This is the sense that "absurd" took on in the theater, where a play like *Waiting for Godot* or *Rhinoceros* seems to break the laws of physics, if not the laws of logic. However, in the context of his overall argument, Camus does not make use of such an extreme notion. Rather, he stresses that the absurdity in this sense largely arises from a mismatch between our expectations and some claim or observation. Thus, it would seem that the epistemic absurd could potentially explain this additional sense of the absurd.

We are left with two puzzles. What precisely is the best interpretation of the epistemic absurd in *The Myth of Sisyphus*? More importantly: is the epistemic absurd wholly independent of the teleological absurd? If so, this would seem to entail that the resulting arguments are themselves unrelated and that Camus is really talking about two quite independent problems with two sets of independent consequences. To see this, consider each potential entailment. Does the teleological absurd entail the epistemic absurd? We know that it does not because we can think of potential ways the world could be where the entailment would fail. One is in fact the modern scientific worldview. On this view, the universe is teleologically absurd. That is, it is true: the universe does not have a justified and sufficient purpose. This is trivially so because the universe does not have any purpose. However, the universe can be explained, and the tremendous success of the scientific method demonstrates this. Consider the converse: must the epistemic absurd entail the teleological absurd? Here again, the answer is that it need not do so. The world of the ancients could be interpreted in this way. The universe could be seen as epistemically absurd because it was largely ruled by the wills of the gods, but these gods had free will and were unpredictable and potentially capricious. As Shakespeare puts it, "As flies to wanton boys are we to the gods; They kill us for their sport." But this mythical world was purposeful; it was not teleologically absurd. Here we have a potential model of the world that is (at least superficially) consistent with the epistemic absurd but not with the teleological absurd.

There is one obvious sense in which the epistemic and the teleological relate: epistemology is fundamentally a teleological enterprise in that it concerns what one should believe. That is, we can interpret it as offering a purposeful account of belief, where the purpose is to believe claims that meet or pass certain standards. This fact, however, will not resolve our puzzle. Camus has suggested that there is some kind of epistemic failure, and thus presumably (in at least some cases) a failure to determine what one should believe. But this still appears to be independent of the question whether I have sufficient reason to continue my existence.

There is another relationship that is relevant here. Some kinds of explanations are fundamentally teleological in the sense that teleology is used to explain a phenomenon. These are explanations of a kind sometimes called "functional." Given that the word "function" is ambiguous and includes both teleological and nonteleological meanings (a mathematical function is not teleological, for example), it will be best to use the term "teleofunctional," which sometimes appears in the literature.

A teleofunctional explanation is one given in terms of purposes rather than causes. If an object falls toward the earth, the causal law of gravitation describes the relationship as a dynamical one where each state of affairs uniquely determines the next one. For many, this kind of dynamical law is the quintessential form of scientific explanation.[9] It refers only to causes as described by lawlike relations, laying out a dynamical development. But in the biological sciences or the human sciences (e.g., psychology, economics), we find ourselves often required to use a different kind of explanation. We say that the purpose of the heart is to pump blood, or that Tom got onto the bus because he wanted to go to his mother's house, or that people are rational agents in a market because they seek to maximize utility. Such explanations require reference to a purpose; they are teleological.

A better interpretation of Camus's epistemic absurd would be that we fail to find adequate teleofunctional explanations of the world. Let us call this the t-epistemic absurd:

x *is **t-epistemically absurd** if and only if there is no teleofunctional explanation of* x *that cannot be replaced with a causal explanation that is at least as successful in explaining* x.

The awkward additional clause is necessary because of course one could offer a teleofunctional explanation of anything. We could say a stone fell to the earth because its telos is to return to the earth. But such an explanation is inferior to, and replaceable by, the causal law of gravitation. Thus, a teleofunctional explanation must be both useful and irreducible to a causal relation, on this accounting.[10]

Let's consider the examples above. We say that the purpose of the heart is to pump blood. This is similar to countless other kinds of explanations one might find in biology or in the medical sciences. It is difficult to imagine how doctors could practice their discipline if they did not understand organs, for example, in terms of their purposes. This concept of purpose is required to distinguish health from disease, for example. Something is a disease only if it impinges on a biological purpose. There are countless possible changes to the heart that can happen, but only those that have the potential to interfere with its ability to pump blood are diseases. Similarly, in the social sciences, we often refer to the motives of agents. Tom got onto the bus because he wanted to go to his mother's house. This attributes to Tom a goal, and we can explain his behavior in terms of this goal. It also allows us to make predictions. We can predict, for example, that at the stop closest to his mother's house, Tom will disembark and walk to her house. Or, if the bus gets a flat tire, we predict that he will seek some other form of transportation. Or consider rational choice theory, fundamental to economics. It is assumed that people have preferences, which are goals held in mind that guide action. Rationality is defined in terms of these states—for example, it typically includes that the preferences are well ordered. These purposes then serve to make predictions of rational agents. Thus, we see that teleofunctional explanations can be essential to key concepts of many disciplines, can generate predictions, and can even serve as a foundation to a methodology.

When Camus calls for explanation of the world, and despairs of achieving it, what he is most longing for is a teleofunctional explanation. Camus claims that if we had "unity"—if our purposes were justified and sufficient because they cohered with some purpose of history or of the universe—we would be filled with joy (1991a, 17). He expresses a similar sentiment regarding knowledge: what he claims we long for is unity in knowledge. Science insults this longing, because it is most successful when it eschews teleofunctional explanations; furthermore, if we want to know about the universe, we turn to a discipline like astrophysics, not economics, and here we find the complete triumph of causal explanations. Teleofunctional explanations play no role in these cosmic explanations. The world is not mine, Camus says. This can only mean: it has no purposes that can make me feel at home in it; it has no purposes that can justify my own purposes or give to me purposes.

This is consistent with his account of revolt in the *The Rebel*. There, Camus writes that "The rebel does not ask for life, but for reasons for living" (1956 [1951], 101) and that "In the eyes of the rebel, what is missing from the misery of the world, as well as from its moments of happiness, is some principle by which they can be explained" (101). But of course such an explanation must be teleofunctional: it must explain purposes in terms of purposes. No causal explanation could justify the misery of the world. Thus, the issue of teleofunctional explanation is one that stretches across the whole of Camus's body of work, uniting it with his enduring concern with the teleological absurd.

Teleofunctional explanations could be realist or anti-realist.[11] One important issue is that, for some of the existentialists, teleological explanation was essentially also a form of anti-realism. Heidegger defends the view in *Being and Time* (*Sein und Zeit*, 1926) that we primarily first encounter the world through our purposes, and we encounter useful beings in a way that actually determines their possibility for being encountered or present. This gives these useful things encountered through use a special ontological status as the "ready-to-hand" (*Zuhandenheit*). This makes the presence of beings dependent on the agent doing the revealing, and in turn dependent on the purposes of that agent. This is where teleofunctional explanation can be seen as a natural precursor to a form of anti-realism. Heidegger embraces this consequence, and perhaps its most obviously problematic consequence is that claims about prehuman eras are rendered paradoxical. Quentin Meillassoux (2010) called this anti-realism "correlationism" because it assumes the world is revealed and accessible only as correlated with the perceiver. This raises an obvious problem. A paleontologist can claim that 250,000,000 years ago trilobites lived in the seas of Earth. Heidegger must translate such a sentence to mean: it is true now (because Dasein exists now to let it be revealed) that 250,000,000 years ago trilobites lived in the seas of Earth. But this move will not solve the problem, since any paleontologist would agree with the following claim: 250,000,000 years ago, it is true that trilobites live in the seas of Earth.

Another aspect of such anti-realism is that different agents with different purposes will have a different "world." This view is not original to Heidegger, who cites in his lectures *The Fundamental Concepts of Metaphysics* the work of Jakob Johann von Uexküll (1864–1944) (1995, 251). Uexküll was a scholar interested in how meaning was created for diverse organisms. He proposed the idea of an umwelt, a "surrounding world," that each organism inhabits and which is unique to that organism because the organism has its own unique purposes and its own unique perceptual abilities. In *The Myth of Sisyphus*, Camus at one point makes claims that could have come directly from Uexküll: "Understanding the world for a man is reducing it to the human, stamping it with his seal. The cat's universe is not the universe of the anthill. The truism 'All thought is anthropomorphic' has no other meaning" (1991a, 13). Camus's t-epistemic absurd, however, need not entail anti-realism. A weaker interpretation of an umwelt is that although we experience the world through our purposes, and often explain the world with reference to our purposes, we can still refer to and speculate about other (possible) phenomena, including phenomena that we cannot directly perceive or "encounter," and thus there can still be evidence-transcendent truths. This is the view, in fact, of strong realists in the tradition of Karl Popper. This position is not open to Heidegger because he equates truth with the revealing of being that Dasein makes possible. Camus makes no such equation and seems to take truth as a primitive. In an interview in 1957, he said, "A press or a book is not true because it is revolutionary. It has a chance of being revolutionary only if it tries to tell the truth. We have a right to think that truth with a capital letter is relative. But facts are facts. And whoever says that the sky is blue when it is gray is prostituting words and preparing the way for tyranny" (1995, 168). I believe here that his statement that "We have a right to think that truth with a capital letter is relative" is merely an assertion that we should allow philosophers and others to continue to raise their skeptical doubts and to make their various epistemic explorations (that is, I believe it is an awkward way of stating epistemic fallibilism). But Camus immediately insists that "facts are facts," which is practically the slogan of realism.

Our puzzle was that the teleological absurd and the epistemic absurd appear wholly independent. Neither entails the other. This would not be a refutation of Camus's views, but it would suggest that he is using the term "absurd" ambiguously and also that his arguments may not apply to all his uses of the term. However, our analysis of the epistemically absurd suggests that we need a refinement of the concept to the t-epistemic absurd, which is formulated in terms of explanation. This provides a solution to our puzzle. The teleological absurd and the t-epistemic absurd are closely related.

First, the teleological absurd would seem to entail the t-epistemic absurd, if our domain of explanation is sufficiently narrow. Thus, if the universe is without any purpose, then it is teleologically absurd; but also this suggests that most likely the best kinds of explanation of the universe (e.g., the kind of thing we see in cosmology) will not be teleological explanations, and so the universe will also be t-epistemic absurd. If history is without any purpose, then it is teleologically absurd, but then most likely the best kinds of explanations of history will not be teleological and so history will be t-epistemic absurd.[12] And if human beings are without any purpose, then they are teleologically absurd, and most likely the best kinds of explanations of people will not be teleological.

Camus's position in *The Myth of Sisyphus* is that the universe and history lack purpose, but he does not assert that human beings are purposeless but rather raises doubt about whether their purposes are justified and sufficient. But even if we adopt his later view that human beings have purposes—even purposes that are justified and sufficient—there is still a fundamental relation between the teleological absurd and the t-epistemic absurd. This is because we continue to long for unity, and this unity would be achieved if we had a teleofunctional explanation of the universe or history that seemed to justify our own purposes. It is in religion that we find a teleofunctional explanation of the universe—for example, the claim that the universe was created in an act of will for specific purposes—that could give us a teleofunctional explanation of our history and our own purposes (which are presumably a product of and serve the purposes of this creator). It is in Marxism, Hegel, and related doctrines that we find a teleofunctional explanation of history, which gives us a teleofunctional explanation of our place in this history that provides a justification for certain purposes (e.g., those deemed to speed communism). But Camus remains adamant that both of these are philosophical suicide; the universe and history lack any purpose, and though we long to explain our place in history or the universe using teleofunctional explanations (that is, we long for unity), we cannot achieve this.

There are important relations in the other way also, from the t-epistemic absurd to the teleological absurd. If we have a successful teleofunctional explanation of some phenomenon, then this is prima facie evidence that the phenomenon is purposeful. Of course, as noted, we are currently in the position where all the human and biological sciences make continual use of teleofunctional explanations. Many scientists presumably expect that these teleofunctional explanations can ultimately be reduced, but no one can yet fully describe such a reduction. As I noted, this would really be an elimination; it would mean that the "purposes" weren't really purposes, with respect to Camus's concerns. But setting aside worries about reduction and elimination, if we explain some event in terms of purposes—if we explain Tom's getting on the bus by saying he is fulfilling his purpose to go to his mother's house—then our teleofunctional explanation entails that Tom has a purpose. It may not be justified or sufficient, but it is a purpose. Thus, from the fact that we have (as yet) ineliminable teleofunctional explanations of human action, but we have eliminated teleofunctional explanations of the universe or history, we have shown that human beings are purposeful, and the universe and history are not. This is precisely the world Camus describes.

It may seem that we have come far afield, from trying to understand the teleological absurd to now trying to understand the t-epistemic absurd. But we must remember that Camus will argue that our understanding of the absurd can and did shape our ethical theories and our political actions. These two notions of the absurd both help us to understand this phenomenon. The teleological absurd will be the primary cause of the threat of nihilism, and thus an important cause of our embrace of extreme theories of historical purpose that get combined with consequentialist decision theories, with disastrous results. The t-epistemic absurd plays an important role in this. Human beings understand each other, and many other phenomena, using teleofunctional explanations. If these are threatened and denied, then the result will be to thrust us toward seeing ourselves and these other phenomena as teleologically absurd. The rise of science played a role in the rise of the teleological absurd precisely because of this effect.

JUSTIFIED AND SUFFICIENT PURPOSES

I have delayed introducing the most important clarification regarding the absurd. As a first draft of the concept, the teleological absurd can be captured with the equivalence x *is **teleologically absurd** if and only if* x *is without purpose.*

This leaves open the question, what things are absurd? One might claim that the cosmos lacks a purpose, or human history lacks a purpose, and so on. Such cases are of special interest to Camus because often we have justified certain social systems, and certain political acts, on the grounds that they served a cosmic or historical purpose. But the claim can be of a smaller scope. We are horrified by the suffering of innocents, such as when a child dies of a disease. "Why?" we ask, a rhetorical question directed at a silent, indifferent universe. The answer, of course, is that it has no purpose. It is absurd.

But a point must be made here about two distinctions that Camus does not make explicit but which are clearly essential to his reasoning. In this, he follows the existentialists, who are concerned specifically with these questions of purpose, but who do not distinguish kinds of purposes or the properties of purposes. The issue here is that it is no doubt true that a person often, perhaps always, can offer some teleological account for his actions. How then can we say that his experience is absurd? That is, if we supposed that some human action was absurd, would such a claim be refuted by the observation that the person completing the action could describe it as serving some purpose?

To help understand this, we need first to distinguish intrinsic and instrumental purposes. Consider the following passage from Camus's *The Myth of Sisyphus*. Camus describes different kinds of endeavors and actions that can come to seem absurd to us. One of his most striking examples is the following: "Men, too, secrete the inhuman. At certain moments of lucidity, the mechanical aspect of their gestures, their meaningless pantomime makes silly everything that surrounds them. A man is talking on the telephone behind a glass partition; you cannot hear him, but you see his incomprehensible dumb show: you wonder why he is alive" (1991a, 14). One could of course go ask this man, "Why did you wave your arm like that?" And he might answer, "Because I wanted to stress my point." That is, he will have a purpose for everything he says and does. But this purpose is instrumental: each act can be explained as being for some other outcome. What then if we follow this chain to its end and arrive at an act or goal for which there is no other act or goal that it aims to satisfy?

For those who are naturalists about purposes, such a method reveals a natural end, an intrinsic purpose. This is the view of Aristotle:

> So if what is done has some end that we want for its own sake, and everything else we want is for the sake of this end; and if we do not choose everything for the sake of something else (because this would lead to an infinite progression, making our desire fruitless and vain), then clearly this will be the good, indeed the chief good. (2000, 4 [1094a16–22])

And furthermore,

> We speak of that which is worth pursuing for its own sake as more complete than that which is worth pursuing only for the sake of something else, and that which is never worth choosing for the sake of something else as more complete than things that are worth choosing both in themselves and for the sake of this end. And so that which is always worth choosing in itself and never for the sake of something else we call complete without qualification. (2000, 10 [1097a30–1097b1])

Aristotle believes that if we follow a chain of instrumental purposes—moving from one to the next by asking, "What is this for?"—we will ultimately come to a purpose that is for itself. That is an intrinsic purpose, and one that Aristotle considers both a good and a natural purpose.

But for the existentialists,[13] what such an analysis reveals is the unfoundedness of our purposes. This is because we see (the existentialists claim) that the final purposes of any such chain of purposes is itself a purpose that is without justification. We are not satisfied by the claim that it is intrinsic, or that it is justified or sufficient as it is. Instead, these purposes at the end of our chain of "what's that for?" questions are themselves like hypothetical or instrumental purposes, but they are bereft of any further goal.

The motive for taking this position seems to be that the existentialists have adopted a kind of foundationalism about purpose. Foundationalism in epistemology is the view that we should secure our knowledge by showing that it is derived from, or in some other way corroborated by, indubitable or otherwise privileged beliefs (these are the foundation). Descartes is the quintessential foundationalist. But there is an analogous move in teleology. Let us call it, "foundationalism about purpose." I define foundationalism about purpose as the view that a purpose is justified and sufficient if that purpose in turn serves some fundamental justified and sufficient purpose. By saying a purpose P_1 serves purpose P_2, I mean that realizing P_1 will assist in (such as, by making more likely) the realization of P_2.[14] An example would be a view that there is a god that has a purpose for the universe, and then our purposes are justified and sufficient if they help in the realization of that god's purpose. The existentialists are foundationalists about purpose, and they accept that the Christian worldview, if true, would offer a foundation for our purposes. But then their atheism entails that this foundation is gone. "The death of God is an embarrassment," Sartre says in his 1946 lecture "Existentialism is a Humanism" (2007). In his notes *The Will to Power*, Nietzsche describes Christian theory and morality as "the great *antidote* against practical and theoretical *nihilism*" (1968, 10). But God is dead, Nietzsche claims, and the result is nihilism. Aristotle's assumptions about teleology do not include the foundationalist assumptions of the existentialists. For Aristotle, it is a fact of our nature that some of our intrinsic purposes are justified and sufficient. The existentialist instead claims that justification of a purpose requires another specific kind of reason (of a kind that Camus has described as a call for "unity"), which they find lacking. As Nietzsche wrote, "What does nihilism mean? *That the highest values devaluate themselves.* The aim is lacking: 'why?' finds no answer" (1968, 9).

In his early work, Camus seems drawn to this foundationalism. We see this in his discussion of "unity" in *The Myth of Sisyphus*. In a secular society, unity would be a state where history or the universe had some purposes and our human purposes served those purposes.

> If man realized that the universe like him can love and suffer, he would be reconciled. If thought discovered in the shimmering mirrors of phenomena eternal relations capable of summing them up and summing themselves up in a single principle, then would be seen an intellectual joy of which the myth of the blessed would be but a ridiculous imitation. (1991a, 17)

This is a longing for a single, enduring, and external purpose that can act as justification to our human purposes. Of course, Camus rejects any such claims, for the simple reason that we have no evidence that they are true: "My reasoning wants to be faithful to the evidence that aroused it. That evidence is the absurd. It is that divorce between the mind that desires and the world that disappoints, my nostalgia for unity, this fragmented universe and the contradiction that binds them together" (1991a, 4950). Unity would provide justification for our purposes, but there is no unity.

I ask you, what do you need your hammer for, and you say to nail down the shingles of your house. I ask you for what purpose will you nail down the shingles on your house? You say, to keep water out of the house. I ask you why you pursue that goal, and keep asking, and ultimately you say something like, because I am trying to ensure a dry warm house that will keep me healthy. If I ask you what health is for, you tell me it is not for anything else. For Aristotle, this indicates that your health is an intrinsic purpose and a natural good, an end-in-itself (a telos) for human beings. It is justified and sufficient. But for Sartre—for example—this merely indicates that there is no justification for the pursuit of health. We may choose it as an end, but we could also choose other ends. (A boxer, for example, chooses ends that are not healthy.)

The later Camus—author of *The Rebel*—has some agreement with Aristotle on this idea of intrinsic purposes. However, the point to be made here is that we should revise our explanation of the absurd in the teleological sense. If we say that something is absurd if it lacks a purpose, then it would seem that many actions that Camus and others identify as absurd would not be absurd; like our man in the phone booth, there will be some instrumental purpose that can be offered to explain the action. But Camus seems to think that some of these instrumental purposes are insufficient. Thus, to claim that something is teleologically absurd includes the implicit assertion that this thing lacks an intrinsic purpose that is justified and sufficient.

In *The Myth of Sisyphus*, Camus sees his method as analogous to Descartes's method of doubt,[15] only, instead of doubting that he knows, he will try to doubt whether he has reason to go on living. He was wise to choose suicide as his theme. There is a certain amount of effort, of work, that goes into living. The question of whether that work is worth doing is the question of whether we have purposes that make it worthwhile. Camus repeatedly reminds us throughout the text that this is his theme. "One kills oneself because life is not worth living, that is certainly a truth" (1991a, 8). Camus's readers were presumably ready to hear his concern. Many shared with him a conviction that the history of the world did not suggest that history had some overarching purpose. And yet one can object that surely human beings do have purposes. If we look at the behaviors of people, we see that they always understand themselves in terms of their own purposes. In what sense then can life be said to "lack meaning," to be purposeless? Camus's brief phenomenological analysis of the man in the phone booth gives us an answer: we wonder about the man's purposefulness, and "This discomfort in the face of man's own inhumanity, this incalculable tumble before the image of what we are, this 'nausea,' as [Jean-Paul Sartre] calls it, is also the absurd" (1991a, 15).

This is at first perplexing. On the one hand, there is clearly a sense in which part of my alienation is that this man does not have purposes that I comprehend and share. But doesn't he have purposes of his own that he comprehends? He does, but it turns out that we can turn that same analysis on ourselves. Camus asserts that we can experience the same alienation from our own lives:

> It happens that the stage sets collapse. Rising, streetcar, four hours in the office or the factory, meal, streetcar, four hours of work, meal sleep, and Monday Tuesday Wednesday Thursday Friday and Saturday according to the same rhythm. . . . But one day the "why" arises and everything begins in that weariness tinged with amazement. (1991a, 12–13)

Essential to this experience is that corrosive "why?" that asks if our purposes are justified and if they are sufficient. I see the man in his phone booth, and he can begin to seem strange—"inhuman"—if I ask, "What is it all about? Why is he alive? Why so animated?" But the same corrosive questioning can be turned against myself: I can look at my own life and question my purposes, embedded in my routine—perhaps a monotonous routine. As a result of such reflection and asking "Why?," my purposes seem no longer justified.

Thus Camus's concerns, and the concerns of the existentialist, were not just whether a purpose is intrinsic, but whether it is justified and sufficient. We can with confidence, for example, assume that the man in the phone booth is speaking and gesturing with purpose. He would explain his own actions by citing those purposes. For the teleological absurd to be consistent with this observation, it must be that what we lack is a purpose, or purposes, that are justified and sufficient.

I have used "justified" and "sufficient" as primitives here, but we can identify a necessary condition of each. Necessary to a purpose being justified is that it does not collapse (we do not judge it as contingent, arbitrary, unjustified—above all, as no better than any other available purpose) when we ask Camus's corrosive "why?" The purpose will not evaporate under interrogation. We may want other criteria and explanation of what justifies a purpose, but at least justification must be such that asking "why?" of one's purposes does not make the purpose seem futile. One necessary criterion for a purpose being sufficient is that it gives one reason to go on living. This is Camus's concern: not whether we have some purpose or other, but rather whether we have a purpose that gives us reason to go on with the effort of living. What we see in these passages is that Camus believes we have an experience in which we doubt whether our purposes are justified and sufficient, and from this looms the question of whether life is worth continuing.

Furthermore, recall that Camus introduced the concept of the absurd tension: the claim that we feel a kind of conflict or tension with the absurdity of the world, in light of our own purposes (or need for purposes). This absurd tension would not exist if we did not have the added expectation that our purposes be justified and sufficient. As we noted, everyone has myriad purposes. You drink a glass of water for the purpose of quenching your thirst, for example. If merely having a purpose, any purpose, was sufficient, then the absurd tension would make no sense. But it does make sense, because of that corrosive "why?" that Camus has identified. Why do I have this purpose? Is this the right purpose? How can I know, when the universe is itself absurd?

Contrast Camus's corrosive "why?" with the teleological conception of Aristotle. On Aristotle's account, my purposes are partially ordered by the relation "____ is for ____." For example, eating is for nutrition, or study is for the acquisition of knowledge. But at the end of each such ordering will be a purpose that has no other purpose; it is reflexively for itself. Aristotle is giving us an implicit method to find such a good. Return to our example above. I ask you why you are nailing shingles on your house, and you say to keep water out of the house. I ask you why you keep water out of the house, and you say because that will be healthy. I ask what is being healthy for, and you say being healthy is for being healthy. Health is a natural end (a natural telos) of a human being. Thus, in this hypothetical analysis, shingles are for keeping a dry house, a dry house is for health, and health is for health. For Aristotle, all our various natural ends came together in the organizing purpose of eudaimonia, living with excellence.

At the time when he is writing *The Myth of Sisyphus*, Camus is in the company of the existentialists in rejecting an account like that of Aristotle. When we reach the end of our ordered purposes, what we find is not an intrinsic and justified and sufficient purpose, but rather a purpose like all the others—but now floating freely, without self-justification and without any further point. (We can say that, for the existentialists, the relation "____ is for ____" orders our purposes, but it is an irreflexive relation.) Heidegger makes this explicit in his own analysis. He observes that every ready-to-hand entity (for example, a tool encountered through its use) has an "in-order-to," and the Dasein[16] using that equipment has a "towards-which" (1962, 99). At the end of a partially ordered chain of such relations of the towards-which is the for-the-sake-of-which of a Dasein: "the 'for-the-sake-of-which' to which every 'towards-which' ultimately goes back" (119). These purposeful relations create a network of meanings and possibilities for Dasein. But, for Heidegger, in the attunement (the mood, *Befindlichkeit*) of *Angst*, one can see that one's for-the-sake-of-which is contingent, is merely a product of one's choices. It is not justified and sufficient. It is "nothing."

Presumably, we need some criteria, independent of our own choices, for when a purpose is justified and sufficient. Aristotle holds that we can know the good is complete because it is a purpose that is not for some other end. A good is thus an end-in-itself. For Aristotle, it is axiomatic that these final ends are justified and sufficient. But for the existentialists, instead, this is just evidence that our justifications don't work; they ultimately are just exhausted with something that is an arbitrary choice.

Consider Sartre's version of existentialism to see how these criteria of justified and sufficient fail to be satisfied in his account of human purposes. Values are wholly the creation of human being: "These considerations enable us to recognize that value arrives in the world through human-reality. Now, the meaning of value is to be that towards which some being surpasses its being: any action that is valued separates itself from its being toward ____" (2021 [1943], 147 [129]). This is Sartre's way of capturing purposefulness in his own metaphysics, in which he claims that the for-itself (the kind of being that you and I are) has none of the kind of essential properties you or I would consider properties (its sole "properties" are highly abstract metaphysical properties, such as being free). Rather, because it is free and therefore without any essence, it is a kind of lack: "human reality is first and foremost its own nothingness. What it negates or nihilates of itself, as for-itself, can only be itself" (2021, 141 [125]). Values negate the world as it is. Values are identical with our striving for a world that is not—a world that we have willed as a goal.

Thus, for Sartre, human values are completely the product of a choice. One chooses to do action A, and in so doing one values A and makes of A a purpose. But is this purpose justified or sufficient? Satisfaction of these criteria would require some measure or criterion that allows us to distinguish the justified and sufficient purposes from those that are not justified and sufficient. For Sartre, the answer must be negative, since there is no other criterion on offer to distinguish one purpose from another. The for-itself that values A by doing A can just as easily choose to hinder all attempts to do action A, and thereby value the opposite. The one criterion that Sartre offers regarding our choices is authenticity, choosing while recognizing the responsibility of one's freedom. However, Sartre avoids saying that one *should* be authentic, and rightly so since this would not cohere with his value theory. Furthermore, this authenticity concerns the state of the acting for-itself; it is not a criterion for purposes themselves. Sartre never denies that one could be an authentic Nazi or an authentic member of the French resistance. It is for this reason that Sartre was never able to complete an ethical theory, although at the end of *Being and Nothingness* (*L'Être et le néant*, 1943) he promised to dedicate himself to this task. I discuss this in chapter 2.

Heidegger, in contrast, is a more difficult case. In our average everyday living, we do not question our purposes, and thus seem to prima facie take them as sufficient and justified. But when in *Angst*, we can come to understand that our purposes are contingent, and therefore presumably unjustified. In response, like Sartre, Heidegger offers only that we can "choose to choose" and form a kind of life (authentic existence) in which we recognize this contingency. But here again, there seems to be no reason to pick one purpose over another, and so it is hard to see how (according to Heidegger's theories) any purpose can be justified or sufficient.

Camus's reasoning, although implicit, is clear enough. We might address his concerns with the following argument:

Argument 1
1. If one has a justified and sufficient intrinsic purpose, then one has reason to continue to live.
2. If one has reason to continue to live, then suicide is not justified.
3. If one has a justified and sufficient intrinsic purpose, then suicide is not justified.

Argument 1 is valid. One could make a very strong case that the argument is sound. The first premise must be true, given the criteria we have adopted for "justified" and "sufficient." The second premise would seem to follow from what we probably mean by "suicide is not justified." But the question that torments Camus is this: What if one does not have a justified and sufficient purpose? Does it then follow that suicide is justified?

From argument 1 it does not follow; to infer it would be to commit the fallacy of denying the antecedent. But this raises a troubling consideration. Is argument 1 misrepresenting our condition? Is our existential condition better captured by the following argument:

Argument 2
1. One has a justified and sufficient purpose if and only if one has reason to continue to live.
2. One has reason to continue to live if and only if suicide is not justified.
3. One has a justified and sufficient purpose if and only if suicide is not justified.

Argument 2 is also valid. If we accept the conclusion of argument 2, then our lack of a justified and sufficient purpose would indeed entail that suicide is justified.

In *The Myth of Sisyphus*, Camus implicitly holds to argument 1 and rejects argument 2. Although Camus is not as explicit in his reasoning as I am above, he makes this point when he observes, "people have played on words and pretended to believe that refusing to grant a meaning to life necessarily leads to declaring that it is not worth living. In truth, there is no necessary common measure between these two judgments" (1991a, 8). Thus, we lack a justified and sufficient purpose, but it does not follow that we should kill ourselves. Rather, Camus argues that more life is a goal that can sustain us:

> If I convince myself that this life has no other aspect than that of the absurd, if I feel that its whole equilibrium depends on that perpetual opposition between my conscious revolt and the darkness in which it struggles, if I admit that my freedom has no meaning except in relation to its limited fate, then I must say that what counts is not the best living but the most living. (1991a, 60–61)

His examples of such a life include such types as Don Juan, an actor, a conqueror, and a creator. There is much in this view that coheres with Nietzsche (one is reminded of the early prototypes of the *Übermensch* described in the third *Untimely Meditation*: "They are those true *men, those who are no longer animal, the philosophers, artists and saints*; nature, which never makes a leap, has made its one leap in creating them" [1997 (1874), 159]). Camus's notebooks are disappointing sites for finding clues to his philosophical development—he rarely reveals his reasoning about philosophical questions in them—but it is of interest that while working on *The Myth of Sisyphus* he refers in the notebooks to reading Nietzsche. There are differences in their approaches here, however. In the *Untimely Meditations*, Nietzsche recognizes that Darwin has shown that we are animals, and he points out that we recognize that animal suffering is pointless (157); the goal of the philosopher, artist, and saint is to make of humanity something super-animal, and in so doing give a meaning to our suffering.

Instead, the early Camus coheres better with Nietzsche's spirit of *amor fati*. Camus's absurd heroes, in *The Myth of Sisyphus*, show heroism by embracing their lives and demanding more life.

During the war, Camus revised his thinking on these matters. In *The Rebel*, Camus endorses the view that there is a human nature, and thus adopts a kind of naturalism along the lines of Aristotle: "Analysis of rebellion leads at least to the suspicion that, contrary to the postulates of contemporary thought, a human nature does exist, as the Greeks believed. Why rebel if there is nothing permanent in oneself worth preserving?" (1956, 16). Indeed, this human nature is revealed to us through the history of our revolt. That we share such a human nature means that there is a fact of the matter about what is better or worse for a human being. It will determine certain human purposes that should be respected. Camus often liked to refer to his views as being rooted in Mediterranean, as opposed to Germanic, philosophy, and this seems indeed true, as his ultimate position is one that is consistent with Aristotle's own. This does not mean that one might not sometimes be plagued by doubts; I hold that Camus remained a fallibilist about purpose throughout his life.

Thus, the primary view of the absurd in *The Myth of Sisyphus*, and the view that explains the consistent concerns of all his work, can be best captured by the following revision of the teleological absurd:

x *is* **teleologically absurd** *if and only if* x *lacks a justified and sufficient purpose.*

A sufficient purpose must be intrinsic, otherwise its justification would rely on the instrumental outcome of the purpose; but not all intrinsic purposes need be justified or sufficient. Although Camus does not make these distinctions, it will greatly clarify his concern with suicide and murder. Suicide stifles one's purposes, but Camus will want to argue that some of those purposes were sufficient reason to go on living.

An important point needs to be made here. One might object that I have missed a distinction: what matters to us is values. A child's death by disease is absurd because we feel the child's death had no value, just as a murder is wrong because it infringes on our values, and so on. But we can understand value in terms of purposes. I have already claimed that we can consistently interpret Camus's account as recognizing that some purposes deserve our respect and the achieving of those purposes is a good deserving of respect. We can add to this interpretation that we value something just in case we have the purpose to respect and to foster that thing.[17] This explanation of value need not be anti-realist: for example, one can claim that something is objectively valuable if the purpose to respect and foster that thing is justified and above all is a purpose that we *ought* to have.

To understand Camus, we must in part understand how his views on the absurd evolved. In *The Myth of Sisyphus*, Camus is exploring the possibility that everything is absurd. He believes that history and the cosmos are both without a purpose. Since we can assert that human history is without a purpose and the cosmos is without a purpose, trivially they have no sufficient purpose, and so human history and the cosmos are both absurd. He considers and does not dismiss the possibility that human life is absurd. But by the time he is writing *The Rebel*, Camus believes that human beings do have justified intrinsic purposes, and some of these are sufficient reason to go on living. This is captured in his new argument against suicide, which I describe in chapter 2.

A CONTRASTING INTERPRETATION

It might be useful to contrast this understanding of Camus's teleological absurd with an alternative one. In an article that responds to Camus's reflections on the absurd, the American philosopher Thomas Nagel offers a view that he presents as corrective of some kind of confusion he ascribes to Camus. His view strikes far from Camus's concerns and fails to offer a plausible alternative interpretation of Camus's work. However, contrasting Nagel's interpretation with our own does offer an insightful distinction.

Nagel begins by claiming that a common form of argument that human life is absurd is not sound. His concern is arguments that depend on such claims as "nothing we do now will matter in a million years" or that "we are tiny specks in the infinite vastness of the universe" (1971, 716 and 717). He claims that because justifications must end, the scale of time involved should not matter. It is interesting that the existentialists had a clear sense that our purposes are essentially temporal; it is for this reason that *Being and Time* concludes with a lengthy analysis of time. But it is sufficient here to note that time scales do matter to the kind of teleological analysis we discussed earlier. A person may have the goal of being a father, and seventy years of life may be sufficient for this, but human beings are also capable of having purposes that extend far in time, past a likely time of death. In such a case, death is an impediment to the realization of those purposes. Camus frequently cites death as an aspect of the absurd for this reason.

But it is another aspect of Nagel's analysis that is more strikingly different. For Nagel, "a situation is absurd when it includes a conspicuous discrepancy between pretension or aspiration and reality: someone gives a complicated speech in support of a motion that has already been passed; a notorious criminal is made president of a major philanthropic foundation; you declare your love over the telephone to a recorded announcement; as you are being knighted, your pants fall down" (718). And, "The sense that life as a whole is absurd arises when we perceive, perhaps dimly, an inflated pretension or aspiration which is inseparable from the continuation of human life and which makes its absurdity inescapable, short of escape from life itself" (718).

Thus, for Nagel, the absurd is a sense of the failure of our lives to live up to some standard that we have. We experience or are aware of the absurd when we take a kind of external or god's-eye view of our lives: "We step back to find that the whole system of justification and criticism, which controls our choices and supports our claims to rationality, rests on responses and habits that we never question" (720). The feeling of the absurd arises "by the collision between the seriousness with which we take our lives and the perpetual possibility of regarding everything about which we are serious as arbitrary, or open to doubt" (719). This has something in common with Heidegger's analysis of *Angst* or Camus's observations about the corrosive "why?" But there is a substantial difference. For Camus, the absurd is not just a product of doubting the entirety of one's system of justifications. Thus, one does not need an external view of all of one's purposes to recognize the absurd. More importantly, Nagel evades the most important issues. For him, something is absurd if it is ridiculous. We laugh—or at least we should laugh—at our folly and pretense. Surely, sometimes we are ridiculous, and perhaps sometimes because of the absurd. But it defies reason to think that the absurd is only the ridiculous.

We can see this by looking to two kinds of examples. First, Nagel argues that the purposes of nonhuman animals cannot be absurd. "A mouse . . . is not absurd, because he lacks the capacities for self-consciousness and self-transcendence that would enable him to see that he is only a mouse" (725). But if the absurd were not dependent on this external, self-transcendent perspective, then a nonhuman animal's life could be absurd. This is precisely the position that Nietzsche adopts in the *Untimely Meditations*. Recognizing that Darwin has shown that human beings are animals, Nietzsche promptly infers that our lives are threatened by the absurd precisely because the lives of animals are often absurd: "More profoundly feeling people have at all times felt sympathy for the animals because they suffer from life and yet do not possess the power to turn the thorn of suffering against itself and to understand their existence metaphysically; one is, indeed, profoundly indignant at the sight of senseless suffering" (1997, 157). Camus does not discuss the purposes of nonhuman animals, but his teleology is closer to Nietzsche's than to Nagel's. An animal's suffering will be absurd if it is not in the service of a justified and sufficient purpose.

Second, a more serious break concerns the status of human suffering. We can illustrate this when we consider an important scene from *The Plague*. In a climactic passage of the novel, a young child dies of the plague while the protagonists of the novel look on, doing their best to try to save the child but unable to do so. The scene is horrific and compelling. One of those present at the death is a priest of the city who had previously preached that the plague was a punishment that the city residents had earned through their impiety. The narrator, Dr. Rieux, in an unusual loss of his temper, angrily tells the priest after the child dies, "That child, anyhow, was innocent, and you know it as well as I do" (1991b, 218). The point is clear: the child's death was not a cosmic punishment. There is no purpose to this child's death. It is absurd. But it cannot be absurd, on Nagel's view, unless we somehow adopt the external transcendent view on our own lives or the life of the child: "absurdity is one of the most human things about us: a manifestation of our most advanced and interesting characteristics. Like skepticism in epistemology, it is possible only because we possess a certain kind of insight—the capacity to transcend ourselves in thought" (1971, 727). And, furthermore, presumably we should recognize our human pretensions in the child's death, as if it were ridiculous to desperately hope he will live.

But there is no issue of such transcendence in this case. We do not need to entertain some kind of super-human perspective to recognize the absurdity of a child's death. We feel it from a perspective well ensconced in our everyday lives and concerns. And there is nothing ridiculous about our sorrow at his suffering and at the loss of his life. As Camus puts it in *The Rebel*, "It is not the suffering of a child, which is repugnant in itself, but the fact that the suffering is not justified" (1956, 101).

Nagel uses his denuded notion of the absurd to criticize Camus:

> Camus—not on uniformly good grounds—rejects suicide and the other solutions he regards as escapist. What he recommends is defiance or scorn. We can salvage our dignity, he appears to believe, by shaking a fist at the world which is deaf to our pleas, and continuing to live in spite of it. . . . This seems to me romantic and slightly self-pitying. (1971, 726)

The reference to scorn is to Camus's claim in the ultimate section of *The Myth of Sisyphus*, where—referring to the victory of Sisyphus over his fate—Camus says, "There is no fate that cannot be surmounted by scorn" (1991a, 121). We see here a notion that is consistent throughout Camus's work: that we can revolt against our fate, and in that way achieve a kind of victory over it. By counseling scorn, Camus is not recommending that we go about with our teeth clenched. A charitable reading makes this obvious.

In his novel *The Plague*, for example, Camus offers a new vision of the absurd hero: this hero does his best to try to promote human flourishing, working in solidarity with other human beings. The absurd hero opposes that which does harm to human beings, even when such efforts are of uncertain efficacy. The scorn is demonstrated through a strength of conviction. It is a refusal to submit to despair. Dr. Rieux, the absurd hero of *The Plague*, expresses this scorn when he is asked by his friend Tarrou whether he believes in God.

> Rieux said that he'd already answered: that if he believed in an all-powerful God he would cease curing the sick and leave that to Him. But no one in the world believed in a God of that sort; no, not even Paneloux, who believed that he believed in such a God. And this was proved by the fact that no one ever threw himself on Providence completely. Anyhow, in this respect Rieux believed himself to be on the right road—in fighting against creation as he found it.
>
> "Ah," Tarrou remarked. "So that's the idea you have of your profession?"
>
> "More or less." (1991b, 127)

Note here that Rieux sees the practice of medicine as his "scorn," his rebellion against creation. For creation harms human purposes—for example, by breeding diseases that kill us, kill even children, for no purpose. To oppose this, to try to protect human purposes, even when one is very unlikely to succeed, is a kind of revolt that asserts our purposes against a universe indifferent to those purposes. Nagel is thus in error when he suggests that by the "absurd," Camus does, or should, mean what Nagel does. They have different and largely incompatible conceptions.

Their solutions are also different. In place of scorn, Nagel claims the right attitude is irony. Philosophers sometimes distinguish between a straight solution to a problem and a skeptical solution. A skeptical "solution" to a problem is in fact is not a solution but rather a claim that there is no solution but we can live with the problem. The stance of irony—too often a temptation in twentieth-century philosophy—is a skeptical solution. Nagel is arguing that there is no solution to the absurd, but we can live with it, although we are changed by feeling now a certain potential distance from our lives. Camus is not tempted by this move. All his work is an attempt to see how we might better understand and respond to the absurd. The issue is urgent: he believes that dangerous political theories were sometimes motivated by the recognition of or reaction to the absurd, and sometimes these theories justified mass murder. (We will see this discussed in the next section, where in the fourth "Letter to a German Friend" Camus in part conceives of the struggle with the absurd as an ethical requirement.) If we see the problem in this way, then to counsel irony toward the death of a child or against fascism or against communism is self-satisfied and unsympathetic—and it is bad philosophy. One can excuse Nagel as perhaps not agreeing with Camus about the effects of the absurd, but we must recognize that he at best egregiously misunderstands Camus.

CAMUS'S CHANGING VIEWS OF THE ABSURD

Camus reiterated that *The Myth of Sisyphus* was an experiment, a work in progress, an attempt at starting on a certain problem. He was impatient with the fact that few seemed to take him at his word about the preliminary and provisional nature of the text. He wrote in his review of *Nausea* in 1938, and thus years before the publication of *The Myth of Sisyphus*, that "The realization that life is absurd cannot be an end, but only a beginning" (1970, 201), and more than a decade later (1950) he reiterated the point: "What is the point of saying yet again that in the experience which interested me, and which I happened to write about, the absurd can be considered only as a point of departure. . . . In the same manner, with all due sense of proportion, Cartesian doubt, which is systematic, was not enough to make Descartes a skeptic" (1970, 159). True to this claim that it is a starting point, Camus's views on the absurd changed during his lifetime.

The distinctions between the senses of "absurd" in Camus's work were overlooked by his contemporaries. In a passage that is likely meant to react to Camus, Beauvoir describes the absurd as a property of "existence," and then she contrasts it with her own view about "ambiguity": "To declare that existence is absurd is to deny that it can ever be given a meaning [*sens*]; to say that it is ambiguous is to assert that its meaning is never fixed, that it must be constantly won" (1948 [1947], 129). Since Beauvoir goes on to claim that "Absurdity challenges every ethics," we can be certain that it is purpose that is her reference here for "meaning [*sens*]." If she means to attack Camus's notion of the absurd, she here misinterprets it—or, rather, she refers only to one view that he experiments with in *The Myth of Sisyphus*. Presumably, she uses "existence" here in the technical sense of Heidegger and the other existentialists, to refer to the being of humans (see Heidegger 1962, 33). (For the existentialists, "existence" referred to the kind of being that is had by beings like us, who make decisions and can question themselves; on such a usage, tables and chairs have being but not existence.) In that case, Camus's later view, expressed quite clearly shortly after Beauvoir wrote this, is that human beings do have justified and sufficient purposes. In any case, this account of the absurd is not the one Camus has by the time he is writing *The Rebel*.

There are two notable changes in Camus's philosophy from *The Myth of Sisyphus* to *The Rebel*. The first was a new recognition of the dangerous implications of believing that the world is teleologically absurd. The second is a renewed concern with ethics, and in particular with justifications of violence. But throughout these changes, his central goal remains the same: to find a way to best live once we recognize the teleological absurd. Thus, both the changes and the continuity in his views concern the teleological absurd. Furthermore, the other uses of the absurd that I have described can be explained in terms of the teleological absurd: the feeling of the absurd comes when we recognize the teleological absurd; the confrontation between our longing for purpose and a purposeless universe is a confrontation with the teleological absurd; and the sense that we lack the right kind of teleofunctional explanations arises because of the teleological absurd.

In *The Myth of Sisyphus*, Camus's proposal for how to live in the absurd tension, and wage metaphysical revolt, is a proposal that he later abandons. It is an ethic of maximizing human experience: "But what does life mean in such a universe? Nothing else for the moment but indifference to the future and a desire to use up everything that is given. Belief in the meaning of life always implies a scale of values, a choice, our preferences. Belief in the absurd, according to our definitions, teaches the contrary" (1991a, 60). To live in this tension, avoiding both hope and despair, Camus suggests that, if there is no right direction for our lives, then we can instead settle for more life. "Knowing whether or not one can live *without appeal* is all that interests me. I do not want to get out of my depth. This aspect of life being given me, can I adapt myself to it? Now, faced with this particular concern, belief in the absurd is tantamount to substituting the quantity of experiences for the quality" (1991a, 60). In *The Myth of Sisyphus*, Camus holds up Don Juan as a possible example of an absurd hero. Don Juan seeks not some form of transcendental love, which can be a self-justifying purpose, but rather to maximize the quantity of sexual experiences that he has.[18]

But, interestingly, the beginnings of the rejection of this proposal were already present in Camus's early work. In an early play (Camus wrote a first version when he was in his early twenties, and the first production was in 1945), Camus portrays the infamous Roman emperor Caligula as an existential hero in the mold of Don Juan. Caligula is tormented by a sense of purposelessness, and as a result he tries to find a purpose in overthrowing deeply held moral conventions. He murders and tortures with impunity. Here we can see the seeds of the philosophical position that Camus ultimately articulates in *The Rebel*. Caligula is miserable: his seeking of a life without limits leads to torment for everyone, including himself. He longs for something impossible to happen—and to force an impossible event, he even demands that his servant Helicon bring him the moon—because he fancies this would somehow give him a new freedom. Furthermore, he imagines that if he could discover some impossibility, it would absolve his crimes against others. But nothing impossible does happen. In the final scene of the play, before he is assassinated, he looks at himself in the mirror and soliloquizes:

> The impossible! I've searched for it at the confines of the world, in the secret places of my heart. I've stretched out my hands; see, I stretch out my hands, but it's always you I find, you only, confronting me, and I've come to hate you. I have chosen a wrong path, a path that leads to nothing. My freedom isn't the right one. . . . Nothing, nothing yet. Oh, how oppressive is this darkness! Helicon has not come; we shall be forever guilty. (1958, 73)

The ethic of quantity over quality, Camus already suspected, is a failure.[19]

In *The Rebel*, Camus identifies metaphysical revolt as another way to live in the absurd tension, in which we honestly recognize that the universe and history are absurd but we strive to foster human purposes in this inhospitable world. Metaphysical revolt can lead to excesses, as we see in *Caligula*, but when pursued in moderation (with *mesure*) it is the assertion of our dignity in an absurd universe.

This change in Camus's work was a consequence of the war: Camus is explicit that his experience during the Nazi occupation, and in support of the opposition, transformed his views. Or, given that he repeatedly insists that *The Myth of Sisyphus* was a kind of experiment and starting effort, perhaps it is better to say that during the war he clarified and developed his view. In the fourth of his letters addressed to a "German friend" (Camus published the first three in the underground paper *Combat*; the fourth was only published later), he writes, "For a long time we both thought that this world had no ultimate meaning and that consequently we were cheated" (1995 [1944], 27). But what are the consequences of this embrace of the teleological absurd? His German friend draws from it an ethical nihilism: "You never believed in the meaning of this world, and you therefore deduced the idea that everything was equivalent and that good and evil could be defined according to one's wishes" (27). This justifies the violence of Nazism: "You supposed that in absence of any human or divine code the only values were those of the animal world—in other words, violence and cunning. Hence you concluded that man was negligible and that his soul could be killed" (27). Here Camus is addressing one possible interpretation of his own embrace of the absurd. But he is clear that his experience of the evils of the occupation lead him to reason that some rejection of those evils must be fundamental.

> You chose injustice. . . . I, on the contrary, chose justice in order to remain faithful to the world. I continue to believe that this world has no ultimate meaning. But I know that something in it has a meaning and that is man, because he is the only creature to insist on having one. This world has at least the truth of man, and our task is to provide its justifications against fate itself. And it has no justification but man; hence he must be saved if we want to save the idea we have of life. (28)

In this one passage, we can see both the continuity in Camus's concerns and also the change in his perspective. His thinking remains focused on the question of what it means to live in an absurd universe. But Camus's revulsion at the evils of the war commit him to grappling with how to argue that the absurd does not entail a rejection of any possible ethics. He also adopts a newly explicit refinement of his views on what is absurd: the universe and history are teleologically absurd, but human life is not.

In his unsent reply to Sartre's open letter criticizing *The Rebel*, Camus calls this change in his work a "discovery," and he adds, "As for me having lived for a long time without morality, like many men of my generation, and having actually advocated nihilism although not always knowingly, I then understood that ideas were not only emotionally moving or pleasant sounding games, and that, on certain occasions, to accept certain thoughts amounted to accepting murder without limits" (2004 [ca. 1952], 207).[20]

Both the change in Camus's views and his enduring central concern are evident in the introduction to *The Rebel*, where he constructs a new argument against suicide. There we see him grappling with the question of how to live in an absurd universe, but also utilizing his new conviction that human beings have intrinsic purposes. I reconstruct this argument in chapter 2; this shows how the teleological interpretation of the absurd allows for a clear and consistent understanding of his philosophical project over time. To illustrate both this continuity of Camus's thought and the power of the concept of the teleological absurd, I shall show that Camus's final argument against suicide is valid, and plausibly it is sound.

TWO

Suicide and Murder

THE NEW ARGUMENT AGAINST SUICIDE

In chapter 1, we saw how Camus's primary use of the term "absurd" concerned the teleological absurd. This allows for a clarification of his concerns and his arguments. We can best illustrate this by showing how it allows us to clarify Camus's revised argument against suicide. This argument provides the foundation of Camus's argument against murder and political violence, and his efforts to develop an ethic from minimal presuppositions. We can contrast his own efforts in this regard with those efforts of Beauvoir and Sartre to pursue a similar project.

In the introduction to *The Rebel*, Camus returns to the problem that was the main theme of *The Myth of Sisyphus*. The rest of *The Rebel* is concerned with the questions of when revolt is justified and how revolt can lead to revolution. But Camus begins with a reassessment of his starting place. He has a new argument, based on the insight that he expressed in the fourth "Letter to a German Friend." This will in turn prove essential to his argument against murder. In *The Rebel*, Camus writes,

> The final conclusion of absurdist reasoning is, in fact, the repudiation of suicide and the acceptance of the desperate encounter between human inquiry and the silence of the universe. Suicide would mean the end of this encounter, and absurdist reasoning considers that it could not consent to this without negating its own premises. . . . But

it is obvious that absurdism hereby admits that human life is the only necessary good since it is precisely life that makes this encounter possible and since, without life, the absurdist wager would have no basis. (1956 [1951], 6)[1]

The first part of this is a reiteration of his idea, expressed in *The Myth of Sisyphus*, that we should live in the absurd tension. But there is a novel addition to the argument, one that Camus sees as a *reductio ad absurdum* akin to Descartes's argument from doubt. Camus repeatedly returns to this idea that his argument is "the equivalent, in existence, of Descartes's methodical doubt" (1956, 8).

Critics have not taken this parallel with Descartes seriously enough. Descartes's argument is concerned with epistemology; Camus is concerned with general teleology. But the analogy is deep, because epistemology is concerned with teleological questions. Descartes is trying to identify what we *should* believe. Camus is trying to identify what purposes we have, which is to say, what, for each of us, we *should* do. Justification of knowledge claims or of purpose claims can have a similar logical structure.

Descartes's method is one of radical doubt about knowing. He supposes, for the sake of argument, a worst-case scenario: an intelligence with power over his perceptions is deceiving him. What he sees, and perhaps even what he remembers and believes, is being controlled by this deceiver. But then is there anything left that one can know with certainty? Descartes's first indubitable belief that he identifies is that he exists. In the *Meditations*, Descartes does not explicitly state his argument as a *reductio ad absurdum*, but his seventh principle in the *Principles of Philosophy* does so.

> In rejecting—and even imagining to be false—everything which we can in any way doubt, it is easy for us to suppose that there is no God and no heaven, and that there are no bodies, and even that we ourselves have no hands or feet, or indeed any body at all. But we cannot for all that suppose that we, who are having such thoughts, are nothing. For it is a contradiction to suppose that what thinks does not, at the very time when it is thinking, exist. Accordingly, this piece of knowledge—*I am thinking, therefore I exist*—is the first and most

certain of all to occur to anyone who philosophizes in an orderly way. (1985 [1644], 194–95)

We can reconstruct the argument for clarity:

Argument 3
1. A is deceived about everything. (Supposition)
2. If A is deceived about everything, then A is deceived in the belief that A exists. (Premise)
3. If A is deceived in the belief that A exists, then it is not the case that A exists. (Premise)
4. A is deceived in the belief that A exists. (Modus Ponens, 1, 2)
5. If A is deceived about everything, then A exists. (Premise)
6. A exists. (Modus Ponens, 5, 1)
7. It is not the case that A exists. (Modus Ponens 3, 4)

We have a contradiction, and we conclude that the error is in line 1: there is at least one thing about which the philosopher cannot be deceived.

How can Camus's implicit argument be similar? The problem for Camus, as he describes it in the introduction to *The Rebel* and earlier in the fourth "Letter to a German Friend," is that recognition that the universe and history are absurd would seem to suggest that we have no reason to be for or against suicide or murder. For example, traditional Christian views entail that suicide is a sin because it destroys human life, which has value because made in the image of God, and because for this reason God values that life. The basic presumption was that our purposes should serve God's purposes, and suicide would be contrary to this. God is thus essential to the value theory in question (God provides all the unity of purposes). A Christian might well conclude that absurdism permits suicide since the universe is absurd if God (as the Christian understands it) does not exist. A Christian could be expected to demand: what could forbid, or speak against, suicide, if God does not exist? And, as I argued in chapter 1, I think this view is shared by the atheist existentialists. In his letter defending *The Rebel*, Camus expresses such a problem as, "Can one, from negation itself and the revolt that it presupposes, draw a rule of life? Can one without recourse to absolute principles escape from a logic of destruction and rediscover, at the level of humiliated man, a promise of pride and fertility?" (2004, 208). Earlier (in his journals in 1943) he put the problem as, "*Can man alone create his own values? That is the whole problem*" (1978, 94).

A point of clarification is required. Many motives for suicide are possible; one might commit suicide to prevent an interrogation, for example; or one might commit suicide to save others in a battle, or commit suicide to end terrible and otherwise continuous pain. Such suicides would not be motivated by the absurd because each of these kinds of suicide would have a purpose that is not revolt against the absurd. Let us call a suicide an "absurd suicide" only if the suicide is motivated by the true conviction that one's life is teleologically absurd. Absurd suicide is thus done *because* of this recognition of the absurd: "Dying voluntarily implies that you have recognized, even instinctively, the ridiculous character of that habit [of living], the absence of any profound reason for living, the insane character of that daily agitation, and the uselessness of suffering" (1991a, 5–6).[2]

But if absurd suicide is a suicide committed in reaction to an absurd universe, what is the *motive* for such an act? To be motivated to be an absurd suicide, one must act in the conviction that suicide is a kind of response to the absurd. The act is a rejection. But then the agent must have the conviction that the thing being rejected is, in some sense, wrong. That is, the individual must have the conviction that the world *should not* be absurd. In his journals, years earlier, Camus put it thus: "But the suicide is selfish too: puts forward a value that seems to him more important than his own life—it's the feeling of that respectable and happy life of which he has been deprived" (1978 [1943], 94). In *The Rebel*, he makes a similar point: "If the world is a matter of indifference to the man who commits suicide, it is because he has an idea of something that is not or could not be indifferent to him"; and if he does commits suicide, then "from this act of self-destruction itself a value arises which, perhaps, might have made it worth while to live" (1956, 7).

The agent, then, acts in the conviction that the world is absurd, but that there should be at least some relevant kind of purpose, such as a sufficient purpose of one's own.[3] From this, Camus claims that absurd suicide is contradictory. As stated, the argument must be an enthymeme. What then are the missing premises? Camus implicitly assumes that if there should be some justified and sufficient purpose, as the absurd suicide asserts by his action, then there is a kind of justified and sufficient purpose: namely, the goal of having a justified and sufficient purpose. This was the claim made in the fourth "Letter": human beings are the creatures that insist on having a purpose, and they have purpose *because* of this insistence. Thus, in committing suicide in the conviction that there is no justified and sufficient purpose, the absurd suicide demonstrates that at least one kind of justified and sufficient purpose exists: his purpose to seek and demand a justified and sufficient purpose. As Camus puts it in his journals in 1942, "Value judgments cannot be suppressed *absolutely*. That negates the absurd" (1978, 66).

Camus is correct to see similarities between his reasoning and Descartes's. Descartes's radical doubt washes away poorly founded beliefs. In contrast, Camus doubts not knowledge but rather whether we have any justified and sufficient purposes. Camus uses radical nihilism as the corrosive that he will apply in his test. He will look at each potential human purpose with doubt about whether we have such a purpose, or whether such a purpose is intrinsic or justified or sufficient. Descartes asked, can universal doubt leave behind any belief? And Camus asks, can universal nihilism leave behind any purpose?

What Camus saw in the evil of Nazism is a nihilism that is only "halfway." His letter to Sartre defending *The Rebel* states:

> There is but a single nihilism, under different guises, for which we are all responsible and from which we can free ourselves only by accepting it with all its contradictions. I will go even further here and say that nihilism is defined less by negation than by the affirmation of a privileged negation that rejects any other kind of negation. It is at the place of the most extreme tension, on the contrary, at the precise frontier where nihilism is turned against itself, and upon which my study is focused, that the contradiction becomes fruitful and makes progress possible. (2004, 209)

These remarks are difficult to understand in the context of his reply to Sartre, but in a close reading of *The Rebel* and his earlier works, they become clear. Nihilism (in this context, the denial that we have justified and sufficient purposes) seems to offer no reasons to contradict suicide or murder. But this is what he is calling "privileged negation." It is privileged because it ignores other facts. If instead we include an additional minimal observation about human being, we will uncover another negation, a contradiction. And this additional observation is that human beings innately strive for, long for, and need a justified and sufficient purpose.

Thus, the motive and cause of the project of *The Rebel* includes to seek out and identify a justified and sufficient purpose that can survive our observations about the absurdity of history and the universe. But wanting to identify the right kind of purpose is thus itself a justified and sufficient purpose. So if we conclude, in light of our demand for a purpose, that we have no justified and sufficient purpose, we have contradicted ourselves. We have the justified and sufficient purpose of seeking a justified and sufficient purpose, and if we deny that we have any such purpose, we have contradicted the fact that the very demand we are making is itself an expression of a justified and sufficient purpose.

We can reconstruct the argument like this:

Argument 4
1. *A* commits absurd suicide. (Supposition)
2. If *A* commits absurd suicide, then *A* wants to have a justified and sufficient purpose. (Premise)
3. If *A* commits absurd suicide, then it is not the case that *A* has a justified and sufficient purpose. (By definition of "absurd suicide")
4. *A* wants to have a justified and sufficient purpose. (Modus Ponens, 1, 2)
5. If someone wants to have a justified and sufficient purpose, then that is a justified and sufficient purpose. (Premise)
6. *A* has a justified and sufficient purpose. (Instantiation of 5, Modus Ponens with 4)
7. It is not the case that *A* has a justified and sufficient purpose. (Modus Ponens 3, 1)

We can conclude that the suicide of *A* is not absurd; rather, it is a kind of mistake. The distinction that I drew between purposes and justified and sufficient purposes becomes relevant at this point. This argument would still be valid if we replaced "justified and sufficient purpose" with merely "purpose." However, it would be far less plausible that the resulting argument is sound. It seems easy to think of purposes, even intrinsic purposes, that one could argue are not sufficient reason to go on living. I may have the purpose to get a drink of water because of innate features of human biology, but it seems that this intrinsic purpose would be insufficient to answer the question posed at the beginning of *The Myth of Sisyphus*. To avert this objection, we need that the purposes in question are justified and sufficient.

The most tentative claim of Camus's argument as reconstructed is the premise at line 5. It may be that Camus simply has to take premise 5 as an axiom. However, we can offer some defense of premise 5 by (1) establishing that we have a purpose to find a justified and sufficient purpose, and then by showing that this purpose is plausibly both (2) justified and (3) sufficient.

(1) We can note that reflection on the nature of a person as understood by Camus offers reason to believe that we are partly constituted by our search for a purpose that is justified and sufficient. There is a common view of purposes that sees them as additional features of a human being. That is, on one view, we can imagine a person having different purposes, and they are still the same person regardless of the purposes that they have—if their purposes change, something would remain that was still the same person. Furthermore, if they had no purposes, they would still be the same person. In one sense, this is not the view of the existentialists. For the existentialist philosophers, a person's purposes are essential to what he is. Heidegger writes that

> Dasein is an entity for which, in its Being, that Being is an issue. The phrase "is an issue" has been made plain in the state-of-Being of understanding—of understanding as self-projective Being towards its ownmost potentiality-for-Being. This potentiality is that for the sake of which any Dasein is as it is. In each case Dasein has already compared itself, in its Being, with a possibility of itself. . . . But ontologically, Being towards one's ownmost potentiality-for-Being means that in each case Dasein is already *ahead* of itself in its Being. Dasein is always "beyond itself," not as a way of behaving towards other entities

which it is *not*, but as Being towards the potentiality-for-Being which it is itself. (1962, 236 [191–92])

On this view, Dasein is essentially constituted by its relation to its purposes, its projects. Similar, for Sartre and Beauvoir, the for-itself has no relevant positive properties, but we can interpret its facticity based on the choices that it makes or the situation in which it exists, and these choices are the expression and formation of purposes and nothing about the situation in which it exists can make it less free. A person strives to be something, therefore, through having purposes. An alternative to this view is one for which a human being is constituted by his purposes but these are not merely chosen; some of them are inherited. Camus was not an existentialist, and instead he believed some of our purposes are inherited. But, like the existentialists (and like Aristotle), Camus believes that our purposes constitute what we are. He also defends the purpose of having a purpose as essential to the kind of beings we are. To believe yourself as absurd is contradictory:

> It is contradictory in its content because, in wanting to uphold life, it excludes all value judgments, when to live is, in itself, a value judgement. To breathe is to judge. Perhaps it is untrue to say that life is a perpetual choice. But it is true that it is impossible to imagine a life deprived of all choice. From this simplified point of view, the absurdist position, translated into action, is inconceivable. (1956, 8)

It seems reasonable that this search for a purpose is a search for a justified and sufficient purpose. Then, in living and making the choices that constitute living, we are asserting that the search for a justified and sufficient purpose is essential to the kinds of beings we are. Camus makes similar observations about the innate purposes of human beings in *The Myth of Sisyphus*, where he writes, "The body's judgment is as good as the mind's, and the body shrinks from annihilation" (1991a, 8). The search for a justified and sufficient purpose thus in part constitutes living. By the time of *The Rebel*, Camus has a view similar to Aristotle's: he believes we have a human nature that entails we have certain purposes; these are not all merely chosen, but rather many are inherited in some sense. For both

Aristotle and the later Camus, our purposes make us what we are. Human nature requires us to choose actions, and activity arises from and expresses our purposes. For this reason, if we share as an essential part of ourselves the purpose of having a justified and sufficient purpose, this purpose will go to partly constituting the very kind of being that we are. To deny it is to deny our nature.

(2) Given that we have the purpose of finding a justified and sufficient purpose, is this purpose itself justified? By the argument above and simplification, we have the purpose to find a justified purpose. Then consider an analogy with epistemology. Suppose one has the purpose of identifying and believing claims that have passed various tests qualifying them as being useful (our equivalent of being justified) and these claims are worthy of continued use (our equivalent of sufficient). Is this purpose itself useful? We can imagine someone saying no, but that seems to undermine the epistemic criteria themselves. It is to say: yes, you have the purpose of finding useful information, but this purpose is not itself useful. At best, if such a position is coherent, it seems analogous to a claim like this: the scientific method is dubious because it is not itself a product of the scientific method. I don't know if the scientific method is a product of the scientific method, but if this claim is to be entertained, I would want to argue that there are deep analogies between the scientific method and our reasons for adopting the scientific method, such that they reinforce each other. Similarly, it seems strange that there could be justified purposes but that our search for those purposes is not itself justified. Remember that "justified" here means stands up to criticism and questioning. If I have as a purpose to find purposes that stand up to questioning, and there are such purposes and I find them because of this purpose, then the purpose that led to the finding of those justified purposes is itself justified by the fact that it leads to this finding. Just as the scientific method is justified by its success.

(3) What about a sufficient purpose? Again, by our first argument above and simplification, we have the purpose to find a sufficient purpose. Camus has observed that we have the innate inclination to go on living, but we also want a reason sufficient to explain and even reinforce this inclination. Consider a case where a person identifies a sufficient purpose, and this is because of the purpose of finding a sufficient purpose. Here also, it seems paradoxical that the thing which resulted in finding the suf-

ficient purpose is not itself sufficient. Perhaps we can say that the purpose to find a sufficient purpose is not sufficient if it fails. But the search for a sufficient purpose often succeeds; few if any people commit absurd suicide. Thus, the purpose to find a sufficient purpose is indeed sufficient *because* it may succeed. That is, if you have this purpose, then there is a significant probability that you will find a sufficient purpose, and this should then give you reason to continue to live.

INTERNALISM

Does Camus's argument offer us motive not to kill ourselves over the absurdity of the universe? That is, should the recognition that we have some justified and sufficient purpose be expected to stop suicide? Recall the criterion for a sufficient purpose: it gives one reason to go on living. Suppose, then, that one has a reason to go on living. Should we expect that having a reason to go on living will make one reject absurd suicide? To answer this, we must understand what Camus's assumptions reveal about his understanding of the link between reason and motivation, and we must evaluate this understanding.

In ethics and in moral psychology, philosophers use the term "internalism" to refer to the idea that belief that one ought to do something is a motive to do that thing. We can also extend it: if one has a reason to do X, then one has a motive to do X (equivalently, we assume reason to avoid X is motive to avoid X). Here I take "motive" as a primitive referring to a motivational state of the organism that can influence the behavior of the organism; we assume a motive to do X increases the likelihood of doing X. There are several versions of internalism, but most of them share this basic form. In the case of the argument against suicide: the argument leads us to recognize we have a sufficient purpose, and if we are aware of the sufficient purpose then we have reason to go on living. And (assuming internalism) if we are aware that we have reason to go on living, then we are motivated by this reason to go on living.

Several defenses of internalism are implicit in Camus's discussion. First, Camus makes reference to the implicit values expressed in our reasoning and our questioning. In asking the question, "Why not kill myself because the universe is absurd?," one is expressing a commitment to being guided by reason. Questions ask for answers, and their answers come through reason; we commit to reason when we ask a question. Camus goes further: to ask such a question is to be motivated by reason. That is, one has already committed to a kind of judgment and a kind of intellectual integrity in asking the question. This commitment then means that one is motivated by reason and by what reason reveals.

Second, Camus's later view includes that reasoning is also a part of human nature, but he already comes close to this claim in *The Myth of Sisyphus*. There, he writes, "I said that the world is absurd, but I was too hasty. This world in itself is not reasonable, that is all that can be said. But what is absurd is the confrontation of this irrational and the wild longing for clarity whose call echoes in the human heart" (1991a, 21). Remember that (as I argue in chapter 1) we must understand this demand for "clarity" as a demand for an understanding of the universe (or, at least, of relevant parts of our experience) in terms of purposes. The absurd, in the sense of the experience we have in encountering a purposeless world, essentially requires our expectation that the world (or some part of our experience) has purpose. The experience of the absurd is available to all human beings; in claiming this, Camus is also claiming that all human beings want the world (or some part of their experience) to answer to reason, in the sense of answering to an understanding in terms of purposes.

Thus, in this quote, the word "reason" is being used in a normative sense. To ask that the world be reasonable is to ask both that it have recognizable patterns and also that we are able to see purpose in those patterns, or at least we are able to relate those patterns to our own purposes in certain ways. As we already noted, Camus is not denying that, for example, science can describe the world successfully; this does not even seem to concern him. Rather, the world that science reveals is indifferent to our purposes and is itself without purpose. "If man realized that the universe like him can love and suffer, he would be reconciled" (1991a, 17). But what science reveals is that much of the physical universe can be explained without purposes.

For Camus, human beings long for an understanding of their lives and environment that explains these through reason and also purposes. This includes in part that they want their lives to answer to reason and purposes. This then includes the motive to be guided by reason. Even absurd suicide is a result of a kind of reasoning—it includes as a presupposition that one should be guided by reason.

Third, another form of internalism that Camus recognizes might be called coherent internalism. It is a brute fact that we have certain motivations. As we noted above, one of these is a motivation to continue living ("The body's judgment is as good as the mind's, and the body shrinks from annihilation"). Camus ascribes this partly to habit: "We get into the habit of living before acquiring the habit of thinking" (1991a, 8). Camus could have added here that we not only have a habit of wanting to live, but that this is a natural or inherent trait of human nature. Such in fact is his later view. Thus, if we reason that we should go on living, this will cohere with the other motives that we already have to go on living. If we prefer such coherence, then the reasons should motivate us.

Fourth, the most important defense Camus can offer of his assumption of some form of internalism is his purpose in writing *The Rebel*. His main concern is to address what he calls "logical murder," this is, the mass murder we saw committed by Stalin and others like him. The essential and distinguishing point of these murders is that they are motivated and justified by philosophical theories. In his essay "In Defense of *The Rebel*" he writes, "I learned that crime, far from having been given birth and burning in a criminal soul only to be immediately extinguished, could justify itself, turning its theoretical system into a powerful force, spreading its adherents around the world, ultimately conquering and ruling" (2004, 205). That is, criminals who do evil out of passion are limited; their influence and the scope of their activity is small and tends to burn out. But there are criminals who use philosophy to spread and perpetuate their evil. Their use of philosophical theories is precisely what distinguishes them. Stalin is one such criminal. Thus, Camus is writing in reply to those who have already committed to justifying their actions through reason. Those he calls "assassins in judges' robes" are already assuming that reason should guide action since they use theory to justify their motive to murder. Also, this logical murder is a kind of murder that scales, that leads to thousands killing millions. Perhaps some who have listened to the justification of murder, claiming to be guided by reason, can hear alternative arguments. And, in any case, we the readers of *The Rebel* would not pick up such a book if we were not open to being guided by reason.

WHY IS MURDER WRONG?

How does Camus reason from his claim that you should not commit absurd suicide to the claim that the absurd does not justify, or permit, murder? He uses one of the oldest tools in ethical reasoning as it has been developed by philosophers: he observes that the reasoning against killing yourself applies just as well to the question of killing another. That is, he appeals to reason again, now in the form of generalization. Like many philosophers before him, he observes that singling out one's self for respect but not applying the same reasoning to other human beings who are otherwise in the relevant ways identical would be contradictory. "From the moment that life is recognized as good, it becomes good for all men" (1956, 6). All humans have the innate longing for a justified and sufficient purpose; this justified and sufficient purpose deserves our respect and should not be undone by the end of that human life, and so all human beings should be treated with this respect and neither kill themselves nor be killed.

Those who are moved by the argument against suicide have already committed to being guided by reasoning. Thus, the reasoning from rejecting suicide to rejecting murder is sound: The argument against suicide offered no morally significant reason to distinguish one's own self from others. A basic commitment to consistency will then require that we treat others as we would treat ourselves.

At the close of his introduction to *The Rebel*, Camus develops another argument for extending our concern for ourselves to a concern for others. He summarizes this with the phrase, "I rebel—therefore we exist" (22). This is somewhat misleading, presumably because he wanted a nice parallel with Descartes claim, "I think, therefore I am." But in the context the meaning is relatively clear. We should remember two things for context: his notion of revolt, and his addition to his argument of the claim that there is a universal human nature. If I revolt against some injustice, I am asserting a value and at the same time I may be discovering a part of my own human nature. Camus claims that this human nature is universal and is invariant over great spans of time (he actually calls it "eternal"). Thus, in revolt, I assert both a value of my own but also a value of yours since you share that human nature. If I revolt against an assault on my dignity, for example, then I am discovering and asserting that some sense of dignity is a universal need for all human beings. And, as a result, I am also now recognizing your own need for dignity. Since we are partly constituted by our purposes, by asserting my purposes I am discovering and asserting who I am, but also who you are.

Camus considers, in this context, the claim of the philosopher Max Scheler, who, following Nietzsche, argues that revolt is generally motivated by *ressentiment*. Here the French term is used with a somewhat technical understanding: resentment of one's superiors. Thus, for Scheler, revolt arises from envy and resentment of one's betters. This kind of revolt is motivated by a desire to reduce the greatness of our betters, for one's own personal satisfaction (this may be an instance of what I call a "negative-sum strategy" in chapter 6). Camus does not deny that *ressentiment* sometimes causes political action, and he grants that the long quote from the Roman Tertullian that Nietzsche gives in his book *A Genealogy of Morals* is indeed an example of *ressentiment*. However, that is not revolt as Camus defines it. The rebel is not asserting some negation—he is not seeking to drag down the person who oppresses him—but rather he is asserting his own value. A suffragette demanding the vote, for example, is in revolt in part because she is not seeking to take the vote away from others. Furthermore, some people revolt against injustices committed against others; that cannot be because of *ressentiment*.

This is nearly enough for Camus. His concern is not to develop a theory of ethics of the kind that would satisfy a philosopher. Rather, he wants to defend his idea that revolt leads us to self-understanding and to moral progress, but more importantly he wants to analyze how revolt can decline into violent revolution. We will consider in the next three chapters this theory of revolt, but in brief summary: Camus's view is that human beings are driven to revolt when something conflicts with their human nature. This conflict may arise from the absurd indifference of the universe—as seen, for example, in a plague. In this case, he calls the reaction "metaphysical revolt." Or the conflict may concern human actions. In this case, he calls the response "historical revolt." All moral progress, on his view, comes from revolt, from human beings asserting their purposes in an inhospitable and purposeless universe and history. This assertion is also a kind of assertion of equality. Not for universal equality of all conditions, nor equality of outcomes, but rather equality in respect for these shared human values (which he recognizes will often result in rights that should be universal). Most importantly, Camus claims that the best explanation of revolt is that we have a human nature (1956, 16).

All of this results in an intriguing additional parallel with Descartes cogito argument in *The Meditations*. Descartes makes minimal use of his proof that he exists. The bulk of his results come from his attempt to prove that a benevolent God exists, and then to infer that this God would not give us deceiving senses and capabilities. From this Descartes derives a theory that we can rely (within limits) on our senses. Similarly, Camus will derive little directly from his argument against suicide. Instead, the bulk of his results will come from his assumption that there is a human nature, which is stable, coherent, and shared among human beings.

Camus's reasoning from revolt to solidarity is valid and plausibly sound. If I revolt, I assert a value. This value may arise from an intrinsic human purpose. But then, if this purpose is part of shared human nature and this purpose is enduring, I should recognize that this purpose is universal. As before, the reasoning generalizes, and if I think of my revolt as justified because of my intrinsic human purposes, I should recognize also those same purposes in my fellow human beings. Furthermore, my demand for respect for those purposes, in human social conditions, should amount to a demand that others receive the same respect (all other relevant factors being equal).

Camus was committed to trying to derive an ethics from minimal presuppositions. Did he break this stricture when he assumed human beings have a human nature? We could charitably argue that he did not. He believed it was true. Facts that we believe for reasons independent of our theory should not count toward the complexity of our theory. When he observed the abuse of human beings during the occupation of France, he could not shake his conviction that this was wrong because it violated something shared among human beings. If one holds to this conviction, then there must be something in those abused human beings that is enduring and that makes their treatment abuse regardless of how that abuse is describe by some theory or other. This enduring and shared thing is, he concluded, their human nature.

It is instructive, in this context, to contrast the failure of Sartre and the partial success of Beauvoir to develop their own ethical theories from minimal presuppositions. We can see that without a stronger claim, like Camus's assumption of a human nature, they are unable to develop successful ethical theories.

SARTRE'S FAILURE AND BEAUVOIR'S ETHICS OF FREEDOM

Philosophers have been constructing ethical theories for several thousand years now and have made much progress in understand the consequences and character of diverse kinds of theories. But I am unaware of any philosophers having asked what the minimum expectations of an ethical theory are, and also the minimum requirements of a theory that can answer those expectations. It is in part for this reason that there is much to find fascinating in the period in which Sartre, Beauvoir, and Camus are developing ethical theories. Because of their different philosophical commitments, each is attempting to build an ethical theory from scratch, assuming just their own philosophical commitments, which are, with respect to ethics, very minimal.

What then should an ethical theory at minimum provide? Given that this philosopher has been able to find no work on the question of the minimum requirements for an ethical theory, I am forced to propose some. An ethical theory should include a value theory and a decision theory. The value theory should satisfy at least these five criteria:

1. Purposes: The theory of value should propose or endorse some purposes.
2. Ordering: The theory of value should be capable of ranking at least some of our potential actions or our potential purposes so that we have reason to pick some over others.
3. Endurance: Some of the endorsed purposes and the rankings must be enduring, by which I mean that the endorsement and ranking last for a significant amount of time.
4. Coherence: The endorsed purposes should not contradict[4] each other—or, if they do, we will need extensive explanation of why this is so and how we should handle it.

5. Commonality: The value theory should be shared, or at least be capable of being shared, by which I mean that more than just one person would share those values.

I am assuming that an ethical theory should be able to allow for planning (both with others but also for an individual to do solitary planning only with himself) and coordination with other people. Without these five criteria above, an ethical theory would fail to allow for planning or social coordination. You cannot plan if your future goals will be different or if they contradict; you cannot coordinate if the relevant goals are not shared. There is no point to planning if you have no ranking of outcomes.

A minimum decision theory should offer a method to determine how we should apply the value theory, in at least some cases. Since Sartre and Beauvoir assume an implicit consequentialism, and since Camus, Sartre, and Beauvoir primarily struggle only with questions of value theory, my primary focus here will be value theory and I will not try to determine minimum criteria for a decision theory.

Let us begin with Beauvoir and Sartre. Scholarship on Simone de Beauvoir's work in philosophy has largely focused on her later work, especially *The Second Sex* (*Le Deuxième Sexe*, 1949). This has led to relatively less attention on her earlier ethical texts. This is unfortunate because *The Ethics of Ambiguity* (*Pour une morale de l'ambiguïté*, 1947) accomplished what Jean-Paul Sartre struggled but failed to achieve: it describes an ethical theory derived from the posits of existentialism that was able to meet our minimum criteria for a value theory.

To understand the significance of Beauvoir's accomplishment, it is helpful first to review Sartre's failed attempts at developing an existentialist ethics. Beauvoir and Sartre had some distinct philosophical views; in particular, Beauvoir did not see all human interaction as confrontational and competitive, as Sartre did. But their fundamental metaphysical assumptions were shared and presumably developed together. For this reason, they both confront the same problem in developing an ethical theory within the constraints of a shared existentialism.

Heidegger, the founder of existentialism,[5] avoids all talk of ethics in his most well-known work, *Being and Time*. He offers advice and uses a value-laden terminology (such as describing some actions as "authentic" and individuals as "fallen"), but he aggressively avoids an explicit ethical theory. There are several plausible interpretations of this. One is that Heidegger is not interested in ethics, or perhaps not ready to address it at the time he was writing those works. Another interpretation is that Heidegger is an ethical nihilist. He sees the consequences of his existentialism and believes that there is no fact of the matter that makes any one purpose better than another. We can authentically choose to choose, but that tells us nothing about what choices are best. Another possibility is that he had an ethical theory and did not articulate it in this early work. This is consistent with his later endorsement of Nazism; he seemed to treat Nazi ideology as providing an admirable ethics. In any case, we can learn nothing from Heidegger to help us respond to this problem.

Sartre did not at first assume a similar evasion. At the end of *Being and Nothingness*, after declaring humanity a "useless Passion" (2021 [1943], 797 [662]), Sartre posed a series of questions about freedom and authenticity. He answers these questions by saying, "All of these questions refer us to pure, and not complicit, reflection. They can be answered only within the domain of morality, to which we will devote a future work" (811 [676]). But Sartre never finished this promised work on ethics, though he left behind very extensive notes (such as those published in English as *Notebook for an Ethics*). Sartre himself admitted ethics is "*difficile*."[6] This outcome is not surprising: Sartre's existentialism is insufficiently strong to satisfy any of the five minimum criteria we have proposed. Of course, others may disagree with this assessment. There have been defenders of Sartre who claimed that he was developing some new and revolutionary understanding of ethics. Furthermore, both Sartre and Beauvoir came to frequently claim that some future ethics must be "concrete" and not "theoretical" or "abstract." This presumably was a call for some radical new formulation of ethics as a kind of situationist ethics. But the point is moot: it is sufficient that we observe that an ethical theory, whatever its nature—revolutionary, concrete, or whatever—must satisfy our five criteria for a minimum ethical theory, and Sartre cannot satisfy a single one of them.[7]

For Sartre, the universe lacks any intrinsic purpose. All purposes are had by the kind of beings that he calls the for-itself (*pour-soi*). Human beings are our only known examples of for-itself (all other kinds of beings—such as stones or tables or chairs—are in-itself, *en-soi*). For-itself entities create values by making choices. As he puts it in *Being and Nothingness*, "value arrives in the world through human-reality" (147 [129]) and man is *"the being through whom values exist"* (810 [675]). Our free will is thus the sole source of value. But there is a problem as a result. Ethics is about more than having purposes. Purposes can conflict, and they do conflict. How shall we choose between purposes? This is the fundamental question of ethics. Sartre has a theory of value: an act is valuable to an agent if he has chosen that action. But what Sartre lacked is a theory of how to value these values. How shall we distinguish between potential actions? That is, how can we say that one should choose one action over another? The answer entailed by Sartre's theory is vacuous: I value choice C_1 over choice C_2 because I choose C_1 over C_2. But is that the right choice?

Sartre is explicit about all this in *Being and Nothingness*:

> It follows that my freedom is the unique foundation of values and that *nothing*—absolutely nothing—can justify my adopting this system of values rather than that one. As the being through whom values exist, I am unjustifiable. And my freedom is beset by anguish at being the foundation—without foundation—of values. In addition, it is beset by anguish because, as values are essentially revealed to a freedom, they cannot be disclosed without at the same time being "called into question," since the possibility of reversing the system of values appears complementarily as *my* possibility. The anguish experienced in relation to values is a recognition of those values' ideality. (77–78 [73])

Thus, his metaphysical theory makes picking out particular values as required or recommended, and the ordering of values, impossible.

Sartre did not complete a work in ethics. Sartre's colleague Francis Jeanson wrote a book, *Sartre and the Problem of Morality (Le Problème moral et la pensée de Sartre*, 1980 [1947]), that is a fine discussion of *Being and Nothingness* but never gets around to describing or even identifying a theory of ethics. This failure is noteworthy but also indicative: Sartre's metaphysics is simply insufficient to solve the problem he set for himself. The closest Sartre comes to answering the question of how his version of existentialism might allow for a ranking of values is in his lecture "Existentialism Is a Humanism" (2007 [1946]). There, he endorsed something similar to a deontological ethics, in which we should choose between acts based on whether we can live with the responsibility that arises from the idea that we are asserting that everyone should act in this way. But Sartre never developed this idea, and he appears to have abandoned this approach—and even perhaps to have thought the lecture was too simplistic. Furthermore, the test seems very weak. Whereas for Kant an act is wrong if universalizing that act leads to a contradiction, for Sartre the test is very subjective. If a Nazi were to assert that he could live with the responsibility of choosing for all of humankind to be Nazis, then there is no further appeal, no further test or criterion that can be applied. In any case, we can see that Sartre abandoned this idea because his notes on ethics are not based on it.

It is important to recognize another issue with Sartre's ethics. Sartre in "Existentialism Is a Humanism" rejects Kant's ethics on the grounds that it cannot decide between whether a young man should join the resistance or stay home to take care of his mother. He first considers this idea in the *Notebooks for an Ethics*: "The problem of collaboration or resistance: there is a concrete moral choice. Kantianism teaches nothing on this subject" (1992, 7). Let us call the demand here a requirement of "completeness," in loose analogy with the logical term. An ethical theory is complete if it answers every relevant kind of moral question. To my knowledge, Kant never addresses directly the question of whether his ethical theory was complete. He seems to believe it is since he does not consider the possibility that his ethics is incomplete, and his notion of the Kingdom of Ends seems to assume his ethical theory if followed would create an ethically perfect society. It is an interesting question whether an ethical theory needs to be complete in order to be adequate. But the theories that Sartre and Beauvoir attempted to develop had no chance of being complete, and so this criticism really cannot distinguish their theories from Kant's; as a result, the criticism is misguided. One might consistently reason that Kant's theory is incomplete but still an excellent theory that we should implement. In any case, I have not assumed completeness is a requirement for a minimum ethical theory.[8]

We should note that Sartre did later suggest that ethics was impossible. In a strange footnote in his book *Saint Genet*, he declares:

> Either morality is stuff-and-nonsense or it is a concrete totality which achieves a synthesis of Good and Evil. For Good without Evil is Parmenidian Being, that is, Death, and Evil without Good is pure Non-being. . . . The reader will understand, I hope, that what is involved here is not a Nietzschean "beyond" Good and Evil, but rather a Hegelian *"Aufhebung."* The abstract separating of these two concepts expresses simply the alienation of man. . . . Thus, any Ethic which does not explicitly profess that it is *impossible today* contributes to the bamboozling and alienation of men. The ethical "problem" arises from the fact that Ethics is *for us* inevitable and at the same time impossible. (1963 [1952], 186n)

I refute that such comments are helpful, given the minimum demand for ethics I am making here. For example, even after the socialist revolution, when "Good and Evil" are reconciled and we are no longer "alienated," people will still need to decide between courses of action, they will need to plan, they will need to coordinate. This will require some ranking of choices, some enduring values, and some shared values. If ethics is impossible in Sartre's judgment, it will not be because of our alienation in our prerevolutionary condition, but rather because his own metaphysical theory is too weak[9]—or, as he claims in this footnote, because his own metaphysical theory makes ethics contradictory and impossible.

Sartre published a work in 1960 that some refer to as a work in ethics, or at least as concerned with ethics: *The Critique of Dialectical Reason* (*Critique de la Raison Dialectique*, 2004b). However, Sartre's task in the work is to give an existential-phenomenological analysis of social organization. Value and ethics are discussed only briefly. He argues that ethics emerges from material scarcity:

> it is the first stage of *ethics*, in so far as this is *praxis* explaining itself in terms of given circumstances. The first movement of ethics, in this case, is the constitution of radical evil and of Manichaeism; it values and evaluates the breaking of the reciprocity of immanence by interiorized scarcity . . . but only by conceiving it as a product of the *praxis* of the Other. (132)

Thus ethics is the arrival of the idea of evil, which is a motivation to fight the other who competes for goods: "the ethical takes the form of the destructive imperative: evil *must* be destroyed" (133). But all this is descriptive. It is a kind of philosophical anthropology offering a hypothesis about how humans come to be in conflict because of scarcity; it offers nothing to meet the five minimum criteria I have offered.

It is not hard to see why Sartre struggled to develop a moral theory. His dual commitment to the idea that human beings are free (in the sense of event freedom) and that free choices alone are the source of value leaves him with no resources to offer a theory of how some choices could be better than others. The very idea of *better* is a value concept, which must then arise (according to his theory) from a free choice. So how can he explain how some choices are better than others? The best he can do is say something like, "I choose to believe this choice is better than that choice." Others, being radically free, could choose differently. The result will lack commonality (there is no reason why human beings, being radically free, will choose in similar ways), endurance (there is no reason why human beings, being radically free, will make the same decisions over time), and coherence (there is no reason why human beings, being radically free, will choose values that cohere).

But in *The Ethics of Ambiguity*, Beauvoir develops an existentialist ethical theory that requires only a few additional posits. That is, she needed to assume only a little more than does Sartre, and as a result her theory is arguably a friendly emendation to Sartre's starting position in *Being and Nothingness*. Her existentialist ethics is developed in a very indirect way in the book; the key moves must be reconstructed and inferred since she never lays out an explicit argument for her presuppositions or conclusion, nor does she make explicit and defend her inferences. But it is possible to reconstruct the essential steps of a valid argument for her ethics.

In her earlier work "Pyrrhus and Cineas," Beauvoir repeatedly rejects realism about value judgements as requiring a "heaven." "We must first turn away from the errors of false objectivity. The serious mind considers health, fortune, education, and comfort as indisputable goods whose worth is written in heaven" (2004 [1944], 126).[10] And "Kantian ethics enjoins me to seek the support of all of humanity, but we have seen that there exists no heaven where the reconciliation of human judgments is accomplished"

(132). The criticism is misguided[11] since standards in "heaven" are not the only way that an objective ethical theory could be developed. What is needed is some standard that gives us a ranking of choices and is coherent, that is stable over time, and which can be widely shared. And, in fact, this is how Beauvoir proceeds. She claims that all human beings share some basic needs that arise from the nature of freedom, she never considers the possibility that these are anything other than enduring and coherent, and these will allow us to rank some values over others. Her notion of what these basic needs are changes over time, as is evident if we contrast "Pyrrhus and Cineas" with *The Ethics of Ambiguity*. Scholarship on Beauvoir's ethics tends to lump together the claims of these two works, but the theories defended in each are distinct, and the key element to Beauvoir's successful ethical theory appears only in the later book.

In "Pyrrhus and Cineas," Beauvoir claims that each human being has a need for the freedom of others, because one has need of others to affirm one's purposes. The arguments of the essay are often evasive, in part because throughout Beauvoir embraces and affirms paradoxes that she claims are essential to human existence, and also because she often indulges in a dialectical method that refuses to resolve "contradictions" between various plausible claims. But her principal argument is this: Human beings have finite, personal purposes. These purposes arise solely from our choices. When we achieve a purpose, it suddenly fails to be a purpose for us anymore; we "surpass" it. This is one of the many ambiguities of human existence that she takes as essential to our kind of being. "The paradox of the human condition is that every end can be surpassed, and yet, the project defines the end as an end. In order to surpass an end, it must first have been projected as something that is not to be surpassed. Man has no other way of existing" (2004, 113). There are no unsurpassable projects. For example, there are no projects that are infinitely far away so that they always remain projects—it is an error to suppose that dedicating oneself to God's will, or to humanity, might provide such a project. Given that she agrees with Sartre that our values arise from our choices, there would seem to be no room here for an ethical theory. But Beauvoir adds the claim that, in the freedom of other people, our project can become something that is not surpassed.

There seem to be two aspects of this. First, we are troubled by the finitude of our projects, but other people in some sense help us overcome this finitude: "I don't know if God exists, and no experience can make him present for me. Humanity never realizes itself. But the other is there, before me, closed upon himself, open onto infinity. If I destined my actions to him, wouldn't they also take on an infinite dimension?" (2004, 116). This is presented as a preliminary judgment, and Beauvoir is careful to argue that we must embrace the finitude of our projects. However, she does repeat in *The Ethics of Ambiguity* the claim that one benefit of others being free is that they can take on my projects. So one aspect of the benefit of the free other seems to be this potential for the additional duration of my project.

Beauvoir also argues—and this seems to be her primary point—that I need others not just to sustain my projects but to verify my projects.

> In order for the object that I founded to appear as a good, the other must make it into his own good, and then I would be justified for having created it. The other's freedom alone is capable of necessitating my being. My essential need is therefore to be faced with free men. My project loses all meaning not if my death is announced, but if the end of the world is announced to me. (2004, 129)

This early version of Beauvoir's ethics, however, has two problems. The first is that Beauvoir never explains the role of time in her value theory. Although it coheres with our everyday experience that we want our projects to continue, we also know that at least some of these projects must end if achieved. Beauvoir argues that my desire that my projects continue after my death should make me interested in other people's freedom. But she also recognizes—and we all know—that ultimately everyone, and even our species, will die. And, in her novel *All Men Are Mortal* (*Tous les hommes sont mortels*, 1992a [1946]), Beauvoir presents the view that immortality would render a human being inert, because the finitude of our projects is required for the projects to be valuable. Hence, she claims that it is a shared goal of all humans for their projects to continue past death; but every project must terminate and a project is not less worthy because it is finite; and a project would be worthless if it continued forever. The role of time here is obscure; it seems one could argue that my project dying with me or dying centuries later are not sufficiently different, and therefore I have no interest in the freedom of others with respect to this purpose.

A second problem is that Beauvoir here seems to appeal to what Sartre called bad faith, a kind of inauthentic existence. She holds with Sartre the view that there is a paradoxical experience we have arising from our freedom: we usually choose to "be something." We choose to attempt to become a good person, or courageous, or something like this. But because a human being is radically free, one can never "be something." A human can only continue to choose. Each choice is new, a starting over. Bad faith arises when one believes one can be, or is, something. Thus, as Beauvoir puts it: "We have seen that the original scheme of man is ambiguous: he wants to be, and to the extent that he coincides with this wish, he fails. All the plans in which this will to be is actualized are condemned" (1948, 23). But for Sartre, one of the clearest examples of bad faith is wanting another to tell you that you are something. It is bad faith to ask another to verify my purpose because I would then be attempting to hand to that person my responsibility for my choices.

Perhaps Beauvoir realized this tension between authenticity and others' verifying one's purposes. That could explain the shift in reasoning between "Pyrrhus and Cineas" and *The Ethics of Ambiguity*. The later work does endorse the role of others in continuing one's project after one's death, but it does not mention again the idea that others justify one's purposes with their judgments.[12] Instead, Beauvoir's primary argument for her ethical theory in *The Ethics of Ambiguity* is based on new key principles. She assumes that human beings are free and that they want their freedom. But, Beauvoir argues—and this is one of the places where she reaches beyond Sartre's presuppositions—we can realize our freedom through the goal of unveiling being: "Man also wills himself to be an unveiling of being, and if he coincides with this wish, he wins, for the fact is that the world becomes present by his presence in it" (23; translation modified).[13] For Beauvoir, the most successful unveiling of being is the recognition that one is allowing being to be present through one's free actions, and when one is also recognizing that one can never be something but can only continue to freely choose how to act.

This concept of unveiling being is taken from Heidegger. In *Being and Time*, Heidegger claims that Being (most broadly understood) needs Dasein to be present. His term, the equivalent here of Beauvoir's "to unveil," is "to disclose" (*erschliessen*). He writes in *Being and Time* that

Disclosedness is a kind of Being which is essential to Dasein. *"There is" truth only in so far as Dasein is and so long as Dasein is.* Entities are uncovered only *when* Dasein *is*; and only as long as Dasein *is*, are they disclosed. Newton's laws, the principle of contradiction, any truth whatever—these are true only as long as Dasein *is*. Before there was any Dasein, there was no truth; nor will there be any after Dasein is no more. (1962, 269 [226])

(This is a concise statement of the correlationism discussed in chapter 1.) Thus, according to Heidegger, phenomena can only appear, and truths can only arise, if there is a Dasein to disclose the world. Beauvoir agrees with Heidegger and adds the claim that our desire for freedom is equivalent to a desire to continue to unveil Being. Just as we want our freedom, we want to unveil being.

Beauvoir also reasons that other human beings must be free in order for me to best unveil beings. So I have an interest in ensuring that other human beings are free. "Thus, every man has to do with other men. The world in which he engages himself is a human world in which each object is penetrated with human meanings. . . . He must unveil the world with the purpose of further unveiling and by the same movement try to free men, by means of whom the world takes on meaning" (1948, 74). Human beings are free in the sense that they can choose. This is axiomatic for Beauvoir. But here she means that human beings can be less "free" in the sense that they can be ignorant or they can be physically restrained. It is these two things—ignorance and political oppression—that we should oppose, she asserts.

The implicit reasoning seems also to include that other human beings create the meanings of beings only when they are free, and we cannot create all or much of those meanings ourselves. Seen in this way, her claims are highly plausible. Suppose that Pierre is a jazz musician. Think about what this entails. He plays the saxophone—an instrument that someone else invented and someone else manufactured. It is designed for Western classical scales. Much of the music he wants to play was written by other people, and all his goals as a jazz musician are to emulate others and (in culturally specified ways) distinguish himself from these others. He wants to play for audiences, and they only come if they already have expectations about jazz.

And so on. Thus, Pierre's project is at every point dependent on the creations and the ongoing activities of others.

There is an important observation to be made here. Beauvoir bases the generalization of her ethics on an appeal to self-interest. She assumes that each of us is self-interested, and then shows how our self-interest in unveiling being, along with the assumptions about the nature of unveiling being, leads to a general principle that we should seek to make others more free. We might draw a rough distinction between recognizably distinct approaches in fundamental ethics. Some scholars like Beauvoir assume self-interest and then appeal to it. Hobbes might be interpreted in this way; he reasons from the self-interest of each person not to be harmed, to their interest in formulating a general social contract. Some other philosophers have instead proposed general principles as the foundation of their ethics and then observed that the principles apply universally to human beings or persons. Camus takes this approach. So does Kant: any rational agent, according to Kant, deserves moral respect because it is a rational agent. No appeal to self-interest is used; rather, the value theory is general. Both approaches are means to develop what I have called "commonality"—that is, they give us reason to believe the ethical theory will have application across a population and that many may be willing to adopt the theory.

Beauvoir does not discuss that this unveiling comes in degrees, but this is necessary to her argument. That is, a tyrant is unveiling being by his tyrannical actions—it cannot be that he fails to make things be present since he is free and his free choices unveil being. So, at most, we can say that the tyrant would unveil more being, or would unveil being more effectively, if he renounced his tyranny and helped liberate his fellow human beings. This would explain why Beauvoir says, "if the oppressor were aware of the demands of his own freedom, he himself should have to denounce oppression" (1948, 96). Since Beauvoir claims that "To will freedom and to will to unveil being are one and the same choice" (78), it must be that not only unveiling being but freedom can be limited (one can be less than wholly free). She needs also that our need for an increase in the freedom of others is general—that is, it does not allow that we might encourage the freedom of some while oppressing others. She does not give an argument for this, unfortunately.[14] With these emendations, we can reconstruct the form of Beauvoir's primary argument, where this additional point is the premise at step 2.

Argument 5
1. Each person wants to unveil being. (Premise)
2. If a person wants to unveil being, then that person wants more unveiling of more being. (Premise)
3. Each person wants more unveiling of more being. (Derived from 1, 2)
4. If a person wants more unveiling of more being, then that person wants it to be more possible for there to be more unveiling of more being. (Premise)
5. Each person wants it to be more possible for there to be more unveiling of more being. (Derived from 3, 4)
6. Each person is more free if and only if it is more possible for that person to help unveil more being. (Premise)
7. If each person is more free if and only if it is more possible for that person to help unveil more being, and each person wants it to be more possible for there to be more unveiling of more being, then each person should want that all people are more free. (Premise)
8. Each person should want that all people are more free. (Adjunction 5, 6; Modus Ponens 7)

This is a valid argument. The substantial work in this argument depends on the claim that the unveiling of being is improved to the degree that others are free. This claim is not defended by Beauvoir; she asserts it, presumably on the grounds that its truth is revealed by phenomenology.

If Beauvoir's argument is sound, it offers a sufficiently strong general principle to ground an existentialist ethics that can achieve the minimum task—required of any ethics—of ranking some actions over others. It also gives us a basic shared purpose: the unveiling of being. Furthermore, it seems possible that it meets our other criteria: because the unveiling of being is helped by social efforts (Beauvoir presents it as a kind of coordination problem), it seems the unveiling of being (and thus what is valuable) will at least in some cases be enduring, common, and coherent.

I confess that I find it hard to reason out how the theory would settle contentious issues. For example, is gun control an increase or a decrease in the potential to unveil being? It is unclear how to answer such a question. And the most pressing questions in ethics concern the costs of community. Does Beauvoir's ethics of freedom allow for taxation? For the punishment of crimes? The reduction of some freedom is involved in such actions. When is this permitted? But I have not claimed a minimal ethical theory must be complete, or easy to apply, so these observations are not a criticism of the theory's ability to meet the minimal threshold.

I do have one substantive criticism of Beauvoir's ethical theory: Beauvoir tries to accommodate her ethics to an ideology of revolution, including violent revolution, and as a result she undermines and contradicts the theory. I will discuss this problem in chapter 5, after we introduce the debate over the nature of revolt and revolution that arises when Camus publishes *The Rebel*.

Beauvoir's theory does do what Sartre could not: it gives us a shared purpose and a way to rank some choices, and if social conditions are enduring, coherent, and common, then it will at least sometimes meet the criteria for a minimum ethics. There will be cases where it is possible to determine in a reliable way how to act based on this general principle. Some choices are indeed better than others, this is true for all beings of our kind, and we can act ethically by choosing correctly in these cases. Does Camus fare better? We will assess this question in the next three chapters.

FREEDOM, PURPOSE, AND ACCOMPLISHMENT

I want to discuss a metaphysical problem that is not addressed by the existentialists or by Camus but that I believe is lurking behind their debate. I believe Camus sensed some of the issues related to this problem and was guided by this tacit understanding. The concern is about freedom as an end-in-itself, and especially with any theory that holds that freedom is the highest or most important end-in-itself.

There are multiple notions of "freedom" in the long history of Western metaphysics. Two are immediately relevant here. One notion of freedom concerns lack of restraint. Closely related to this is the idea that one is free in doing action A if one could have done otherwise than A. Let us call this "event freedom." This is a suitable name because we are defining freedom in terms of the event, the action A. Another notion of freedom is that the agent is free when the agent is the source (including the cause) of his action. The agent chooses certain outcomes and then uses his own capabilities to act to achieve those outcomes. Call this "agency freedom."[15]

My contention is that the metaphysical theories of Sartre and Beauvoir represent the purest realization of event freedom. Camus, instead, had a conception of freedom consistent with agency freedom. Neither side makes this explicit, and so they often talk past each other.

The question of the nature of metaphysical revolt touches on a problem that Camus does not raise but which is relevant to his notion of the role of human nature. Camus is opposing a view that human beings are very highly malleable—that they can be changed and redefined by theory or social convention or economic conditions or choice. This is a perennial battle, colloquially referred to as the debate over nature versus nurture. We can think of the battle as fought on a continuum where we can imagine two limit positions. At one limit, human beings are complete blank slates. For convenience alone, let us call this the "nurture" limit of the continuum. At the other limit, the human being is fully determined by his inherited character; we can call the "nature" limit of the continuum. Perhaps few people take positions at these extreme limits. Those who believe much of human character is inherited, for example, will grant that customs and language are learned and so on. However, in fact, Sartre adopts the extreme "nurture" limit of this view.

Sartre and Beauvoir are important philosophers in part because they are the exemplars of the full realization of certain tendencies in the tradition from which they arise. Sartre's theory includes the claim that a person is a blank slate, choosing all his purposes. But Sartre also respects that aspect of the philosophical tradition that recognizes a person is his purposes. For an extremely pure conception of event freedom, any predisposition or purpose inside the agent (it would be more accurate to say, any intrinsic purpose that constitutes the agent) would actually be an impediment to the agent's freedom. If Pierre is making certain choices because he has as an essential part of himself certain purposes, then these purposes will limit him. It won't be true that he could have done otherwise because then he would be someone else—he wouldn't be Pierre. Put these together (that is, join [1] the claim that people are constituted by their purposes with [2] the claim that such constituting purposes limit your freedom as understood by event freedom, and finally [3] the claim that people are wholly free in the sense of event freedom) and you get as a straightforward logical implication that a person is nothing. This is precisely Sartre's position: nothingness "is right inside being, in its heart, like a worm" (2021, 57 [56]). We are that worm. Our freedom arises from the nihilation of being; the future arises from the nihilation of the present. "The for-itself cannot support its nihilation without determining itself as a *lack of being*" (137 [121]). Given that it's something—it has some kind of being—Sartre is forced into paradoxical descriptions of this being that is a little pool of nothingness, nihilating the world: "its way of being is such that it is not what it is and it is what it is not" (129 [115]). The most perfect, the most pure form of the idea of event freedom combined with the recognition that we are constituted by our purposes puts us at the extreme "nurture" limit of the nature-nurture continuum. This agent has no internal structure and therefore cannot internally cause any limit on event freedom.

Beauvoir presumably has these same beliefs, but also clearly articulates the ethical theory that freedom (understood as event freedom) is the sole end-in-itself (all other ends are merely chosen). This addition motivates opposition to any claim that human beings may have some innate purposes, other than this purpose to be free and so unveil being. Claims that we have any other nature amount to a denial of the possibility of unlimited event freedom, and as such the existentialists reject them.

There is some leeway here, in that Sartre adopts Heidegger's concept of facticity. This is the recognition that there are contingent facts about oneself that one did not choose. Many of these cannot be changed through your choices. I cannot choose to flap my arms and fly. I cannot choose where I am born and what language I first am taught. And so on. But for Sartre, freedom is all and only concerned with the kinds of things that the agent can do, given its current facticity. Furthermore, the examples of facticity tend to be one's location, one's social condition, and the brute physical facts of the body. There is nothing inside the for-itself that acts as facticity; this follows directly from the fact that there is nothing inside the for-itself. The for-itself has no properties of the kind that you or I would think of as constituting a person or character. Thus, Sartre believes facticity is not relevant to the role of the for-itself in event freedom.

Without facticity, consciousness would be able to choose its attachments in the world, in the manner in which souls, in *The Republic*, can choose their condition: I could decide to be "born working-class" or "born bourgeois." But, on the other hand, my facticity cannot constitute me as *being* bourgeois or as *being* working-class. Strictly speaking, my facticity is not even the *resistance* of facts, since it is by taking it up within the infrastructure of my *prereflective cogito* that I endow it with its meaning and its resistance. My facticity is only an indication that I present to myself of the being I am obliged to keep company with, in order to be what I am. (2021, 134 [119])

Facticity is never described as including things like cognitive capabilities, character predispositions, inherent preferences, or inherent purposes. It is like a set of opportunities and tools presented to a radically free agent, which then decides without limitation what to do with these opportunities and tools.

For Beauvoir's ethics, these concerns reappear in what we can call the *initial choice* problem. Beauvoir's theory makes all values, other than the value of freedom, rest on an arbitrary choice. Let us suppose that Pierre decides to be a jazz musician, and as a result a series of free possibilities opens to him, and there will be more possibilities open to him if others are free. But no degree of freedom (either for himself or others) is at stake in his choosing to be a jazz musician. He could spontaneously choose some other course of action, such as giving up on music and dedicating himself to farming. It is unclear how there can be a ranking between these choices. Thus, it appears that Beauvoir's theory ranks options *after one has made some initial arbitrary choice*, but it cannot rank those initial choices. Another way to recognize the same problem is to return to our example of Pierre and recognize that the behaviors that are made possible by the freedom of others are, on Beauvoir's account, just arbitrary social conventions. The reason a jazz musician strives to play in a certain way or to have an audience or even to make sound is because there is such a social convention, arising purely from a free choice that could have gone in any other way. This may seem an extreme claim, but remember that for Sartre—and presumably for Beauvoir, who claims to be consistent with Sartre—there is no human nature. Human beings have no positive properties (other than very abstract metaphysical properties, like being free). Thus, there can be no fact of the matter about what is better or worse music for a human being, for example. There can only be the free choice of various standards. Ethics thus turns out to be a question of how we freely follow and modify some existing social conventions.

Recall also that many of the intellectuals around Camus are committed Marxists. The Marxists are not at the "nurture" limit of our continuum. But they are far toward that end. They argue that human nature is highly malleable, and that a strong determinant of human character is the economic condition of the individual. Thus, the communists promise a new kind of human being will arise when living in the conditions of communism. For example, this new person will never be susceptible to adopting a free-riding strategy on the labor of others.

There is debate about to what degree Marx is an "economic determinist." However, there is no doubt that many of his followers were. For an example, consider the debates between "humanists" and the conservative Maoists in China after Mao's death. The debate has the air of religious interpretation, but the important point is that, like many Marxists, Mao seemed to reduce human nature to being a product of social—and in particular class—activity. Mao writes:

> Is there such a thing as human nature? Of course there is. But there is only human nature in the concrete, no human nature in the abstract. In class society there is only human nature of a class character; there is no human nature above classes. We uphold the human nature of the proletariat and of the masses of the people, while the landlord and bourgeois classes uphold the human nature of their own classes, only they do not say so but make it out to be the only human nature in existence. The human nature boosted by certain petty-bourgeois intellectuals is also divorced from or opposed to the masses; what they call human nature is in essence nothing but bourgeois individualism, and so, in their eyes, proletarian human nature is contrary to human nature. (1967 [1942], 90)[16]

Stalin had expressed similar views.[17]

Camus argues that the instantiation of a Marxist state—or any instance of what he calls a historical revolution—requires this blank-slatism.

Camus interprets Marx as believing some strong form of economic determinism, but also as hiding from this problem: "Any kind of coherence that is not purely economic between the past and the future of humanity supposes a constant which, in its turn, can lead to a belief in a human nature" (1956, 236), which Marx evades. But once implemented, the Marxist state under Stalin requires a violent enforcement of blank-slatism. "The Empire [by which Camus means totalitarian socialism] supposes a negation and a certainty: the certainty of the infinite malleability of man and the negation of human nature" (237). Camus observes a similar extreme in Stalinism to the one we observed in Sartre's philosophy: "If there is no human nature, then the malleability of man is, in fact, infinite" (237).

As we have observed, for the existentialists, human beings are infinitely malleable. Beauvoir writes:

> We must first turn away from the errors of false objectivity. The serious mind considers health, fortune, education, and comfort as indisputable goods whose worth is written in heaven. But he is duped by an illusion: ready-made values whose hierarchy is imposed upon my decisions do not exist without me. What's good for a man is what he wants as his own good. (2004, 126–27)

Health, for example, is not intrinsically good. We simply tend to choose it as such, and we might change our minds and see it as a bad thing if we so choose—and in doing that, health would become bad.

In a closely related view, Heidegger proposed that Dasein is always entirely a social creation. This general social condition is *Das Man*, the They. It shapes the individual into a kind of version of itself, called a "they-self." Heidegger summarized this with the phrase "Dasein is a modification of the they-self." And authenticity is always also a modification of the they-self—it is recognizing the contingency of the purposes that have been given to you by *Das Man*.

In both the quotes above, we see Mao and then Beauvoir resort to a false dilemma. The claim that there is a fact of the matter about what is good or bad for a human being is not equivalent to the claim that such facts are "written in heaven" or are "transcendent."[18] Camus is not committed to this human nature being heaven-sent or otherwise "transcendent." He does not describe it this way, but it would be fully consistent to interpret Camus's human nature as our biological inheritance. On the standard Darwinian view, our biological inheritance is an accident, in the sense that it was not planned by any intelligence, and it is wholly a product of history (and prehistory), in the sense that we evolved as social beings. Another example of a similar attack can be found in the claim by Francis Jeanson that Camus endorsed an ahistorical morality. Jeanson does this in his review of *The Rebel*: "[*The Rebel*] offers us many examples of this Manicheanism that situates Evil within history and Good outside of it and that requires consequently that we choose *against it* in every possible way" (in Sprintzen and van den Hoven 2004, 97). Camus is not committed to the view that justice lies outside history. He is only committed to the view that history does not have a purpose, and that therefore we cannot justify our actions by appealing to some theory that our actions are serving history's purpose. Jeanson thus mistakes—perhaps, one ought to suspect, willfully misinterprets—Camus's denial that history can provide a justification for our political choices for a claim that there are justifications for our political choices that are somehow "outside" of history. But that is not at all Camus's claim. Rather, it is the human search for purpose, and human nature, that determines what is good and bad for human beings. Our human nature does not transcend history; it is a material fact that stands wholly grounded in history. But on such a view our ethics will never be justified by appeal to the ends or purposes of history. Instead, we can evaluate our actions on whether they help or hinder human flourishing, and this we determine with reference to human nature. In light of this, it would be far more fair to accuse Jeanson of having something like a belief in transcendental justice: for him, history can have a direction, and this is something that transcends any particular human life.

From the perspective of those who have the agency freedom conception of free action, one problem with the event freedom account is that it is indistinguishable from randomness. If Pierre acts randomly, then he could have done otherwise. If he is not acting randomly, but rather is pursuing certain innate purposes, then his actions are guided by those purposes and event freedom is not true of the resulting actions. What the agency freedom theorist wants from an account of human freedom is not the claim that humans are acting randomly, but rather that they are themselves the masters of their choices. Thus, there is a fundamental difference in perspectives; Camus and the existentialists have incompatible conceptions of agency. This comes out when Sartre criticizes Camus's conception of agency on the grounds that it requires limits (albeit internal limits in the form of the agent's purposes and choices) on freedom. Sartre claims Camus is confused about what freedom is; freedom "is or is not; but if it is, it escapes the chain of causes and effects, being of another order" (in Sprintzen and van den Hoven 2004, 145).

This problem lies behind a concern we could raise for Beauvoir's ethical theory. On the event freedom account of freedom, the individual has no agency (in the sense of their purposes being the cause of their actions) because he has no innate purposes. Sartre and Beauvoir hold that one can inherit from one's culture certain purposes, but they also claim that one can recognize this and then freely decide whether to adopt those purposes (this is what Heidegger calls "authenticity" and is arguably equivalent to what Sartre calls "good faith"). And, in any case, one is completely free (in the event freedom sense) to choose other purposes. So why choose one purpose or another? We saw that Beauvoir solves this puzzle by arguing you should choose the purpose that will unveil more being, and she claims this is the purpose that makes others more free. But as we also saw, this criterion only applies after one has chosen some course of action. If Pierre chooses to become a jazz musician, then certain things follow from the contingent social facts constituting jazz musicianship. But should he choose instead to be a classical pianist?

The claim I am making follows from metaphysical theory. That is, if one has the view that I have called event freedom, and you adopt a position at the "nurture" limit of the nature-nurture continuum, then it follows that people cannot be guided by innate purposes. Put equivalently, if you have innate purposes, these will be incompatible with event freedom, because you will limit your own actions in order to pursue your purposes. But if a person is not guided by innate purposes, then they are nothing and their actions are random.

During the war, Camus was driven to the conclusion that human beings have a shared and enduring human nature. This human nature is shared and enduring purposes. Not all of our purposes are innate, but many are. This axiom allows for him to begin the construction of a minimum ethics, and it allows him to outline a theory of how we can make progress in revising our institutions so that they grow better at respecting and fostering these human purposes. Thus, freedom lies not in being nothing, nor in being a purely socially constructed agent, but in being empowered to pursue and realize one's purposes in one's own ways. This also means that the realization of one's purposes can result in order, in the form of institutions or conditions that help realize or sustain one's purposes: "The most elementary form of rebellion, paradoxically, expresses an aspiration to order" (1956, 23).

The minimum ethics that Camus develops is akin to Aristotle's virtue ethics in the following regard: human flourishing is to be understood as realizing human purposes. For Aristotle and for Camus, some of these purposes constitute a shared human nature. The question of where we fall on this nature-nurture spectrum is highly relevant to the question of human purposes. For the farther we are to the "nurture" limit of the continuum, the more contingent and malleable human choices become. From the perspective of someone holding such a theory, there is some threshold on the nurture side of this continuum past which this ethics collapses (that is, past which an ethics of human flourishing based on a conception of human purposes is no longer viable).

The point here is a general one about human purposes and teleology. If we agree that flourishing requires the achieving of one's purposes (there may be much more to ethics, but if this is a necessary part of it), then human beings with only arbitrary purposes will likely fail to have an ethics that meets our minimum criteria. Instead, on the view of someone like Camus, if agent A has purpose P and achieves that purpose, this is some contribution to their flourishing. Perhaps this purpose is to have and enjoy the company of friends. Achieving it means an increase in flourishing; if the purpose is frustrated, it is a decrease in flourishing. For the sake of simplifying the argument, let P be the only purpose so that achieving it means one flourishes. Now, if we are far to the nurture side of our continuum, past the threshold I described, then P will be a choice and there will be no inherent character of the agent that requires P. The agent could later choose (or economic conditions could later instill in the agent the tendency to choose, etc.) some purpose that is contrary to P. Call this purpose *anti-P*. Maybe (to use our example of friendship) it is a goal to demonstrate self-reliance and independence by fighting and insulting and rejecting all other human beings. Then achieving *anti-P* is flourishing. Obviously, then, flourishing is wholly arbitrary. There can be nothing about it that makes it worth having, nor can there be anything in our purposes that makes them worth achieving—other than the simple claim that we might choose to choose (as Heidegger put it). Under this view, any purpose is as good as any other, and, obviously, they will not have endurance, coherence, or commonality.

It is logically possible to adopt a view far to the nurture side of our continuum and still claim that there is a fact of the matter about which purposes are better than others. This is Beauvoir's position. But note several things. First, this has not typically been the position of those on that side of the continuum. Sartre, as we saw, says that our values arise from our choices, and only our choices can rank those values. Second, those who adopt the agency freedom view and are more toward the nature side of our continuum have nearly all assumed that it is possible to have a coherent set of better purposes. Aristotle never even considers the possibility that we could have innate purposes, which are ends-in-themselves, but which cannot be achieved to some degree together. For him, eudaimonia, a flourishing life, is excellence in the achievement of many of one's purposes. From the perspective of logic, this is an additional assumption. But Camus makes it, and it can be justified on the grounds that one observes people achieving many of their purposes and having a coherent, flourishing life. But then, if this principle is true, what makes it true? It seems that it in part relates to facts about the purposes that constitute a flourishing life. That is, something about our purposes will contribute to the possibility that they can be achieved together (e.g., it is hard to make and enjoy friends if your health is severely failing).

If one believes that different kinds of lives can be compared, then we cannot be far to the nurture extreme on this continuum, past the indeterminacy threshold. For beyond that threshold, one can chose any kinds of purposes. It seems plausible that one could piece together a set of purposes that we would recognize as cruel sociopathy (such as Camus's character of Caligula), and a set of purposes that we would recognize as similar to some of those that Aristotle valued. Is one better than the other? If the answer is yes, then there must be some facts that make some purposes better than others. Presumably, social and biological pressures have carved humans into beings who have some of these better purposes, and in achieving these we can lead lives that are objectively better. But if our purposes are all and always just a choice or product of shifting social conditions, then it would be dumb luck if these resulted in a better form of life—and it is unclear how this concept of "better" would fit the account.

There is another threshold to the nature side of our spectrum. If all of our nature is inherited, to the point where every action were determined by some unchanging and simple algorithm, we would not be persons. Camus values liberty, and this value is not a purpose so much as a condition on our nature. Camus's account requires some happy medium, where there is some role for choice and self-determination in diverse ways, but also an inherited human nature that determines what is better or worse for a human being; and also it is true that those purposes together when achieved with excellence can cohere to form a flourishing life.

Note that to say we inherit some purposes that constitute our human nature can be consistent with other theories about those purposes. They may be good for other reasons. They may satisfy some objective moral evaluations that we have not yet discovered. But if value is nothing but choice, if we rule out any other reason to have a certain kind of character or to have certain kinds of purposes, other than choice or social convention, then that road is cut off.

There is another important issue that is closely related to these observations. For someone like Aristotle, achieving one of your intrinsic purposes is good and remains good. You can take lifelong satisfaction in having achieved that goal; its achievement is something that endures and marks an increase in your eudaimonia, in your striving to live with excellence. Let us call this the "accomplishment" hypothesis:

Accomplishment hypothesis: *For some intrinsic purposes, achieving that intrinsic purpose is an enduring good for the agent who achieves the purpose.*

But in the world of radically free humans with little or no internal structure and no intrinsic purposes (other than greater freedom), there seems to be no enduring benefit of the achieved purpose. Purposes are like the empty calories of junk food; you enjoy chewing the junk food, but there is no benefit when it is over, and you can only therefore maintain any satisfaction by continually eating the junk food. If every purpose is an arbitrary choice, achieving the purpose appears to have no enduring benefit. Rather, you must find another purpose, which is then to be achieved, discarded, and replaced, ad nauseum.

Beauvoir makes this explicit. In "Pyrrhus and Cineas" and other works, Beauvoir struggled valiantly against a series of paradoxical implications arising from her views on temporality and its relation to telos. She assumes that the realization of our purpose is our only source of value. But our purposes are merely chosen—there is nothing about realizing them that makes them inherently good. Thus, when we realize our purposes, they are done and evaporate. There is a kind of nihilism that results from achieving a goal. Furthermore, we realize that we will die, and so some of our purposes will not be achieved. She proposes we can achieve some kind of benefit from ensuring others continue our projects after we die, but she does not ever reflect on the fact that those people will die, and even eventually the human race might die. The result is that both achieving a goal and not achieving a goal are a kind of failure. And, as we noted, she also claims immortality would be no benefit. Beauvoir wrote a novel, *All Men Are Mortal*, about an immortal man, Fosca. The main theme of *All Men Are Mortal* is that an immortal life renders one purposeless. This is interesting because it offers something like the opposite view of the pronouncement of Dostoevsky's character Ivan in *The Brother's Karamazov*; Ivan claims that if there is no eternal life, then all life is meaningless. For Beauvoir's protagonist, immortality breaks the illusion that life has a purpose; one cannot enjoy the fiction that one's purposes matter, because one sees (as Beauvoir presents the story) no progress but just repetition ending always in death (for all others).

Thus, Beauvoir recognizes that purposes are essentially temporal, but she also holds that achieving a purpose is a kind of failure, not achieving the purpose is a kind of failure, death is a failure, and immortality would be a failure. As Sartre put it in *Being and Nothingness*, "man is a useless passion." I submit that this paradoxical situation in which she finds herself is a direct result of the purposes not being ends-in-themselves but rather just being choices. For Aristotle, a purpose is not undone by its realization;

the human character that gave one that purpose endures and is satisfied by this achievement. But if these purposes have nothing to recommend them other than being arbitrarily chosen, then their achievement just means that one has to move on and choose something else now.

As a consequence of this view, Beauvoir held that there can be no progress. The potential for progress requires that there is, in fact, a human nature of the kind that Camus posits. For if human beings are highly malleable, if their preferences are social constructions, then there is neither a common set of motivating forces nor shared and enduring human preferences. In "Pyrrhus and Cineas," Beauvoir called the belief in objective values an "illusion" that "dupes" those who believe in intrinsic goods. As a result,

> One can surpass one project only by realizing another project. To transcend a transcendence is not to effectuate a progress, because these different projects are separate. The transcendent transcendence can in turn be transcended. No instant joins up with the eternal. Ecstasy and anguish still take their place in time; they are projects themselves. Every thought, every feeling is a project. Thus the life of man does not appear as a progress but as a cycle. (2004, 140)

Beauvoir is correctly following out the implications of her existentialism. There is no human nature; there are only human choices. We choose some end as our project, and if we achieve it, then we "transcend" it. It no longer is there as an end. We must choose again. No aspect of life is the achieving of intrinsic ends, and so there is no measure we can use to identify something we might call progress or any enduring benefit. Thus, for Beauvoir, "The words 'utility,' 'progress,' and 'fear' have meaning only in a world where the project has made points of view and ends appear" (2004, 141), where each such project is an arbitrary choice. Those points of view are free to change in any way, and so there really can be no enduring individual notion of progress, and there can be no enduring and shared notion of progress. After all, I could choose to build a house, and then choose to tear it down, and both choices have value—both choices are the only source of value for me—because they are choices. So life can never be measured as anything more than the cycle of choosing and then pursuing one arbitrary project after another.

Fosca, the immortal protagonist in *All Men Are Mortal*, ultimately sees this continual repetition of human life as revealing no changes, no progress. As a result, he struggles constantly against a lethargy caused by nihilism. Fosca's belief that there is no progress extends even to science. At one point in his centuries of living, he takes up an interest in chemistry, but he comes to see any potential discoveries as worthless:

> I would never break through the crusty surface of the apparent world. Even with the aid of microscopes and telescopes, it was still only with my *eyes* that I saw things; objects existed for us only because they were visible, tangible, prudently situated in space and time amid other objects. Even if we were to fly to the moon, or go down to the bottom of oceans, we would still be men in the heat of a human world. As for those mysterious realities which revealed themselves to our senses—forces, planets, molecules, waves—they were hidden by words and protected by the yawning gap of our ignorance. Never would nature deliver up to us her secrets; she had no secrets. We were the ones who invented questions and then formulated the answers to them; in the bottoms of our retorts we would never discover anything but our own thoughts, thoughts that might in the course of centuries multiply, become more complex, be formed into vaster and more subtle systems. . . . Never would anything be *something else*, never would I be someone else. (1992a [1946], 276)[19]

If, however, there is a human nature, then real progress is possible. Recall the accomplishment claim was the claim that achieving an intrinsic purpose was an enduring good. I had the purpose to be a father; the achievement of this goal is a benefit to me for the entirety of my remaining life; it is not something that became worthless the moment it was achieved, but rather constitutes a step toward having lived a good life. But if the accomplishment claim is true, then it is also possible to improve the living conditions of humans so that they can better realize their innate purposes. Thus, both personal and social progress are possible.

I began by claiming I believe Camus had some tacit understanding of these facts. I claim this because it coheres with his central concept of limits, *mesure*. He calls on us to choose to limit our freedom and to act within those limits. What are these limits? They are respect for the most important human purposes—if not in oneself, at least in others. The person who takes freedom as the only value, or as the highest value, inevitably calls for the *demusuree* action. If our purposes are merely chosen and can be replaced at any time by any other purposes, then we are no longer persons—because a person is constituted by his purposes. Without those purposes, there can be no stable ethics and no stable political goals. And without those purposes, there can be no progress, since any measure of progress is arbitrary and replaceable and soon to be replaced. But respecting human purposes instead means that we need to act with *mesure* and can create a shared ethical theory, and we have the possibility of shared progress.

CAMUS'S MINIMUM ETHICS

Camus does not provide what a philosopher would typically call an ethical theory. Some critics have suggested this is because his thinking was vague and undeveloped. A more charitable interpretation is that the preliminary state of his ethical theory is consistent with his caution and fallibilism; furthermore, his theory is focused on how morality is possible, rather than on the specific details of morality. He is suspicious of formal moral theories, but more importantly he has a theory that our morality emerges slowly through the struggle of individuals. "*The Rebel* proposes neither a formal nor a dogmatic morality. It only affirms that a morality is possible and that it costs us dearly" (Camus 2004, 217). He is more specific when he describes the needed constraints on revolt, which in turn act as the method by which the moral theory will evolve; I discuss these in chapter 5. But he has provided us with an account that shows how it is possible to meet our criteria for a value theory of a minimal ethics.

Camus's position is that there is an enduring and shared human nature that determines what is better or worse for human beings. If we grant this claim, it is possible to identify enduring, shared, and coherent values. It is the task of revolt to reveal these human purposes to us. Camus is not aiming for a complete catalog of innate human purposes. Instead, he is eager to observe the most basic facts that we can recognize together. But, from *The Rebel* and from his other works, we can discern the kinds of things that he believes are essential to human beings. We can tell, from the kinds of values that he defends, what he believes human beings share. These include that all human beings seek and need health, friendship, love, dignity, a useful social role, the experience of beauty, and to have and pursue worthwhile purposes.

We might criticize such a list as little more than platitudes. But, if one were to argue that these are platitudes, then Camus's point would be made: that human beings need these things to thrive is a simple truth that we should all recognize. Only someone corrupted by theory, and unable to stop and look at the simple facts of human life, would deny that a human being is better off with his health or a sense that he is pursuing valuable purposes that he has chosen (all other things being equal). Furthermore, these are highly general claims. So much so that we can expect that many of Camus's Marxist peers, and perhaps some who identify themselves as existentialists, would accept that these were consistent with their own choices. Again, so much the better for Camus's approach. He is trying to draw our attention to facts; if we admit that they are facts, he has accomplished his end.

Camus offers no explicit decision theory, other than a deep suspicion of consequentialism and a conviction that over time revolt will lead to the establishment of norms and institutions that will guide us in our decision-making. In this regard, he offers an interesting variation on the kind of evolution of institutions one sees proposed by contract theorists like John Locke. Locke proposes a human nature that for him is a kind of assumed source of minimum values. Then, Locke relies on the belief that from our contractual arrangements and other social interactions there will emerge a decision theory and other norms. Because government requires the consent of the governed, there is also an error-correction mechanism built into the development of these laws and norms. For Camus, instead, there is not a contract but rather an emerging set of institutions that arise from countless successful instances of revolt.

Camus's value theory rests on the belief that human beings have a shared and stable human nature. This human nature includes many purposes the human being aims to achieve. The good for Camus, as for Aristotle, is the achievement of these ends. We must then structure society so that it can support and allow for this flourishing. But, according to Camus, both the discovery of our purposes and most moral progress arise from revolt. As noted, Camus distinguishes metaphysical revolt and historical revolt. Metaphysical revolt is the individual asserting his purposes in a purposeless universe and history. Historical revolt is the individual asserting his purposes against some social infringement of those purposes. In both cases, Camus believes that one must have a human nature in order for revolt (as he understands it) to be possible in the first place (recall his plea, "Why rebel if there is nothing permanent in oneself worth preserving?" [1956, 16]).

Camus also recognizes that the denial of human nature is the source of many justifications of tyranny, which arises from revolution:

> Absolute revolution, in fact, supposes the absolute malleability of human nature and its possible reduction to the condition of a historical force. But rebellion, in man, is the refusal to be treated as an object and to be reduced to simple historical terms. It is the affirmation of a nature common to all men, which eludes the world of power. History, undoubtedly, is one of the limits of man's experience; in this sense the revolutionaries are right. But man, by rebelling, imposes in his turn a limit to history, and at this limit the promise of a value is born. It is the birth of this value that the Caesarian revolution implacably combats today because it presages its final defeat and the obligation to renounce its principles. (1956, 250)

If we recognize that it is human nature to need and to pursue these and other things, then we have made the essential step of recognizing that there is a fact of the matter about what is better or worse for human beings. And we therefore have introduced objective, pancultural normative standards. Such standards can help us distinguish and evaluate kinds of action.

Camus does not offer an account of human nature, because it reveals itself through revolt. He has epistemic humility; we are learning, over long stretches of time, our own nature. This means that history can (but need not) result in the emerging self-understanding and self-assertion of human beings. Thus Camus writes:

> Rebellion with no other limits but historical expediency signifies unlimited slavery. To escape this fate, the revolutionary mind, if it wants

to remain alive, must therefore return again to the sources of rebellion and draw its inspiration from the only system of thought which is faithful to its origins: thought that recognizes limits. If the limit discovered by rebellion transfigures everything, if every thought, every action that goes beyond a certain point negates itself, there is, in fact, a measure by which to judge events and men. In history, as in psychology, rebellion is an irregular pendulum, which swings in an erratic arc because it is looking for its most perfect and profound rhythm. But its irregularity is not total: it functions around a pivot. Rebellion, at the same time that it suggests a nature common to all men, brings to light the measure and the limit which are the very principle of this nature. (1956, 294)

Camus's analogy is apt. A double pendulum, for example, is practically unpredictable. And yet it acts in deterministic ways. The principles that underlie its unpredictable motion are orderly and simple. Working with a double pendulum alone, we would need time and many false starts to understand the nature of motion. Just so, through the revolts of history, Camus argues, we have the potential to come to better understand human nature. Revolt reveals our essence.

Human progress, where society comes to respect more of human nature and to allow for more human flourishing, is thus possible. It is a logical possibility of Camus's theory that human beings might be able eventually to achieve a sufficiently just society so that they no longer found it necessary to revolt against that society. But in fact he does not expect this ever to happen. As he said in a speech at a monastery in 1948, "Perhaps we cannot prevent this world from being a world in which children are tortured. But we can reduce the number of tortured children" (1995, 73). And, even if a sufficiently just society were achieved, human beings would always find metaphysical revolt necessary: condemned to live in a universe without purpose, and to participate in a history without purpose, they must act in defiance of that purposelessness, and create and foster human purposes.

We might call this a tragic view of ethics: a recognition that we will never achieve a perfectly just state or condition. It is interesting to note that Camus's idea that our ethical understanding will emerge from revolt, and will be corrected and revised through revolt, is tantamount to a kind of fallibilism about ethics. He never uses such technical terminology, but I believe it is fitting here. On this view, there is no final state of complete knowledge but rather an endless search for improvement. This is consistent with his contention that we will never achieve a world without unjust suffering, but we can strive to ever improve and create an ever more just society. The denial of fallibilism is the theory that one could ultimately achieve perfect and complete knowledge. This is the view that utopians have: they ultimately find it necessary to deny any possibility of revision of their theories and predictions.

Historical revolt then is an act by a person who asserts a value and opposes a social practice. Camus describes this as a seeking for equality, and he seems to mean by this equality of privileges and rights to be recognized by society. There must be some kind of inequality of this kind for there to be historical revolt, since if the deprivation were not one arising from social deprivation of some kind but rather arising from the conditions of the world, the revolt would be metaphysical revolt.

There are social actions that might get called "revolt," in the everyday use of that term, that we have now ruled out on Camus's use of the term. The "rebellion" of the South against the North in the Civil War of the United States, for example, was not a revolt. By Camus's standards, the abolitionists are the rebels.[20] Similarly, we might in colloquial English use the word "revolt" for some violent response that had no goal. But here again, the term would not be used as Camus intends. From here on, we will use "revolt" in this normative sense: it is a kind of reaction, a kind of activity, that meets certain standards. (We should note here that Camus writes as did many scholars of his time using equivocal terms in an equivocal way, depending on us to determine their meaning by the context. Thus, sometimes in *The Rebel* he will refer to "revolt" in a context where he means someone else's concept of revolt. The book must be read carefully to separate out these uses. However, I will strive to use the term only in his full, normative sense in this text.)

Similarly, there might be some actions that satisfy many of these criteria that we are not inclined to call revolt. If one votes in a referendum that one perceives as having the possibility of increasing human freedom or otherwise benefiting human flourishing, for example, we would not typically call such an orderly participation in civics a "revolt." Probably, there is no benefit in attempting to draw a hard line between such acts of reform or civic activity and revolt. Camus is concerned with revolt that is a strong action against an unjust force, when such action seeks significant change in social mores or government institutions. But there will be no harm in allowing that there is no clear border between revolt and other kinds of action that meet many of his criteria.

Camus is primarily concerned with revolt that is undertaken by people who are well aware of the reasons for their cause. He refers to the rebel as explicitly saying, "This far but no farther." This suggests we might conclude that one criterion of just revolt is that the rebel be aware of his reasons. Camus does not explicitly consider this issue; he does in at least one place in *The Rebel* suggest that revolt can sometimes be a kind of pretheoretical reaction: "It is no more than incoherent pronouncement" (1956, 106). And indeed, it seems we can imagine a group of people who revolt and are caused to revolt in part because of the inequality in rights and privileges that they suffer, but they are not at first able to articulate the reasons for their frustration. It may be useful to be able to say that they are justified by Camus's criteria, setting aside as a separate issue their own understanding of their actions. However, ultimately the revolt would need to be articulated, since to be revolt as Camus understands it, it must lead ultimately to greater understanding of the human condition and even to change in institutions.

Revolt, so understood, could be conceived as an essential determinant of some forms of moral progress; in particular, it is an essential determinant of moral progress in the modern West. People who revolt assert greater equality of rights, assert limits to social wrongs, and increase the likelihood that others will flourish in light of their human nature. To the degree that they and others like them succeed, there is moral progress. On Camus's view, then, history has no direction or single purpose; but, from our perspective, it is possible that things can get better for human beings if we revolt against injustice and continue to establish and improve the institutions of our societies.

Perhaps the most challenging aspect of Camus's conception of revolt is that it is not a purely descriptive concept; he clearly includes normative constraints in his theory of revolt. For example, he distinguishes revolt from a reaction that is driven by *ressentiment*. Revolt is by definition for him not motivated by *ressentiment*. Furthermore, revolt is an assertion of shared human purposes—or, as he puts it, "rights." There cannot, as he describes it, be a revolt that arises because the agent is seeking some particular and unshared good. There is some difficulty here. Camus also argues—very plausibly, I believe—that it is through revolt that we come to realize some of the shared human purposes that we later defend with the concept of a right. But then we have a circularity: an action is revolt when it arises from and recognizes a shared, enduring, common human purpose; but we discover the shared, enduring, common human purposes through revolt. "What is at stake is humanity's gradually increasing self-awareness as it pursues its course" (1956, 20). Equivalent to this worry is that Camus does not give us a method to distinguish actions that are not revolt but claim to be from true revolt (as he understands the term). I discuss this in chapter 5. But as for the circularity here: I believe this circularity is not pernicious. It can be that we try out certain ideas of our humanity, and that over time some of these fall away and others are recognized as genuinely human universals—perhaps, for example, because the revolt appeals to many other people or proves to cohere with our other recognized human values. We might call this the iterative process of ethical progress: we try out revolt, and when it really is motivated by defense or realization of a human universal, this helps us all discover that human universal. But presumably this process is not perfect, and Camus is instead focusing on the successful cases.

We might summarize the view as something like this:

Revolt hypothesis: *Sometimes, if an intrinsic human purpose is offended, this motivates a defiant reaction.*

Here the phrase "defiant reaction" is meant to be a neutral term that includes revolt. I need the neutral term "defiant reaction" because I am not defining "revolt," nor am I offering necessary and sufficient conditions for revolt (as Camus understands revolt). It seems obvious that there are some defiant reactions that are not motivated by an offense to an intrinsic human purpose. That's why the hypothesis is a conditional and not a biconditional; the converse of the hypothesis is not true.

This small clarification draws our attention to an interesting fact about Camus's theory. He is assuming that there is something shared between metaphysical revolt and historical revolt. This is plausible, but it is also nontrivial. In the case of metaphysical revolt, the defiant reaction (referred to in our definition) is presumably the continued striving to support and foster human purposes, in defiance of a universe indifferent to those purposes and in defiance of despair. In the case of historical revolt, the defiant reaction is retributive. The reaction is something like civil disobedience, refusal to participate in social norms, or another retributive act. The essential point is that it puts a cost on others with the intent of forcing a change in the social order to reduce the offense. In both cases, Camus assumes there is a common motivational mechanism underlying the two forms of revolt.

We can see how Camus's theory is strikingly different than Beauvoir's theory. For Beauvoir, some action is permissible as long as it will increase freedom. For Camus, the question will rather be whether some action allows for, or promotes, human purposes. These human purposes are not arbitrary, and at least some of them are not chosen. There will be a fact of the matter, then, whether some action does promote or hinder human flourishing. Camus's concern is to respond not primarily to existentialism—I am unaware of whether he even read *The Ethics of Ambiguity*—but rather to totalitarian Marxism. But here too his ethic will rule out the cruel excesses of Stalin's USSR. The totalitarian Marxists understood human nature as a malleable product of economic conditions. For Camus, instead, there will be an objective fact of the matter about whether some action by the state will promote, or hinder, human purposes and therefore human flourishing.

But why did revolt slip into revolution and then violence and cruelty? Why did the Marxists, who spoke of a better world, create the horror of Stalinism? This is Camus's primary concern. We turn to these issues in chapters 3 and 4.

THREE

Metaphysical Revolt

REVOLT

Most of the *The Rebel* is dedicated to describing revolt: Camus argues that revolt is essential to our moral development, but also it can lead to revolution. Here we are presented with a terminological difficulty. Camus often uses the term "revolution" for extreme social movements where an abstract and totalitarian ideology dominates political action. This can happen because revolt loses sight of its original motives and becomes disconnected from the human purposes that were being asserted through the initial acts of revolt, or it can happen because the pursuit of some particular human purpose becomes exaggerated and is pursued in a way that harms other human purposes. In either case, theory, or some other extreme drive, replaces the revelation of our human nature, and human beings are seen as malleable and subservient to this other cause.

Strictly speaking, then, there can be revolutions that do not have the failings that Camus is concerned to identify. In his short essay "In Defense of *The Rebel*," Camus says this explicitly:

> I have simply said that revolt without revolution ends logically in a delirium of destruction and that the rebel, if he does not rebel on behalf of everyone, ends up by reaching an extremity of solitude where everything seems permitted to him. Inversely, I have tried to show that revolution, deprived of the incessant control of the spirit of revolt, ends by falling into a nihilism of efficacy, resulting in terror. (2004, 210)

Presumably, "revolt without revolution" here means revolt that does not seek to build institutions or widely shared and enduring mores that ensure the rights of other human beings. We might introduce some term like "totalizing revolution" for the cases of revolution that are harmful and have lost connection to the spirit of revolt. Recall that, for Camus, "unity" is when a set of purposes can order and make sense of our place in the world; ideally, these would justify our other purposes and guarantee that they are sufficient. Totality is a kind of attempt by the state or ideology to create and enforce a form of unity: "Totality is, in effect, nothing other than the ancient dream of unity common to both believers and rebels, but projected horizontally onto an earth deprived of God" (1956, 233). The harmful form of revolution aims to assert this dominating purpose, indifferent to other human purposes.

In passages like the one above, Camus recognized that "revolution" was an ambiguous term, and that if some people thought that any substantial change in social conditions that endured should be called "revolution," then he was not against revolution in that sense.[1] In fact, "revolution" would then be the aim of revolt, which seeks to create institutions respecting human purposes. As long as we keep these observations in mind, we can—for the sake of brevity—use the term "revolution" in the remainder of this book as a technical term, meaning totalizing revolutions of the kind that Camus aims to criticize. This is consistent with most of Camus's use of the term, especially in *The Rebel*.

Camus's primary task will be to show how we might prevent revolt's decay into revolution. Revolt is necessary, but can it be controlled? Camus describes two aspects of revolt, which he calls "metaphysical revolt" and "historical revolt." Historical revolt is what most of us mean by "revolt": some kind of movement or reaction to a social condition. Metaphysical revolt instead concerns not the social but the metaphysical. Camus's own explanation is clear:

> Metaphysical rebellion is the movement by which man protests against his condition and against the whole of creation. It is metaphysical because it contests the ends of man and of creation. The slave protests against the condition in which he finds himself within his state of slavery; the metaphysical rebel protests against the condition in which he finds himself as a man. The rebel slave affirms that there is something

in him that will not tolerate the manner in which his master treats him; the metaphysical rebel declares that he is frustrated by the universe. For both of them, it is not only a question of pure and simple negation. In both cases, in fact, we find a value judgment in the name of which the rebel refuses to approve the condition in which he finds himself. (1956, 23)

The slave in the passage of course exemplifies historical revolt.

It is because his notion of revolt is partly normative that Camus argues that revolt is a Western phenomenon. This may shock a contemporary reader, but it is important to remember he is using "revolt" as a technical term. Camus reckons that most non-Western societies are religious. He may be wrong about that; if so, it is possible that we could replace "Western" with "secular" in his formulation while still preserving his intent. The important point is that in a traditional religious society, or in a society where myths are taken seriously as guiding truths, "all the answers [have] been given" (1956, 20). In terms of metaphysical revolt, this means that one does not judge and reject the universe as one finds it. One already knows the answers to all questions about teleology and ethics: these are given in religion or myth, or at least can be derived from the first principles already given in religion or myth. In contrast, those in the West can feel their world is ill-made (if it were to be made) and deserving of condemnation and resistance. This resistance is the source of progress, and also at any time our values are open for improvement and revision. Similarly, historical revolt is a Western phenomenon because in a traditional, religious culture, one sees injustice as a failure to live up to the deity's strictures. In a Western, secular society, instead, injustice is a call for debate about theory. We are not only reacting to the injustice, but we are as a result also striving to develop a better theory of justice. Here again, the iterative but fallible realization of justice over time is perhaps the best way to understand this.

There is an interesting parallel here with some of the work of Karl Popper. (To my knowledge, Popper and Camus never read each other's work; thus, the parallels are interesting for showing independent but similar approaches.) Popper draws a distinction between open societies and closed societies. Modern Western societies would all qualify (at the time of this writing) as what Popper calls "open societies." Closed societies for him are "organic": "A closed society resembles a herd or a tribe in being a semi-organic unit whose members are held together by semi-biological ties—kinship, living together, sharing common efforts, common dangers, common joys and common distress" (1963 [1945], 173). In such a society, Popper claims, "There are few problems in this form of life, and nothing really equivalent to moral problems" (172). Surely revolt (as Camus understands it) would not be a phenomenon of this closed society but only the open society. (In chapter 4, I make additional comparisons between Camus's account of revolt and Karl Popper's account of the open society.)

This chapter serves three purposes. First, we will examine Camus's explanation of metaphysical revolt and how this revolt tends to descend into revolution and cruelty. Second, there is an important question about the relation of freedom to purpose, which is not made explicit in Camus's account but underlies it. I argue that there is a paradox to taking freedom as the highest end-in-itself. I show that Camus has recognized what we can call a new paradox of liberalism; this is the first of two new paradoxes that Camus recognized (the second paradox is discussed in chapter 6). Third, I try to answer the questions that Camus's account raises: does metaphysical revolt really matter? Camus believes metaphysical revolt influences historical revolt, and he gives us the novel idea that some of our social problems arise from the concerns human beings have about their metaphysical condition. Is this plausible? Is it true?

WHAT IS METAPHYSICAL REVOLT?

Metaphysical revolt is the active rejection of some aspects of one's metaphysical condition. If someone rages against the prospect of death, for example, they are engaging in metaphysical revolt. It is a metaphysical condition that a human must die; to reject this, to judge it as an injustice, to denounce it and call for it to end, is to engage in metaphysical revolt. As such, metaphysical revolt will often be akin to attacking the sea: a futile gesture. Camus's earliest description of metaphysical revolt may be in his essay "The Dessert," where he describes his reaction in a Florentine cloister:

I was carried away by something I mistook for distress, which was only anger. It was raining. I was reading the inscriptions on the tombstones and ex-votos. . . . Nearly all of them, according to the inscriptions, had resigned themselves to dying, doubtless because they accepted their other duties. . . . Everything in me protested against such a resignation. "You must," said the inscriptions. But no, and my revolt was right. . . . I said no. I said no with all my strength. The tombstones were teaching me that it was pointless, that life is *"col sol levante, col sol cadente."* But even today I cannot see what my revolt loses by being pointless, and I am well aware of what it gains. (1970 [1938], 98–99)

Rejection of death is perhaps the most common and basic form of metaphysical revolt, but there are other forms. Any rejection of our metaphysical condition, motivated by a sense that it impedes our purposes, can qualify. The rebel "attacks a shattered world in order to demand unity from it" (1956, 23–24).

Camus argues that Christianity was essential to metaphysical revolt. "The only thing that gives meaning to human protest is the idea of a personal god who has created, and is therefore responsible for, everything. And so we can say, without being paradoxical, that in the Western World the history of rebellion is inseparable from the history of Christianity" (1956, 28). This claim is both plausible but problematic. It is plausible because Camus convincingly describes cases of metaphysical revolt where the bad features of our metaphysical condition are taken as personal affronts. And, of course, human beings are more angry at agents who harm them than at chance events. Indeed, arguably it is irrational to be angry at chance events. Thus, a personal god who failed to make a suitable world could merit our wrath. Furthermore, many of the examples of metaphysical rebels whom Camus will describe are explicitly dedicated to opposing and blaspheming Christianity. They aim to judge God.

However, although this may be true as an explanation of some motives, it cannot be that metaphysical revolt is only available to the lapsed Christian. As we saw in chapter 1, Camus's later model of an absurd hero is Dr. Rieux in his novel *The Plague*. Rieux is an atheist, but he is also a metaphysical rebel. He fights death even when he knows he cannot defeat death. Thus, it may well be that Christianity has shaped much of metaphysical revolt, and perhaps even was essential to the development of the idea that one should judge and reject (rather than accept as impersonal but inevitable chance) one's metaphysical condition, but there can now be metaphysical rebels who are not Christians or even lapsed Christians.

There is at stake here an important metaphysical issue. In chapter 1, I discussed foundationalism about purpose: the view that our purposes are justified and sufficient if they serve certain fundamental purposes that are taken to be self-evidently justified and sufficient. It is plausible that what Camus is identifying in Christianity is that it formed the most common form of foundationalism about purpose in the West. God's purposes served as the foundation for our purposes. In this case, then, any adoption of foundationalism about purposes, coupled with the belief that we have lost those foundations, will cause us to view the world or history as absurd, and this in turn is a condition in which a certain form of metaphysical revolt arises. This is consistent with Camus's criticisms of Hegel and Marx, whom he recognizes as having a fundamental similarity to the Christian worldview. Marx replaces God with history and sets a future utopian state of communism in place of redemption and heaven. Furthermore, Camus's constant calls for a philosophy that is Mediterranean, rather than German, seem to turn on the observation that our human purposes do not need to unify with cosmic purposes in order to be sufficient and justified. He sees this as a Greek and Mediterranean belief. Thus, his claim that revolt is founded in Christianity could be interpreted as being a recognition that many instances of metaphysical revolt are motived by the adoption of foundationalism about purpose.

Camus considers several examples of kinds of metaphysical rebels. For each kind of metaphysical revolt, he picks one or more examples of a rebel whose revolt went to excess, leading to metaphysical revolution—"What is the bitter end of metaphysical rebellion? Metaphysical revolution" (1956, 58). These include Sade; the poets Rimbaud, Baudelaire, and Lautréamont; Nietzsche; and the surrealists. He describes these different individuals as going through different progressions from revolt to revolution, but there is a shared pattern that emerges: each in his own way rejects any limit on his own freedom. Each seeks a life that is *démesure*, without measure. These metaphysical revolutionaries seek some ultimate or total solution, which ends up being a kind of substitute for God. These substitutes include freedom, or humanity, or history. But in each case, it is lack of restraint that characterizes their creed. Lack of restraint means not curbing the pursuit of one purpose in order to develop other purposes, and it often also means individualistically pursuing a purpose in a way that is a harm to the purposes of others. Lack of restraint always leads to a kind of failure. Let us consider some of these rebels.

Sade is the writer who presents, Camus claims, "the first coherent offensive" against a hostile heaven. Sade claims to be an atheist, but it is hard to believe him: he is so concerned with blasphemy that he is always reacting to, rather than escaping from, Christianity. His large body of work offers us a vast repetition of one man's imagination of endlessly satisfying his desire to oppress and humiliate others. For Sade, Camus claims, "Freedom, particularly when it is a prisoner's dream, cannot endure limitations. It must sanction crime or it is no longer freedom. On this essential point Sade never varies" (1956, 40). This kind of reasoning characterizes all the metaphysical revolutionaries: the goal to surpass limits on their freedom leads inevitably to crime. Camus uses the word "crime" frequently, and it is clear from his usage that what he means is immoral harm to other human beings. The term represents for him a way to refer to immoral action, infringing on the purposes of other human beings.

For the metaphysical rebel there is this constant lurking danger: one perceives the world as unjust or otherwise offensive. This might be conceived as an offense against one's freedom. Death, for example, is an ultimate limitation to freedom. If one makes this leap, then the appropriate reaction might seem to be the pursuit of more freedom. And thus, ever greater freedom can become the dominant goal of the metaphysical revolutionary.

Camus sees in Sade a kind of movement in reasoning that he believes is typical of metaphysical revolt when it turns toward the ideal of a life without limits. This notion of having, or being without, limits must be carefully clarified. Camus is not describing metaphysical constraints when he says freedom with (or without) limits. He means rather to refer to the kinds of norms that one chooses to follow. Living without limits is to live without obedience to norms (or, rather, it is actively trying to live without obedience to norms). Equivalently, "extreme freedom" is to exercise one's freedom in ways that break and disobey (many) norms. In contrast, to live with measure (*mesure*) is to live in voluntary obedience to certain norms

(Camus will later describe it as recognizing that freedom must include responsibilities—and greater freedom means greater responsibilities). Camus shows that any such goal of a life without limits, if pursued, ultimately leads to an embracing of power and domination, which then inevitably declines into cruelty.

Camus's reasoning is sound. We express values with our limits. When we say that there should be no murder, we express our valuing of (other) human lives. When we say that there should be no theft, we express our valuing of property rights. And so on. In each case, there are no values without corresponding limits on freedom. But it follows now from basic logic that if someone wants to attempt to go beyond all limits, then they must attack every value.[2] Many of these values concern the respect of other human being, and so the metaphysical revolutionary who takes increasing freedom as the most important end-in-itself ultimately commits to violating the integrity of other human beings. Furthermore, a life without values is a life without purpose. There is a straight line from the goal of limitless freedom to complete nihilism (in this context, meaning a refusal to respect any values).

But there is one complication to this reasoning from unlimited freedom to nihilism, and it suggests a kind of tentative value that might survive the drive toward nihilism. A life without limits requires force. One lives in a society, and one must have the power to resist and oppose social norms. After all, by definition, if there are social norms, then other people will strive to maintain those norms. And even one's own inclinations—such as values acquired and still held by habit—might lead to motivations to maintain social norms. To overcome all norms in order to express a limitless freedom, one must even overcome one's own implicit values. This sounds like a version of what Nietzsche called "overcoming" oneself, which is one of Nietzsche's favorite concepts. But if we aim simply to always overcome ourselves and others, there is implicit in this a kind of metavalue: this metaphysical rebel of excess can measure his progress only in terms of how much he succeeds in overcoming. And that means he can have one stable goal: ever more power. And, indeed, Nietzsche attempted to reduce our lives to the will to power.

Some metaphysical rebels celebrated solitude; Nietzsche's Zarathustra lives in a cave with only nonhuman animals for company. This is one way to escape the limits that other human beings create. But it is a brute fact that a human being is a *zoon politikon*. We are social animals and live in relation to each other. Thus the exercise of power, for no other purpose but more power, leads to the requirement that we overcome and oppress others. It leads to cruelty. For how else can we measure our success in overcoming limits but by overcoming the limits of those around us? And those limits are their values. The goal of a life without limits becomes a goal of taking away from other people what they value.

Camus often calls this valuing of power an endorsement of "efficacy." The reason is clear: to assert a limitless freedom, one must be effective at overcoming limits. And, as we noted, those limits are ultimately the values of other people. So the only measure of success in the pursuit of limitless freedom is the effectiveness of one's domination of others.

Sade would oppose any appeals to respect other human beings because this would require restraint. Sade's literary work has as a fundamental goal the portrayal of lives without limits. In his discussion of Sade, Camus cites a section of Sade's *Philosophy in the Bedroom* in which the character Dolmance reads from a pamphlet he claims to have found. The fake attribution fools no one—this is Sade's vision we are reading. Written as an appeal to his fellow revolutionary republicans, Sade herein describes the appropriate new laws and mores that the revolution of 1789 should institutionalize. What does he offer? Legalized murder, when it is committed in passion between citizens—but the state shall be forbidden to use capital punishment. Calumny and theft shall also be legal. All this is prelude to what Sade really cares about: in the republic of his dreams, rape shall be legalized. A man may rape any woman he chooses, whenever he chooses. This is justified because the man is, according to Sade, the more powerful; in this way, Sade corroborates Camus's claim that the metaphysical rebel who respects no limits must resort to power and oppression as the sole measure of success. Also, Sade argues, the state should provide facilities that allow these rapes to be conveniently done on the street. And, in the coup de grâce, Sade argues that there shall be no limit, no limit of any kind, to the age of a child that can be legally raped. Camus does not mention this last criterion for Sade's republic, but it is essential. We are most protective of children; metaphysical revolution, in its drive to overcome all norms and limits, must ultimately always seek to transgress the protections we put around children. This can be taken as its most reliable indicator.

Camus sees in this text—and in Sade's many novels, plays, and stories—a vision of life without limits (*demesuree*). This extreme form of metaphysical revolution takes the kind of worry that is later expressed by Dostoevsky's Ivan in *The Brother's Karamazov*—that if there is no divine plan expressed through immortal life, then "all is lawful"—and transforms it into a goal. Sade wants to overcome every social constraint to satisfy his own desires. His goal is to assert his own human freedom against any social law and anyone else's desires.

In his novels, Sade's fantasies often take place in medieval fortresses where the libertines are able to rule without restraint over sexual slaves. And Camus argues,

> For Sade, man's emancipation is consummated in these strongholds of debauchery where a kind of bureaucracy of vice rules over the life and death of the men and women who have committed themselves forever to the hell of their desires. His works abound with descriptions of these privileged places where feudal libertines, to demonstrate to their assembled victims their absolute impotence and servitude, always repeat the Duc de Blangis's speech to the common people of the *One Hundred and Twenty Days of Sodom*: "You are already dead to the world." (1956, 42)

But what about the libertine who rules this world? Camus observes that "In Sade's fortress republic, there are only machines and mechanics" (43). The victory of these libertines becomes their defeat. They are doomed to a mechanical repetition. "The masters of these tortured communities do not find the satisfaction they so desperately desire. . . . This leads to that dreary accumulation of erotic and criminal scenes in Sade's novels, which, paradoxically, leaves the reader with the impression of a hideous chastity" (43–44). Camus concludes that the metaphysical revolutionary will never achieve his own goals, or any stable goal.

There is a parallel here with the observations I made in chapter 2. I argued that if we have no intrinsic purposes, and all our purposes are chosen, then we have as a consequence the precise condition that Beauvoir described: we get no satisfaction from achieving a purpose, but rather just must move on to making another choice, choosing a new purpose and trying to achieve that. The result is a world without progress: things cannot get better. Each person is merely undertaking the cyclical task of achieving arbitrary purposes until death. This was in contrast to the accomplishment claim that achieving an intrinsic purpose is an enduring benefit. Camus identifies in Sade's metaphysical revolution a condition equivalent to rejecting the accomplishment claim. If we take freedom as an end-in-itself and the most important goal, we can predict a similar deflation of our purposes. The goal of being more free finds its realization in an endless seeking to overcome new limitations to freedom. Once one has overcome some limit to freedom, you have not achieved some stable and enduring state of freedom. Rather, you have just earned some temporary incremental proof that you have expanded your freedom. But the quest must continue since expanding freedom is the highest goal. Thus, there is no progress, just an endless cycle. In Sade, his fantasies of sexual violence are not titillating or satisfying but rather an endless dull repetition of the assault of one person after another. There can be no enduring benefit from the accomplished purpose. There is only the endless moving on to the next increase in freedom, the next assault.

It is worth noting also that Camus is indicating a kind of revelation of failure in Sade. We who live a life within limits cannot reason with Sade. We could not reason with someone who found attractive this idea of a life that had no limits and expressed this by overcoming others and oppressing them. But we can look at what they imagine such a life would be like and see that what is portrayed here is not a flourishing life. The life envisioned is a grim failure. Sade's dream is meant to show the exercise of godlike power, and this is supposed to give to the sadist godlike satisfactions. And yet, even in fiction, even when freed to imagine his ideal life as some kind of glorious victory of his personal desires, all Sade can muster is a portrait of failure and mechanical misery. Sade's fantasies should be his strongest persuasions; instead, they damn his vision. In the next section of this chapter, I will assess one reason why this must be.

What about the other metaphysical revolutionaries? They fare no better. Camus turns next to the French romantic and decadent poets (such as Baudelaire and Rimbaud). He understands these poets as celebrating crime as some kind of expression of transgression, but the core motive, Camus uncovers, is "outraged innocence." They are angry that the world is not living up to some ideal of unity, and in response they celebrate spiteful condemnations of this failure. The romantics take Milton's Satan as their model. "Since God claims all that is good in man, it is necessary to deride what is good and choose what is evil. Hatred of death and of injustice will lead, therefore, if not to the exercise, at least to the vindication, of evil and murder" (1956, 47). Camus offers us an insightful challenge: "compare the Lucifer of the painters of the Middle Ages with the Satan of the romantics" (49). This is an inspired demand. Consider the grotesque figure in Michael Pacher's pre-Rinascimento painting *The Devil Presenting St. Augustine with the Book of Vices*. Satan is unnatural, grotesque, with a head like a sickly dog and a second face howling from his rectum. The figure is perfectly ugly. Contrast this with a painting by a French romantic, created during Baudelaire's lifetime: *Fallen Angel* by Alexandre Cabanel. The figure is in form and beauty modeled on the Greek ideal. The wings are not bat wings but the pale wings of some raptor, if not of a dove. Satan has been transformed from loathsome bricolage of unfunctional monstrous elements into a beautiful young man to be admired. In these two images we see the transformation from the conviction that evil is ugly and must be rejected to evil instead becoming a model to be admired and followed. Satan becomes the archetype for "The romantic hero [who] considers himself compelled to do evil by his nostalgia for an unrealizable good" (48). Thus we see again the movement we saw in Sade: metaphysical revolt celebrates the attack on restraint or balance (*mesure*). This inevitably becomes a celebration of the infringement of those last limits: the integrity of other human beings. It becomes the celebration of crime.

Camus's observation that metaphysical revolutionaries celebrate crime is well supported by his examples, and also highly plausible. These revolutionaries see criminals as transgressive, and so they celebrate criminals for this transgressiveness. On this view, the victim merely represents the status quo. This explains why the metaphysical revolutionaries have no sympathy or concern for the victims.

For Camus, many other poets and artists end up in a similar place, though for different starting motives. He is particularly harsh on the surrealists, who were of course his contemporaries and who unsurprisingly resented his attack. The surrealists represent the more pure form of metaphysical rebellion that emerges: freedom explicitly solely for freedom's sake.

Camus quotes Breton: "Incapable of accepting the fate assigned to me, my highest perceptions outraged by this denial of justice, I refrain from adapting my existence to the ridiculous conditions of existence here below" (92). Again, the slide from metaphysical revolt to metaphysical revolution ends in the celebration of, and call for, the violation of others. Breton sums up his philosophy as

> The simplest Surrealist act consists of dashing down the street, pistol in hand, and firing blindly, as fast as you can pull the trigger, into the crowd. Anyone who, at least once in his life, has not dreamed of thus putting an end to the petty system of debasement and cretinization in effect has a well-defined place in that crowd with his belly at barrel-level. (1975, 125)

Ironically, Breton eventually identifies as a Marxist. This is ironic because Marxism does not cohere with the surrealist philosophy. But in another sense it is predictable: most of the intellectuals of Camus's generation in France became Marxists, regardless of whether this creed was consistent with their other beliefs. And the motion is one that Camus predicts and explains: the metaphysical revolutionary is hungry for some substitute for God. One substitute is the deification of human beings. But a substitute that proves more compelling is the deification of history, and the siren song of a future utopia to be achieved through violence in the present. These two paths are not unrelated since the Marxist promises a new, and better, human being in the communist future.

Camus claims that Nietzsche is our best example of the attempt to replace God with man. Camus's primary source in his discussion of Nietzsche is *The Will to Power*. This is a controversial choice because this text is a collection of Nietzsche's notes for an unfinished book on his concept of the will to power. Some scholars believe it is possible that Nietzsche would have said something very different in the final text. I won't address this issue here. To some degree, this issue is irrelevant since Camus is assessing influence, and *The Will to Power* was influential. There is a kind of coherent vision that emerges in *The Will to Power*, and it is not unreasonable for Camus to interpret it as an example of metaphysical revolution, and not unreasonable to associate that form of metaphysical revolution with Nietzsche or at least with the followers of Nietzsche.

Camus sees Nietzsche's struggle with nihilism as leading to his embrace of *amor fati*. This is a replacement for the *odium fati* that (Nietzsche believes) was the product of Christianity. This is a twist on metaphysical rebellion since it calls for a kind of complete embrace of the world, whereas metaphysical rebellion is defined as a form of rejection of some aspect of our world or our condition. "The Nietzschean affirmative, forgetful of the original negative, disavows rebellion at the same time that it disavows the ethic that refuses to accept the world as it is" (1956, 77). But it is not enough to accept the world; one must also strive to produce something new, something that sets human beings apart. The only antidote to nihilism is the creative tyrant, and Nietzsche prefers the tyrant to the Christian's image of the hero: we should strive "even for a Cesare Borgia rather than for a Parsifal." Here we see again the kind of movement that Camus claims to find in metaphysical revolt that is without *mesure*: from rejection of past ethical theories and rejection of our condition, to a celebration of power and "efficacy," which ultimately can only express itself in cruelty and the celebration of cruelty. Camus sees in Nietzsche's concept of the *Ubermensch* the project to replace God with man. Comte had a similar project. But Camus sees in this movement also a predecessor to a kind of thinking that will reach its apex in applied Marxism. The *Ubermensch* is a future man; a replacement for God that will come later. Under Marxism, we will find ourselves waiting for the communist man. But this results in the replacement of God with history: that is, they have a theory that history has a direction, and the end of this history becomes the primary value and justification for a consequentialist ethic. "The rebel whom Nietzsche set on his knees before the cosmos will, from now on, kneel before history. . . . Nietzsche, at least in his theory of super-humanity, and Marx before him, with his classless society, both replace the Beyond with the Later On" (79).

Camus considers other metaphysical rebels. These include the poet Lautrémont, other surrealists, the figure of Ivan Karamazov from Dostoevsky's *The Brothers Karamazov*, and the theorist of absolute selfishness Max Stirner. The patterns that Camus discovers are different in their details but the same in their ends. Metaphysical revolt, if not restrained, if not pursued with *mesure*, leads to metaphysical revolution. In metaphysical revolution, the desire to overcome all limits entails that efficacy will become the only measure of success, and cruelty to other human beings is the final opportunity to expand one's exercise of freedom.

THE FIRST NEW PARADOX OF LIBERALISM

I contend that Camus has here recognized a new paradox of liberalism, one of two that can be found in his work (the second new paradox is described in chapter 6). Camus does not use such terminology, so I am translating from his own idiom. But the implications of his criticism of metaphysical revolution are clear.

To understand what I mean by a "paradox of liberalism," we can refer to Karl Popper's description of the paradox of tolerance in *The Open Society and Its Enemies*, a book that (as I will discuss at some length in chapter 5) shares many concerns with *The Rebel*. Popper argues that Plato describes several paradoxes of freedom, which he summarizes as "the so-called *paradox of freedom*": "the argument that freedom in the sense of absence of any restraining control must lead to very great restraint, since it makes the bully free to enslave the meek" (1963, 265n4). But Popper writes that there is another kind of paradox for freedom or liberal society: "Less well known is the *paradox of tolerance*: Unlimited tolerance must lead to the disappearance of tolerance. If we extend unlimited tolerance even to those who are intolerant, if we are not prepared to defend a tolerant society against the onslaught of the intolerant, then the tolerant will be destroyed, and tolerance with them" (265n4). For Plato, the primary cause of tyranny—or perhaps rather, of the genesis of tyranny—is a leader who had not cultivated his virtues, and thus he acts without restraint on his most base desires. This arises because we have different kinds of purposes and desires: "the soul of a man within him has a better part and a worse part, and the expression 'self-mastery' means the control of the worse part by the naturally better part" (1961, 672). Thus there is a kind of paradox. The freedom to allow these more base desires to reign can result in less freedom for everyone.

Popper's paradox of tolerance is a more general claim: he needs no reference to the motivations of those who oppress others. Rather, consistent with the way that Popper thinks about these issues, his focus is on the social structure. He warns us that we must be able to remove bad leaders in an effective way. The motive of those leaders (the internal constitution of their souls, for example) won't concern him, but rather he is concerned with the institutions that can avoid oppression and bad leadership. In the paradox of tolerance, he has identified a kind of impediment to the best methods for avoiding such tyrannies: criticism. For Popper, we must structure society so it is as easy as possible to remove bad leaders. This will rest on a culture of social criticism. We keep criticism alive by tolerating diverse theories about our social condition. But this opens the door to his paradox: if we must in a liberal society tolerate diverse ideas and theories, then prima facie we should tolerate the kinds of ideas and theories that (if implemented) lead to the end of social criticism and therefore to oppression. The challenge becomes how to balance free speech with assaults on the liberal order.

When Camus describes Sade, he identifies him as having the tyrannical impulse to place his desire over the integrity of others. His metaphysical revolution leads to a result that is, at first, similar to the model of Plato's tyrant.

> Sade denies God in the name of nature—the ideological concepts of his time present it in mechanistic form—and he makes nature a power bent on destruction. For him, nature is sex; his logic leads him to a lawless universe where the only master is the inordinate energy of desire. This is his delirious kingdom, in which he finds his finest means of expression: "What are all the creatures of the earth in comparison with a single one of our desires!" (1956, 38)

But ultimately Camus identifies a more fundamental problem, more general than the problem of Plato's tyrant motivated by base desires. When one makes freedom both an end-in-itself and the highest good, then how will one pursue and increase that freedom? The drive to find ever greater freedom results in a race for power and domination; *bellum omnium contra omnes*.

> In a world that knows no other rule than murder, beneath criminal heaven, and in the name of a criminal nature, however, Sade, in reality, obeys no other law than that of inexhaustible desire. But to desire without limit is the equivalent of being desired without limit. License to destroy supposes that you yourself can be destroyed. Therefore you must struggle and dominate. The law of this world is nothing but the law of force; its driving force, the will to power. (41)

The extreme limit of metaphysical revolution is "complete totalitarianism, universal crime, an aristocracy of cynicism, and the desire for an apocalypse" (46). Camus also identified what he believes is a later form of metaphysical revolution, captured by Dostoevsky in the character of Ivan Karamazov. Ivan starts from a position of "outraged innocence," but in judging God sets up human beings as God.

> The master of the world, after his legitimacy has been contested, must be overthrown. Man must occupy his place. "As God and immortality do not exist, the new man is permitted to become God." But what does becoming God mean? It means, in fact, recognizing that everything is permitted and refusing to recognize any other law but one's own.... To become God is to accept crime. (88–89)

What Camus identifies in the excesses of metaphysical revolution is the equivalent of a more general and fundamental paradox of liberalism, although it is closely related to these paradoxes described by Plato and Popper. Let us call it the "Paradox of Freedom as the Highest End-in-Itself." When we take freedom as an end-in-itself, and most importantly when—like Beauvoir—we take it as the highest end,[3] then we enter a regime in which the motive will be to ever increase one's freedom. What are the limits to freedom that must be overcome in order to increase one's freedom? One must find some limit to freedom and then overcome that limit. At first, the limits to freedom may well be injustices. But if the march for ever greater freedom is to continue, eventually the limits to be broken must be traditions, things such as the mores of family or marriage. It may even include attacking and denying the limits of the body—that is, the limits that are inherited through our evolutionary history. But when our social traditions are destroyed and the body is altered, what is next? How does one keep increasing freedom? The outcome of metaphysical revolution must be the pursuit of violating the integrity of other human beings, since this will be the last set of barriers to the relentless pursuit of ever greater freedom. This then is the Paradox of Freedom as the Highest End-in-Itself: if we take freedom as the most valued end-in-itself, then the integrity of other human beings will be seen as a limit to freedom and the integrity of other human beings will be attacked. It is paradoxical because if universally adopted, each person would be the subject of violence and have their freedom profoundly diminished.

The metaphysical revolutionaries that Camus discusses are not liberals. Neither Sade nor Nietzsche nor Breton pays any allegiance to any principle of universalizability. As they seek ever greater freedom, Sade asks for state support of the rape of children and Breton celebrates the idea of murdering people out on their daily walk. While contemporary liberalism takes freedom as an end-in-itself (perhaps not the highest), one might hope that John Stuart Mill's proposal in his essay *On Liberty*—which many of us consider as partly defining "liberalism"—that freedom does not include the right to harm others would undo such a paradox (e.g., see 2015 [1859], 12–13). A similar sentiment was expressed by the French National Assembly in the Declaration of the Rights of Man: "Liberty consists in the freedom to do everything which injures no one else; hence the exercise of the natural rights of each man has no limits except those which assure to the other members of the society the enjoyment of the same rights. These limits can only be determined by law."[4]

Mill's principle is typically referred to as "the harm principle": liberty must stop at the limit where it harms other people. A liberal society that adopts such a principle might find it sufficient to prevent the Paradox of Freedom as a Highest End-in-Itself. But there is room for doubt. Any vagueness or ambiguity in the definition of "harm" or "injury" leaves the door open to allowing some people to define the integrity of others as a kind of harm. If another does not use the words I want him to use, is that a harm? If another does not respect or celebrate my choices in life, is that a harm? If another does not agree with my values, is that a harm? Many people answer yes to all three of these questions, and many nation-states are aggressively willing to enforce such assessments. So, unless "harm" is rigorously defined and that definition is rigorously enforced, Mill's harm principle cannot allow us to escape the Paradox of Freedom as the Highest End-in-Itself. Obviously, the situation is worse for those theories without a principle like the harm principle.

DO IDEAS ABOUT PURPOSE SHAPE HISTORY?

Does metaphysical revolution matter? Camus has given us a series of examples of metaphysical rebels who slide into *demesuree* metaphysical revolution. But are these few, albeit famous, cases representative of some larger (that is, widely influential) trends? After all, these poets and philosophers and painters were not the leaders of political parties, and—with the exception of Sade, who attempted at least once to torture and rape a servant—did not seem to pursue the crime and cruelty that they celebrated.

Implicit in Camus's account is a radical claim: a tacit metaphysical theory that spreads in modern secular society can have significant effects on how people act in that society. As an instance of this claim, Camus believes that one contribution—perhaps not sufficient, but necessary and important—to the catastrophes of the twentieth century is the sense of the teleological absurd that the new secular society created. Speaking of the Nuremberg trials, Camus writes "When the English prosecuting attorney observes that 'from *Mein Kampf* the road led straight to the gas chambers at Maidenek,' he touches on the real subject of the trial, that of the historic responsibilities of Western nihilism and the only one which, nevertheless, was not really discussed at Nuremberg, for reasons only too evident" (1956, 181). The sense of the teleological absurd led to metaphysical revolt, and this in turn failed and (in some influential people and movements) became metaphysical revolution; metaphysical revolution then influenced and supported violent radical political movements. This is a novel hypothesis: that our sense of the teleological absurd is, or at least has been, a powerful influence on human politics.

It is fascinating to contrast this hypothesis with a short work by George Orwell: his review in 1940 of Hitler's *Mein Kampf* in the first English-language edition. The timing is interesting since the translators apparently began their task with a favorable view of Hitler, but by the time of publication, war had begun and sentiment had changed. As is often the case with Orwell, his insight is profound and prescient. It is worth quoting at some length from the review:

> Suppose that Hitler's programme could be put into effect. What he envisages, a hundred years hence, is a continuous state of 250 million Germans with plenty of "living room" (i.e. stretching to Afghanistan or thereabouts), a horrible brainless empire in which, essentially, nothing ever happens except the training of young men for war and the endless breeding of fresh cannon-fodder. How was it that he was able to put this monstrous vision across? It is easy to say that at one stage of his career he was financed by the heavy industrialists, who saw in him the man who would smash the Socialists and Communists. They would not have backed him, however, if he had not talked a great movement into existence already. Again, the situation in Germany, with its seven million unemployed, was obviously favourable for demagogues. But Hitler could not have succeeded against his many rivals if it had not been for the attraction of his own personality, which one can feel even in the clumsy writing of *Mein Kampf*, and which is no doubt overwhelming when one hears his speeches. . . . The fact is that there is something deeply appealing about him. One feels it again when one sees his photographs—and I recommend especially the photograph at the beginning of Hurst and Blackett's edition, which shows Hitler in his early Brownshirt days. It is a pathetic, dog-like face, the face of a man suffering under intolerable wrongs. In a rather more manly way it reproduces the expression of innumerable pictures of Christ crucified, and there is little doubt that that is how Hitler sees himself. The initial, personal cause of his grievance against the universe can only be guessed at; but at any rate the grievance is here. He is the martyr, the victim, Prometheus chained to the rock, the self-sacrificing hero who fights single-handed against impossible odds. If he were killing a mouse he would know how to make it seem like a dragon. One feels, as with Napoleon, that he is fighting against destiny, that he *can't* win, and yet that he somehow deserves to. The attraction of such a pose is of course enormous; half the films that one sees turn upon some such theme. (1968, 13–14)

Let us note that Orwell, writing independently and a decade before *The Rebel*, has just described Hitler as taking on the mantle of metaphysical revolt. The motive of outraged innocence that Camus saw in the romantics is deftly described here by Orwell.

Orwell goes on to observe that Hitler understands what liberal theories like Mill's utilitarianism miss: the importance of a telos, a purpose. The greater the sense of telos, the more people find it compelling. This means that even grand and deadly purposes can be of widespread and powerful appeal:

> [Hitler] has grasped the falsity of the hedonistic attitude to life. Nearly all western thought since the last war, certainly all "progressive" thought, has assumed tacitly that human beings desire nothing beyond ease, security and avoidance of pain. In such a view of life there is no room, for instance, for patriotism and the military virtues. The Socialist who finds his children playing with soldiers is usually upset, but he is never able to think of a substitute for the tin soldiers; tin pacifists somehow won't do. Hitler, because in his own joyless mind he feels it with exceptional strength, knows that human beings *don't* only want comfort, safety, short working-hours, hygiene, birth-control and, in general, common sense; they also, at least intermittently, want struggle and self-sacrifice, not to mention drums, flags and loyalty-parades. However they may be as economic theories, Fascism and Nazism are psychologically far sounder than any hedonistic conception of life. The same is probably true of Stalin's militarised version of Socialism. All three of the great dictators have enhanced their power by imposing intolerable burdens on their peoples. Whereas Socialism, and even capitalism in a more grudging way, have said to people "I offer you a good time," Hitler has said to them "I offer you struggle, danger and death," and as a result a whole nation flings itself at his feet. Perhaps later on they will get sick of it and change their minds, as at the end of the last war. After a few years of slaughter and starvation "Greatest happiness of the greatest number" is a good slogan, but at this moment "Better an end with horror than a horror without end" is a winner. Now that we are fighting against the man who coined it, we ought not to underrate its emotional appeal. (14)

We must remember that the Nazi party received 44 percent of the vote in 1933, and that Hitler was elected chancellor.

Prima facie, the perspectives of Orwell and Camus are related but different. Orwell here observes that people are moved by a call for grand purposes, and that this call can shape human social events.[5] Camus is describing a process where the threat of nihilism left people susceptible to a call for grand purposes, and it also left them susceptible to consequentialist reasoning where power is a goal in itself. But arguably the insights are related and mutually consistent. If the grand purposes offered by people like Hitler are often a response to metaphysical revolution—they give us purpose in a world that seems hostile to all our purposes, and they give us purpose when the previously socially approved purposes ("happiness") seem unjustified and insufficient—then we have Camus's hypothesis providing one possible explanation for Orwell's observation. Camus's analysis of metaphysical revolt should be understood in this context and in light of such examples. Camus is proposing that our sense of our own purpose is essential to who we are and will influence our actions. Part of this, very important in the modern secular West, is the sense that we don't have any justified and sufficient purposes—or, at least, that such a state of nihilism threatens us. A sense of purposelessness is particularly dangerous; grand purposes appeal far more than does a sense that one has little or no purpose in this world. Camus's examples of metaphysical revolution are localized cases that help us to see and understand a greater malady: how a sense of purposelessness can lead to a kind of extremism, by way of the natural human need to assert one's purposes against an indifferent universe. This remains a hypothesis that we continue to ignore. Few assess the trends and threats of our politics in light of the sense of purpose—and the threats to the sense of purpose—that human agents may feel. Camus has provided a primer on why we should care.

METAPHYSICAL REVOLT AND PROGRESS?

When he describes historical revolt, Camus holds out the prospect that historical revolt can sometimes lead to progress. He is always eager to point out that he is not a utopian, and he thinks we will never achieve a perfectly just society. But it is possible to make a more just society, and revolt is an individual contribution that can drive that improvement. But what then about metaphysical revolt? Can it lead to a kind of progress?

To my knowledge, Camus never suggests that it does. However, it seems plausible to me that metaphysical revolt could be the motivating force for a kind of progress. As we have seen, the most fundamental form of metaphysical revolt is the rejection of death. In a sense, this is futile, since all human beings die. In *The Plague*, Dr. Rieux sees his vocation as a rejection of creation as he found it. His ability to treat the disease sweeping Oran is very limited, but he continues to fight unrelentingly against the disease. But not all medicine is futile. The same motivation that drove Rieux also drives the scientific endeavor to find cures for disease. Perhaps it is not unreasonable to describe much of the progress in medicine as motivated by the metaphysical revolt against death. Camus gave us a tragic view of social progress, arguing that we will never have a world in which no one suffers, but we can strive to reduce suffering, and sometimes succeed at reducing suffering. Just so, we could have a tragic view of the kind of progress driven by metaphysical revolt: we will never have a world without death and disease, but we can strive for a world where we live longer and healthier lives, and we can sometimes succeed.

More difficult are those cases of metaphysical revolt concerned more generally with a sense of the teleological absurd. Suppose someone is motivated to metaphysical revolt not by a rejection of death but by a rejection of their sense that there is a lack of unity (a lack of justification for one's purposes). Can progress be made here? It is harder, I grant, to make the case as we did with medicine. But it is at least possible that human beings could make philosophical progress, of a kind that reassured us that some of our purposes are justified and sufficient. Arguably, *The Rebel* is precisely an attempt at this very project.

FOUR

Historical Revolt

REVOLUTION

Camus's stated theme for *The Rebel* is how revolt declines into revolution, and thereby results in mass murder—in particular, mass murder that is justified by bad philosophical theories. Recall that for Camus, metaphysical revolt is "the movement by which man protests against his condition and against the whole of creation" (1956, 23). "Historical revolt" is Camus's term for revolt against social conditions—it is what we usually mean by "revolt." Metaphysical revolt can be a solitary act; the person revolts against what he perceives to be the injustice of the cosmos. Historical revolt is essentially a social act: the person revolts against a perceived injustice, typically seen as a morally relevant form of inequality.

The section on historical revolt in *The Rebel* is thus the most relevant to his task. It is the largest section in the book, making up nearly half the text. In it, Camus attempts to identify the development of ideas and reasoning (of a kind that we already saw in metaphysical revolt and revolution) that lead from revolt to revolution: "the purpose of this analysis is not to give, for the hundredth time, a description of the revolutionary phenomenon, nor once more to examine the historic or economic causes of great revolutions. Its purpose is to discover in certain revolutionary data the logical sequence, the explanations, and the invariable themes of metaphysical rebellion" (1956, 108).

Camus places a slightly different stress on historical revolt than he did on metaphysical revolt: what most distinguishes historical revolt from historical revolution is that each revolt is an incremental rejection of a particular injustice, and thus implicitly a demand for one particular kind of remedy. But revolution is total, and this is why it must be guided by some grand theory:

> Rebellion is, by nature, limited in scope. It is no more than an incoherent pronouncement. Revolution, on the contrary, originates in the realm of ideas. Specifically, it is the injection of ideas into historical experience, while rebellion is only the movement that leads from individual experience into the realm of ideas. While even the collective history of a movement of rebellion is always that of a fruitless struggle with facts, of an obscure protest which involves neither methods nor reasons, a revolution is an attempt to shape actions to ideas, to fit the world into a theoretic frame. That is why rebellion kills men while revolution destroys both men and principles. (106)

Camus's concerns, and to some degree this project, were shared by others in his time. Late in World War II, and during the decade after the war, a series of remarkable books critical of revolution appeared. Presumably, these can all be interpreted as works aiming to understand the phenomenon of totalitarianism arising during this time. These included Karl Popper's *The Open Society and Its Enemies* (1963 [1945]), Hannah Arendt's *The Origins of Totalitarianism* (1985 [1951]), Eric Voegelin's *The New Science of Politics* (1952), Czeslaw Milosz's *The Captive Mind* (1990 [1953]), and Raymond Aron's *The Opium of the Intellectuals* (1962 [1955]). There is a remarkable consistency in some of the views of the other critics of revolution writing independently at this time. For example, Milosz reported that the Eastern European communist is "accustomed to living in a society in which law exists exclusively as a Party tool, and in which the sole criterion of human action is its effectiveness, [and] he finds it hard to imagine a system in which every citizen feels himself bound by the sanction of the law" (1990, 31). Karl Popper argued that Marx evades moral theory and stakes the normative dimension of his philosophy on his prophecy, and this results in what Popper calls "moral positivism": "the theory that there is no moral standard but the one which exists; that what is, is reasonable and good; and therefore *might is right*" (1963, 206). Although their analyses are different, there seems to be independent agreement among these critics of revolution with Camus's primary claim: revolution led to an abuse and embrace of power as an end-in-itself.[1]

It is interesting to note that Camus sees revolution as being driven by theory and by a host of beliefs related to the relevant theory. As we noted before, he leaves open the possibility that revolt is sometimes, perhaps often, nontheoretical. On his view, revolt can arise as a response to an offense of a human purpose, and then interpretation can follow that revolt. Ultimately, a revolt must be understood in theoretical terms so that one can use it to establish a norm or institution. But the initial impulse can be atheoretical.

I will review some of Camus's discussion of revolution, and then contrast it with Popper's own.

MAN AND THEN HISTORY

Camus's analysis of historical revolution considers several historical cases: the French Revolution, Russian revolutionaries in the nineteenth and twentieth centuries, the fascists, and the USSR. He also discusses the two most influential theorists of these revolutionary visions: Hegel and Marx.

Camus begins his analysis of revolution with the French Revolution. He sees in the justifications and explanations of the decision to kill the king a desire to attack the old order, which held that the king was God's appointed leader. In killing the king, they were killing God and replacing divine justice with human justice. This is the kind of movement he had already described in metaphysical revolution: the revolutionary does not believe in a god, but he judges and rejects the Christian God. Rousseau's conception of the General Will becomes the replacement for the divine right of kings. Rousseau makes of the people a unified entity, and "It is evident that, with *The Social Contract*, we are assisting at the birth of a new *mystique*—the will of the people being substituted for God Himself" (Camus 1956, 115).

Remember that for Camus "unity" is the idea that some order outside the human sphere would have purposes with which our own purposes can cohere and be justified and found sufficient. This was long God's purposes, but now in atheist Europe we see a striving for other candidates. I called the underlying metaphysical view "foundationalism about purpose"—the view that our purposes are justified and sufficient if and only if they serve some other purpose, presumably beyond and independent of us, which is taken to be self-justified and self-sufficient. I do not believe that Camus was an adherent of this foundationalism about purpose. Rather, it was primarily an outgrowth of Christianity, but the decline of Christianity was not accompanied by a rejection of foundationalism about purpose. Camus recognized this foundationalism was a strong and enduring impulse in human beings, and when the foundation falls away these foundationalists aggressively sought a replacement. The first replacement is humanity. The second replacement is "history," by which Camus means some belief that a future condition (e.g., the communist utopia) is the greatest purpose and all our current purposes must be based on this prophesied outcome. This latter move includes or encompasses the earlier one since the future state is portrayed as one where humanity is perfected. For this reason Camus will say that "Russian Communism, on the contrary, has appropriated the metaphysical ambition that this book describes, the erection, after the death of God, of a city of man finally deified" (186).

The General Will is a theoretical embodiment of the first step in this development; it explicitly replaces God with humanity. Rousseau argues that this General Will cannot be wrong, and thus he infamously concludes that compelling submission to the General Will is to compel freedom. The result of this kind of reasoning is of course the Terror. The Terror creates some of the key ideological precepts that will become normal in twentieth-century tyrannies: "Whoever criticizes is a traitor, whoever fails to give open support is a suspect" (126). Murder becomes a tool to ensure compliance.

Where the Jacobins imagined a new rational order to replace the old, the Russian revolutionaries of the nineteenth century developed a vision of total revolution and replacement of the old order. Men like Bakunin, Nechaiev, and Pisarev imagined a complete overthrow of the existing order. Their view was that something more free must arise from the ruins. In retrospect, this was obviously naive.

Pisarev justifies Bakunin. Certainly, the latter wanted total freedom; but he hoped to realize it through total destruction. To destroy everything is to pledge oneself to building without foundations, and then to holding up the walls with one's hands. He who rejects the entire past, without keeping any part of it which could serve to breathe life into the revolution, condemns himself to finding justification only in the future and, in the meantime, to entrusting the police with the task of justifying the provisional state of affairs. (159)

Camus is more sympathetic to the early twentieth-century Russian revolutionaries who recognized that violence was an evil and therefore were willing to be punished for their choice of undertaking violent revolution. His discussion of fascism is brief since he does not place fascism in the historical developments that he is tracing; in particular, he believes fascism did not arise from revolt. Its initial impulse is not to seek some kind of moral equality but rather to seek domination and war.

But Camus's most important arguments concern Hegel and Marx. They are the theorists who give us the ideology that, as he has put it earlier, replace God with history; they replace "the Beyond with the Later On." Camus's reading of Hegel appears to be profoundly influenced by Alexandre Kojève, who had given famous and influential lectures in Paris on Hegel. But regardless of the accuracy of the details (Sartre, for example, was dismissive of Camus's interpretation of Hegel), Camus succeeds in identifying the essential element of Hegel's influence that is relevant to the history of revolution. "Hegel's undeniable originality lies in his definitive destruction of all vertical transcendence—particularly the transcendence of principles" (142). By "transcendence" here Camus means some set of principles or purposes that are not subjective human principles but rather in some sense independent of the beliefs of human beings. These would be a foundation or other kind of justification for our purposes that is not just a human choice. By "vertical" here Camus means independent of history. It would be "above" history, and thus as relevant now as it would be at any other time. God was of course a source of vertical transcendence: his purposes for us are not our choice, not affected by our beliefs or perceptions, and are relevant and the same at all points in history. For Hegel, on his reading, our values and principles are all just historical events essential to the progress of history but not in any way objective, and they serve only to provide a step in the battle of the development of our destiny. "Values are thus only to be found at the end of history. Until then there is no suitable criterion on which to base a judgment of value. One must act and live in terms of the future. All morality becomes provisional" (142). This leads to the kind of movement in revolutionary reasoning that will reach its apex, after Hegel, in Marx. Where the earlier revolutionaries replaced God with humanity, these revolutionaries replace God with history.

In terms of the analysis that Camus is providing, Marx does not add much to Hegel's theory. For him, the essential influence of Marx arises from the particulars of his prophecy: Marx predicts the utopia of communism and invites revolutionaries to pursue this utopia with consequentialist reasoning. However, what Marx does add and change is decisive: he claims his theory about the direction of history is scientific. He replaces Hegel's *Geist* with economic conditions, and then tries to link his prophetic revolutionary theory with his economic analysis of capitalism. In an era of great scientific progress, this lends his theory a veneer of plausibility and results in much greater influence. Marxism is the most significant development of the historical lineage that Camus describes:

> The Jacobins destroyed the transcendence of a personal god, but replaced it by the transcendence of principles. Marx institutes contemporary atheism by also destroying the transcendence of principles. Faith is replaced in 1789 by reason. But this reason itself, in its fixity, is transcendent. Marx destroys, even more radically than Hegel, the transcendence of reason and hurls it into the stream of history. (200)

The result is that revolution will have no restraint. Its slide into tyranny is inevitable, and the tyranny is new and more powerful than anything seen before. All revolutions have resulted in a state with more power over its citizens, Camus claims. But Marxism will result in the states with greater power over citizens than has ever previously been seen.

Thus, for Camus, we see in the twentieth-century revolutions—or calls for revolution—the same impulse to replace God with man or to replace God with history. Of course, this is essential to the Hegelian tradition that spawns the Marxist tradition: tens of millions will live in states where some future utopia stands as the highest possible value and justifies any action taken to speed the coming of this utopia. But it is easy to underestimate the power that this kind of thinking had in the West, and especially among Camus's intellectual peers. For example, Sartre explicitly endorsed these sentiments. Sartre wrote in his *Notebook for an Ethics* that "Ethics must be historical: that is, it must find the universal in History and must grasp it in History" (1992, 6). But remember that Sartre is a foundationalist about purpose, and our anguished condition is specifically because that foundation is gone—that is, because God is dead. Thus, Sartre saw ethics as floundering precisely because of the death of God. Again, in the *Notebooks for an Ethics* he writes, "At the moment [of realizing that God is dead], the maxim 'act ethically in order *to be* moral' becomes poisoned" (1992, 3). Sartre also never doubts that revolution to overthrow our own governments and replace them with utopian socialism should be our goal. His comment on colonial revolutions is representative: "nothing less will do than the demolition of every existing structure. If it triumphs, the national revolution will be socialist" (in Fanon 2004 [1961], xlvi–xlvii). My point here is not to criticize Sartre but rather to say that Camus's assessment of the state of much political reasoning was not unrealistic.

It is important to make an observation here. Contemporary readers—perhaps most especially contemporary philosophers—may be inclined to underestimate the power of Camus's observations about revolution. The revolutionaries have some fantasy utopia that is their only value, and they combined this with a consequentialist decision theory. In several different governments, this fatal combination led to mass murder, torture, and injustice. But I suspect it is hard for people to grasp the importance of this consequentialism. Philosophers are well used to criticisms of utilitarianism (a common ethical theory that has a consequentialist decision theory), and they may as a result be inclined to sigh and mutter that all these problems about consequentialism are solved with what we call "rule consequentialism." Rule consequentialism is a theory that posits that maintaining certain rules is the best way to ensure the right kind of consequences. But such a reply would be misguided. It is anachronistic to suppose that Camus's concerns are not insightful or urgent but can be addressed with this theoretical move. The revolutionaries that Camus is addressing had a total consequentialism, in part because revolutionaries in the twentieth century, and especially those in the Marxist tradition, often dismissed ethical reasoning as a ruse of the bourgeoisie. The danger, and the reasoning, is captured well by the Soviet writer Lev Kopelev when he describes his small role in the millions of deaths by starvation in the Holodomor:

> With the rest of my generation I firmly believed that the ends justified the means. Our great goal was the universal triumph of Communism, and for the sake of that goal everything was permissible—to lie, to steal, to destroy hundreds of thousands and even millions of people, all those who were hindering our work or could hinder it, everyone who stood in the way. And to hesitate or doubt about all this was to give in to "intellectual squeamishness" and "stupid liberalism," the attributes of people who "could not see the forest for the trees." (1977, 11)

Furthermore, in Camus's own circle, philosophers like Sartre provided metaphysical justifications to add to the Marxist ones. Thus Sartre could write, in his essay "Materialism and Revolution" (published in 1946) that

> a revolutionary philosophy ought to set aside the materialistic myth and endeavor to show: (1) That man is unjustifiable, that his existence is contingent, in that neither he nor any Providence has produced it; (2) That, as a result of this, any collective order established by men can be transcended towards other orders; (3) That the system of values current in a society reflects the structure of that society and tends to preserve it; (4) That it can thus always be transcended toward other systems which are not yet clearly perceived since the society of which they are expression does not yet exist—but which are adumbrated and are, in a word, invented by the very effort of the members of society to transcend it. (1955, 219–20)

Thus humans have no intrinsic values or goals, those values or goals that currently bind our society are all a trap set by the rulers, and the revolutionary vanguard can invent whole new values and future societies through their violent revolutionary action. There is nothing here that could act as any constraint on consequentialism. A rule consequentialist argues that if we had rules of such and such a kind, then we would have better consequences. But in Sartre's view above, which was shared by countless Marxists, all the values that should be respected are yet to be created. They will exist only in the "transcendent" future. Any consequentialist activity in the present that will lead to this creation cannot be constrained by any values because the values that are being sought do not yet exist. To call for such constraints would be, as Kopelev notes, "intellectual squeamishness" and "stupid liberalism"—or, worst of all, bourgeois.

The consequentialism of many revolutionaries, such as the Bolsheviks, was extreme and total; it was focused on a distant fantasy that entitled quite literally any action in the present that they could justify as speeding the arrival of that fantastic utopia. Worse, the standards for justification were wholly unstated and unconstrained; basically, the revolutionary vanguard used its special prophetic powers to determine what action will have the right consequences.[2] Consider Lenin's explanation of what the dictatorship of the proletariat would entail; it is worth quoting at length:

> The scientific term "dictatorship" means nothing more nor less than authority untrammeled by any laws, absolutely unrestricted by any rules whatever, and based directly on force. The term "dictatorship" has no other meaning but this—mark this well, Cadet gentlemen. Again, in the analogy we have drawn, we see the dictatorship of the people, because the people, the mass of the population, unorganised, "casually" assembled at the given spot, itself appears on the scene, exercises justice and metes out punishment, exercises power and creates a new, revolutionary law. Lastly, it is the dictatorship of the revolutionary people. Why only of the revolutionary, and not of the whole people? Because among the whole people, constantly suffering, and most cruelly, from the brutalities of the Avramovs, there are some who are physically cowed and terrified; there are some who are morally degraded by the "resist not evil" theory, for example, or simply degraded not by theory, but by prejudice, habit, routine; and there are indifferent people, whom we call philistines, petty-bourgeois people who are more inclined to hold aloof from intense struggle, to pass by or even to hide themselves (for fear of getting mixed up in the fight and getting hurt). That is why the dictatorship is exercised, not by the whole people, but by the revolutionary people who, however, do not shun the whole people, who explain to all the people the motives of

their actions in all their details, and who willingly enlist the whole people not only in "administering" the state, but in governing it too, and indeed in organising the state. (1965 [1920], 51)

The revolutionary vanguard must suffer no limits to its power; ethics is a thing for after the revolution. This is essential to the nature of the revolution; it will not be revolutionary dictatorship if it is constrained by rules.

Thus, the fact that philosophers know of ways to mitigate the dangers of consequentialism does not change the fact that these revolutionary movements that Camus is criticizing endorse none of those mitigations— *and cannot endorse those mitigations.* Camus is correct to recognize that the revolutionary's fantastic vision of a future utopia, coupled with unconstrained consequentialism, resulted inevitably in cruelty, oppression, and mass murder.

THE OPEN SOCIETY

It is interesting to contrast Camus's discussion of Hegel and Marx with the more extensive criticisms we find in Karl Popper's *The Open Society and Its Enemies*. It is remarkable that the two books, written by very different philosophers from very different traditions, and completely independently (Popper's book was not available in French until after Camus completed *The Rebel*) come to so many similar conclusions about Hegel, Marx, and revolution.

The first volume of Popper's work is primarily dedicated to an attack on Plato. Popper sees Plato as one of the most influential enemies of an open society. By "open society," Popper means a society where individuals make their own decisions (in distinction from a closed society, where the group or tribe is meant to take precedence in all decision-making). Open societies allow for change, debate, and improvement. Closed societies strive to stop any change, and they strive to limit debate. The implicit premise of the first volume is that Plato's arguments against the open society both influence later attacks on the open society (including in our own time) and also may help us to understand the stronger forms of reasoning against the open society.

The second volume is concerned with Hegel and Marx. Popper is dismissive of Hegel as a philosopher; he considers him a fraud who created bad philosophy for the motive of pleasing the dominant powers of his time and earning their patronage. But Popper does recognize the unfortunate influence of this bad philosophy. Popper's primary criticism concerns what he calls "historicism." Here he uses the word differently than the term is perhaps more typically used today. In his short book *The Poverty of Historicism*, he defines historicism as "an approach to the social sciences which assumes that *historical prediction* is their principal aim, and which assumes that this aim is attainable by discovering the 'rhythms' or the 'patterns,' the 'laws' or the 'trends' that underlie the evolution of history" (2002, 3). And thus, "the belief in historical destiny is sheer superstition, and . . . there can be no prediction of the course of human history by scientific or any other rational methods" (ix). This historicism tends to be coupled with a defense of a closed society. In Plato, we find arguments that aim to predict and describe the best historical outcome, and then enforce this. In Marx, we find utopianism and grand social schemes that are naively assumed to be possible and even practical, if not inevitable. Both arise from historicist theories. Hegel's importance is that he is the most influential historicist, and he is responsible for motivating later historicist projects like Marxism and the communist states.

Popper's view of Marx is more laudatory. He believes much of Marx's work was valuable. Camus read Marx as an economic determinist: "Marx's position would be more properly called historical determinism. He does not deny thought; he imagines it absolutely determine by exterior reality" (1956, 198). But Popper instead understands Marx as having shown that economic explanations are useful and irreducible (that is, they are not replaceable by other kinds of explanations). In particular, Popper holds that Marx made a valuable contribution in showing that we cannot answer many economic or social questions with solely psychological explanations; we will need explanations that take economic factors as their fundamental posits. Popper claims Marx did not believe economics wholly determined our social condition; it can affect our social condition, but it cannot be the sole or even the most important determinant. As Popper puts it, "Some knowledge of economic conditions may contribute considerably, for example, to a history of the problems of mathematics, but a knowledge of mathematics themselves is much more important for that purpose; and it is even possible to write a very good history of mathematical problems without referring at all to their 'economic background'" (1967, 107). Popper has a conclusive argument showing that knowledge must be more important than economic conditions in determining social outcomes.

> Imagine that our economic system, including all machinery and all social organizations, was destroyed in one day, but that technical and scientific knowledge was preserved. In such a case it might conceivably not take very long before it was reconstructed (on a small scale, and after many had starved). But imagine *all knowledge* of these matters to disappear, while the material things were preserved. This would be tantamount to what would happen if a savage tribe occupied a highly industrialized but deserted country. It would soon lead to the complete disappearance of all the material relics of civilization. (1967, 107–8)

We should note, however, that it is possible that in this regard Popper grants too much to Marx. If Marx did not believe that economic conditions were an overwhelming influence on human society, it is hard to see how he could have believed in communism in the way that he does. Marx reasons that under communism human beings will have a number of remarkable traits, such as abandoning specialization of labor, not being prone to the temptation of free riding, and not feeling any group animosities (because there will be only one class). All this is supposed to arise from the change in economic conditions alone. Perhaps Marx himself was inconsistent on this point, sometimes adopting a weak hypothesis, sometimes a strong one, about the relation between economic conditions and social and personal outcomes.

For Popper, the key problem for Marx is his historicism. His predictions simply did not come true. Capitalism did not collapse. The poor did not get more poor. The government was indeed able to create suitable welfare policies. And so on. Marx's theory of what life under communism would be like was undeveloped and false; in particular, it was false to suppose that if there were only one social class, antagonisms would melt away. Camus makes similar observations. Although he was rarely the kind of person to delve into technical issues like economics, Camus rightly observes a host of empirical failures for Marx's theory: "Economic crises, which should have occurred with increasing frequency, have, on the contrary, become more sporadic" (1956, 212); capital has not only concentrated but small industries have continued, and new small industries have arisen; the complexity of modern production has favored a proliferation of diverse specialized industries; agriculture has not consolidated as Marx predicted; and so on.

In chapter 6 of *The Open Society and Its Enemies*, Popper sketches his own view of political progress. It follows his epistemic theory: just as you cannot predict or prophesy new knowledge, you cannot predict or prophesy new successful social orders. He draws a contrast between utopian engineering and a "piecemeal" engineering. Utopian engineering, he supposes, is based on the following reasoning:

> Any rational action must have a certain aim. It is rational in the same degree as it pursues its aim consciously and consistently, and as it determines its means according to this end. To choose the end is therefore the first thing we have to do if we wish to act rationally. . . . These principles, if applied to the realm of political activity, demand that we must determine our ultimate political aim, or the Ideal State, before taking any action. (1963, 157)

Popper quickly points out a host of problems with this reasoning. Utopian engineering requires strong centralized power and so is likely to lead to dictatorships, but dictatorships punish criticism and so cannot improve. Succession will be a problem since the project will not be realized in one lifetime and the successor may have a different project to pursue. Worst of all, it is unlikely the original blueprint of the utopian society will remain the working final blueprint, but this undermines the reasoning of the argument for utopian engineering.[3]

In contrast Popper offers piecemeal engineering, in which a free people suggest and try out various solutions to current concrete problems. Many of these solutions will fail, but we can then learn from our failure and try something else. In this way, social progress will emulate scientific progress. Just as with science, what we need to do is try things out and reject them when they fail. To ensure that piecemeal engineering can flourish, we adopt methods in politics like those we have adopted in science. This means our efforts should be toward ensuring we have a governmental system that makes it easy to reject bad politicians, bad administrators, bad policies, and bad laws. This combination of fallibilism with a defense of criticism is consistent with Camus's theory of revolt. But it is interesting to note that Camus came close in his journals to articulating a view very similar to Popper's here: "I choose liberty. For even if justice is not realized, liberty maintains the power of protest against injustice and keeps communication open" (1978 [1945], 104).

The Open Society and *The Rebel* have different solutions to the problems they consider. And yet, the works are similar in that they evaluate social and political problems in terms of the ideas of the theories that contributed to those social and political problems. It may be fruitful to debate to what degree, and in what manner, the ideas of Hegel or Marx influenced events, and to debate what history would look like without them. But it is highly plausible that their ideas had significant influence on the catastrophe of communism. One is reminded of the warning with which Czeslaw Milosz opened his book *The Captive Mind*: "It was only toward the middle of the twentieth century that the inhabitants of many European countries came, in general unpleasantly, to the realization that their fate could be influenced directly by intricate and abstruse books of philosophy" (1990, 3). Understanding the ideas of Hegel and Marx, and other thinkers before them, will allow us to evaluate their influence but also identify their errors. This holds the hope that we could develop the methods to avoid another era of what Camus called "philosophical murder."

What can we say about the methods of Camus and Popper, which appear similar in various ways? Camus makes no effort to claim his sample of historical events is representative. Indeed, a real challenge for his view would have been to consider a wider range of revolutions (such as in the United States or in Haiti). Similarly, neither Camus nor Popper try to establish in any empirical way that they have identified the philosophical ideas that had the most influence on politics. However, it does seem that their method is plausible and valuable if we see it as an account, looking backward, based on their assessment of the dominant character of revolutionary ideas as they observed them in their time. Then, although the sample is narrow and incomplete, it is an attempt to trace out the development of certain ideas that they recognize having been influential.

A PROCEDURAL THEORY

Camus has not offered something like a traditional ethical theory so much as a theory of how we can best proceed and ensure at least the possibility of continual improvement of our condition. There are aspects to his theory that have parallels in other theories of ethics and political philosophy. But I believe Camus does make an original contribution, which arises from the idea of revolt as the mechanism of social change.

Camus's distrust of utopian projects might lead one to group him with such conservatives as Edmund Burke. Let us call the relevant view here "cautionism." The idea of cautionism, which is clearly an element in Burke's philosophy but not the sum of his view, is that we should distrust grand social engineering. There is no more grand social engineering project than utopian revolution (or, as Popper called it, "utopian engineering"). From the French Revolution to the Soviet revolution, a distant and fantastical goal empowered a consequentialist reasoning that called for wholesale replacement of many existing norms. This led to the Terror for the French Revolution and to mass murder of untold scale for the Russian revolution. Camus's caution against revolution and great-and-distant purposes is consistent with Burke's cautionism and with Popper's own rejection of historicism and grand social engineering.

Another aspect of Camus's view we've seen was his distrust of centralized power. Every revolution, he claims, has strengthened the state—often it has strengthened the state enormously. Popper developed a novel potential solution to the impetus for the closed society: we have made the mistake of constantly asking the questions, Who should rule? And what laws should we have? But the better question is: How can we construct the state so that it is easiest to get rid of bad rulers and bad rules and replace them with alternatives? Camus does not have such a prescription, but he is clear in his hope that we should take bottom-up movements, such as trade unionism, as our model. Such movements attract him in part because they are (or at least, in his experience, had been) distributed and not centralized forms of power. The two concerns are different, but what they share is a distrust of centralized power when that power cannot be revised by citizens.

But Camus is adding something new to these two factors. Camus's proposal that human social progress is driven by revolt offers us a mechanism that can both explain some social change but also make certain predictions. Recall the revolt hypothesis: sometimes, if an intrinsic human purpose is offended, this motivates a defiant reaction. Contrast this hypothesis with cautionism. Cautionism (in the simple way that I have defined it) recommends incremental change because changes often do more harm than good, they need to be tried out and rejected if they fail, and large changes are most likely to be failures and more likely to do the most harm and more likely to be difficult to undo. But cautionism does not explain why moral progress should be possible. If we made small changes at random, progress might be impractically slow. There is nothing in cautionism to explain how incremental changes can be assisted to lead to better outcomes. It can explain why we mitigate potential harm by keeping that potential harm small, but we want more than mitigation; we want help determining which incremental changes are good bets. Popper's own view is relevant here; he seemed to take as some undefined primitive our ability to eventually sort changes (or at least, to sort some of the changes) into the good and the bad. After a change is made, we evaluate it and then undo the change if we decide it was a failure. The way that we evaluate the change is not made clear, but it is some form of after-the-fact evaluation (which may arise from debate).

Instead, Camus's theory of revolt adds something to cautionism. The theory explains why incremental changes can tend to be better. Those incremental changes can often be driven by revolt, and revolt is human beings finding their intrinsic purposes and creating their basic rights. This allows us to predict that revolt, when successful, will have a tendency to lead to moral progress. The system is evolutionary, in a sense, but the selection mechanism is such that what is getting selected for are incremental benefits (or, at least, good guesses at incremental benefits) to human well-being. In this regard, Camus does something Popper does not. Rather than an assumption that, after the fact, we will through debate evaluate the outcomes (where the standards of debate are not defined), instead the mechanism that drives some change will tend to produce beneficent changes—if and only if we respect the restraints on revolt that keep it from declining into revolution. I describe some of these constraints in the next chapter.

I would make one other observation. Camus's theory is distinct from classical liberalism. If we reduce liberalism down to the principle that each should have freedom consistent with the harm principle, then liberalism is quite like existentialism in that it cannot offer any advice on how best to live. John Stuart Mill's version of liberalism was coupled with his utilitarianism, and thus had a value theory that could offer such advice: we should structure society in order to maximize utility, and each of us should serve this project. But Camus instead has a view closer to a kind of virtue ethics. Our innate human nature determines our intrinsic purposes; we partly discover these through revolt; realizing these purposes will be to live a better life; and we should strive for a society that better enables people to achieve these ends.

FIVE

Just Revolt

HOW CAN REVOLT REMAIN JUST?

Camus has proposed that human beings have a shared and innate human nature, which means that there is a fact of the matter about what is better or worse for a human being. We are not blank slates or products of our economic conditions. We partly discover this human nature through revolt: when we are done a harm, sometimes we revolt against that harm. We revolt against our condition in the universe, but we also revolt against social injustice. Our revolt can be influenced by our sense of purpose—or of purposelessness. Revolt against human injustice demands changes in our social conditions, and it establishes a kind of solidarity with others because the revolt reveals a shared human nature. But there is a danger that revolt can accelerate and expand into revolution, in which the revolutionaries replace the goal of respect for human purposes with some distant or extreme goal. The result of revolution is a consequentialism that prioritizes power and inevitably ends up acting with great cruelty.

If Camus is correct about this, then it is important to understand how revolt can proceed without declining into revolution. If this is possible, then revolt could lead to a more just condition, without resulting in mass violence and cruelty.

Camus does not offer a systematic account of how revolt can remain balanced or measured. This is true to his method and his epistemic humility. He always seems cautious and suggests that we will have to discover the answers over time. But in *The Rebel* he does offer a few guidelines for how revolt can remain *mesuree*. He provides at least nine criteria for a just revolt.

1. Revolt recognizes and asserts some limits on "freedom."

> Rebellion is in no way the demand for total freedom. On the contrary, rebellion puts total freedom up for trial. It specifically attacks the unlimited power that authorizes a superior to violate the forbidden frontier. Far from demanding general independence, the rebel wants it to be recognized that freedom has its limits everywhere that a human being is to be found—the limit being precisely that human being's power to revolt. (1956, 284)

Revolt is always a rejection of a kind of freedom, in the thinnest sense of the word "freedom." For example, one can say that the slave revolt seeks to overthrow the "freedom" to own another human being. To revolt against slavery is to reject such a "freedom" and to demand constraints on the treatment of other human beings. Those who defended slavery sometimes spoke of themselves as defending liberty. Similar claims can be expected in defense of other wrong acts. A just revolt will seek to assert some limitation, some *mesure*.

This applies also to metaphysical revolt. Camus argues that those who seek total freedom through metaphysical revolt end up endorsing cruelty. They make freedom an end-in-itself, and this ends up being a call for power over others. To prevent metaphysical revolt from descending into the cruelty of metaphysical revolution, one must adopt restraints on one's actions. One must rebel against one injustice, but in order to establish a kind of limitation.

In chapter 6, I discuss an idea that Camus develops later in his notebooks of the "aristocrat." The aristocrat, as he uses the term, is the person who sees that each of his freedoms comes with responsibilities. These responsibilities are of course limitations. He explores the idea that we need to become such people, who recognize that with each liberty we achieve we have also earned another set of responsibilities.

How is this advice to the rebel? That is, how can one extract constraints on practical action from it? The rebel must resist the lure of an ideology of total liberty, and the rebel must oppose such an ideology when he sees it. He must recognize and explain that revolt in part aims to establish institutions that prevent some kinds of behavior. This is what Camus means by "revolt puts total freedom up for trial" (1956, 284).

2. Fallibilism.

> If, on the other hand, rebellion could found a philosophy it would be a philosophy of limits, of calculated ignorance, and of risk. He who does not know everything cannot kill everything. (1956, 289)

"Logical murder," the use of bad philosophical theories to justify the oppression and killing of millions, is founded on a certainty about one's theory. Often this misplaced certainty is a belief that one understands a direction or telos for history—what Popper called "historicism." Thus, the rebel must thread a path between justifying revolt based on plausible (and presumably near-term) outcomes, while resisting certainty and any grand theories about the ends of history.

Camus also associates this with the pursuit of limited ends. Paradoxically, those seeking total justice then use their certainty and their grand historical theories to assault human beings. He calls this a kind of mystification, which "contrives, by the promise of absolute justice, the acceptance of perpetual injustice, of unlimited compromise, and of indignity" (290). The rebel acting with *mesure*, aiming to achieve near-term and limited goals, will lack the justification for such undertakings. The rebel must embrace individual skepticism about his own political theories and the expected outcomes of his actions.

I understand "fallibilism" to be the view that it is always possible that one's beliefs (including one's theories) can be improved. I have suggested there are some parallels between the reasoning of Popper and Camus. Here I think Popper was insightful and his own view is more clear and developed than Camus's, but complements it. For Popper, we should build our political structures so that it is easy to correct our mistakes: above all, we should construct governments so it is easy to get rid of bad representatives, bureaucrats, and laws. Camus does not suggest such an idea, but it would be a useful emendation to his theory here. The call for humility can be made practical by adding systems in which we can more easily do error correction.

It is not necessary to the fallibilist to make the following observation, but I think it can be missed in simply describing Camus's position as one of recognition that any political or ethical claim could possibly be revised. Camus thinks that human beings are complex, their history is complex, and our understanding of ourselves and of how we should live together is making halting progress that will never be final. Thus, all of human progress comes from revolt, but that revolt should never be thought of as being final; we should never suppose some current theory will do all the work that future revolt will do.

> The history of man, in one sense, is the sum total of his successive rebellions. . . . What was devoutly called, in the nineteenth century, the progressive emancipation of the human race appears, from the outside, like an uninterrupted series of rebellions, which overreach themselves and try to find their formulation in ideas, but which have not yet reached the point of definitive revolution where everything in heaven and on earth would be stabilized. (1956, 107)

Thus we see that Camus's theory of revolt is actually very closely analogous to fallibilism in epistemology. There is no end point to be achieved and then preserved. We make progress, but it is progress from question to question in our search for knowledge, and from rejection of injustice to rejection of injustice in ethics. The ideal of revolution hearkens back to Plato's mistaken idea that we can achieve sufficient wisdom and then should dedicate ourselves simply to fighting any change that might cloud or adulterate that wisdom. Camus puts it: "if there had ever been one real revolution, there would be no more history" (107). The point is that the revolutionaries are so certain of their theory they undertake mass violence and cruelty to realize their theory. They are not open to revision of their theory, and so their goal is tantamount to a static final condition.

3. Freedom of speech.

Camus asserts that just revolt "would preserve as an absolute law the permanent possibility of self-expression" (1956, 290). We must note here that Camus assiduously avoids any positive use of such unequivocal words such as "absolute" and "permanent." That he uses them here shows how he perceived this constraint on revolt to be perhaps the most essential and important one.

Camus does not elaborate much on this claim. However, it is not hard to understand his reasoning. It would appear commensurate with his embrace of revolt recognizing its "ignorance." Mill's defense of free speech is based on this principle. Perhaps Camus can add another, albeit closely related, defense. Revolt is the expression of the individual against injustice, and revolt is necessary to moral progress. But revolt will often require free speech in order to be possible. And the motion from revolt to shared institutions must be one that arises through debate and forming a new consensus. Thus, speech must be allowed for revolt to possibly succeed.

Camus does provide one explicit account of the direct role of free speech, this time for its role in the establishment of rights, which are also essential to revolt.

4. The recognition of rights.

> There is no justice in society without natural or civil rights as its basis. There are no rights without the expression of those rights. If the rights are expressed without hesitation it is more than probable that, sooner or later, the justice they postulate will come to the world. (1956, 290–91)

Camus uses "rights" in the colloquial sense of shared expectations for liberties that nearly all recognize and respect. This is evident in his ecumenical use of "natural or civil." The important thing is that certain rules are treated as axiomatic. One can then appeal to these rights to defend against the relevant forms of inequalities. More general and fundamental than institutions, we have a notion of rights that applies more broadly than legal or institutional rules, and as such our revolt should seek to articulate and create widespread recognition of such rights.

What kind of rights should the rebel seek to establish? Given Camus's commitments, these should be both positive and negative rights. That is, rights to certain goods or access, and also rights that prevent certain kinds of harms. With respect to positive rights, it is important to remember that Camus is a socialist, in the most general sense of the term "socialist," or he was at least always sympathetic to socialism. It seems that in his ethics and in his rejection of Marxism, he shares the view articulated by George Orwell:

> Indeed, from one point of view, Socialism is such elementary common sense that I am sometimes amazed that it has not established itself already. The world is a raft sailing through space with, potentially, plenty of provisions for everybody; the idea that we must all co-operate and see to it that everyone does his fair share of the work and gets his fair share of the provisions, seems so blatantly obvious that one would say that no one could possibly fail to accept it unless he had some corrupt motive for clinging to the present system. (1958, 171)

Positive rights would include rights to things like food, health care, and economic opportunities.

But Camus also shares a respect for the negative rights that characterize liberalism. These include rights like the right to free speech or the right to not be interfered with by the state in matters of personal behavior that do not affect others.

The question of rights raises an important issue—one that Camus does not address but which can only be resolved in one way for Camus. This is the issue of those cases where there is a conflict between rights and democracy (or, more generally, between liberalism and democracy). A demos, a people, could decide that certain rights are to be removed. Camus certainly is a democrat, but in such cases the most consistent interpretation of Camus's philosophy is that rights take precedence over democracy. Even if a majority supports some infringement of rights, the opinion of the majority is wrong. If that is correct, then revolt in a democracy can be justified, and often is justified. That Camus held such a view is consistent with his criticism of Rousseau; he roundly rejects the idea of the General Will.

5. Skin in the game.

> Absolute non-violence is the negative basis of slavery and its acts of violence; systematic violence positively destroys the living community and the existence we receive from it. To be fruitful, these two ideas must establish final limits. In history, considered as an absolute, violence finds itself legitimized; as a relative risk, it is the cause of a rupture in communication. It must therefore preserve, for the rebel, its provisional character of effraction and must always be bound, if it cannot be avoided, to a personal responsibility and to an immediate risk. (1956, 291–92)

It is peculiar that some scholars have claimed that Camus was some kind of pacificist and that *The Rebel* is a pacificist work. Camus's experience in the war convinced him (if he was not already convinced) that violence would be necessary to fight injustice in some, perhaps in many, instances. What Camus does not do is glorify violence, as for example Sartre did. Rather, he sees it as an evil, and it should be treated as such, even when necessary.

Furthermore, Camus was appalled by the bureaucratic nature of much injustice. He had lived to see both the Nazis and the USSR hide murder and torture and other forms of oppression behind paperwork. In contrast, he claims that those who undertake revolt should share in the dangers, if any, of that revolt (or, for that matter, revolution).

It is not hard to understand Camus's reasoning. One might be less likely to order a murder or torture if there were some chance that one might have to be directly involved. There is a section of *The Rebel* where Camus speaks with much sympathy of one group of assassins of prerevolutionary Russia, rebels who in turn were the subjects of his play *The Just* (*Les Justes*)—a play that Camus considered his most important. He admired both their efforts to avoid civilian casualties and their willingness to be killed by the state for their political actions. He saw in this a kind of personal responsibility; these revolutionaries were willing to act on their principles and face directly the consequences of their actions. He holds up the Russian revolutionary Kaliayev as a model in the play. He portrays, as the culminating victory of the play, Kaliayev's acceptance of his death as punishment for his revolutionary violence. Over the course of *The Rebel*, Camus often offers the view that the rebel must be willing to share in all the danger that violence requires and must accept the consequences of it.

In our time, Camus's reasoning here might be less compelling. We might doubt whether this demand would reliably have the effect that Camus hoped for it. We are now well familiar with suicide bombers. They not only are indifferent to innocent casualties, but they also seek them explicitly. The criterion of personal risk is therefore surely not sufficient to ensure a just revolt. However, perhaps it is necessary. It is arguably the case that if someone were willing to follow the other constraints on just revolt that Camus outlines, then this additional constraint would help ensure that they were aware of, and responsible for, their actions; and it plausibly will make them weigh those actions more accurately than they would if they bore no cost.

I believe there are also two other aspects of this "skin in the game" principle. First, Camus loathed how a faceless bureaucracy allowed evil to disperse its origins and undo any responsibility. In his description of fascism he writes:

> If the superhuman microphones give orders only once for a crime to be committed, then the crime is handed down from chief to subchief until it reaches the slave who receives orders without being able to pass them on to anybody. One of the Dachau executioners weeps in prison and says: "I only obeyed orders. The Fuhrer and the Reichsfuhrer alone planned all this, and then they ran away. Gluecks received orders from Kaltenbrunner and, finally I received orders to carry out the shootings. I have been left holding the bag because I as only a little *Hauptscharführer* and because I couldn't hand it on any lower down the line. Now they say I am an assassin." (1956, 182–83)

The principle he is calling for here is one that would directly attack such institutional diffusion of responsibility.

Second, there is here something of a tragic view of human existence. In the classical view, tragedy arises when an individual has two absolute and conflicting duties. Thus Orestes, in Aeschylus's *Oresteia*, has a duty both to avenge his father's death and a duty to obey and respect his mother; since his mother is his father's assassin, his duties are in irresolvable conflict. Some philosophers have argued that such conflicts of duties are impossible; such would be the view of Kant, for example. But Camus sees this as a real possibility for each of us. And one such tragic possibility can arise in resistance to injustice. In 1947, the journal *Caliban* reprinted a series of articles by Camus titled "Neither Victims nor Executioners." The title describes well the intent: Camus argued for a third path, an alternative to helping injustice or being a victim of injustice. A reply from a fellow resistance veteran accused Camus of quietism. Camus's response—an open letter to Emmanuel d'Astier de la Vigerie—argued that this was not so. Camus wrote, "I merely say that we must refuse all legitimacy to violence, whether it comes from raison d'état or totalitarian philosophy. *Violence is both unavoidable and unjustifiable*" (quoted in Judt 2008).

This position is not contradictory; Camus explores it carefully in *The Rebel* and in his play *The Just*. This is part of a tragic conception of history and human existence. Camus, having worked in the underground against the Nazis, believed that deadly violence could be necessary to prevent far worse outcomes. But he is continually against justifications of murder. And a goal shared by any just revolt, he argues, should be abolition of the death penalty: "A revolution is not worth dying for unless it assures the immediate suppression of the death penalty; not worth going to prison for unless it refuses in advance to pass sentence without fixed terms" (1956, 292).

These are ideas that Camus had in his earlier work also. In *The Myth of Sisyphus* he holds up as an admirable feature of Don Juan that he does not seek to explain away and justify his actions. "He would consider it normal to be chastised. This is the rule of the game. And, indeed, it is typical of his nobility to have accepted all the rules of the game" (1991a, 74). Camus would not, in his later work, endorse Don Juan's ethic of more is better. But Camus will always retain this idea that those who offer consequentialist reasons must also be willing to suffer for those consequences. In his introduction to his collected plays, Camus says of *The Just* and its two protagonists:

My admiration for my heroes, Kaliayev and Dora, is complete. I merely wanted to show [in this play *The Just*] that action itself had limits. There is no good and just action but what recognizes those limits and, if it must go beyond them, at least accepts death. Our world of today seems loathsome to us for the very reason that it is made by men who grant themselves the right to go beyond those limits, and first of all to kill others without dying themselves. Thus it is that today justice serves as an alibi, throughout the world, for the assassins of all justice. (1958, x)

These two aspects—rejection of bureaucratic diffusion of responsibility, and acceptance of the tragic—can be illustrated with a contemporary example. After the 9/11 attack on the United States, Vice President Dick Cheney wanted to adopt torture as a tool for United States intelligence. Cheney's immediate action was to seek the legalization of torture.[1] To follow Camus's stricture here[2] would be to tell Cheney that torture can never be justified, but if Cheney truly believed that it was necessary then he should give the orders and accept responsibility for doing an evil thing. To seek the legalization of torture is really a way of seeking to avoid responsibility for the action. It is a shift from personal responsibility to faceless bureaucracy that Camus rightly loathed. If Cheney had been right that torture was necessary, then Cheney would have had no escape option. His least worst option would have been to order that torture be done, and then accept the legal punishment that would come to him for his choice. This is the harsh demand from Camus, but this example makes clear it would also result in better outcomes.

6. The rebel recognizes that the ultimate goal of revolt is institutions.

"Every historical crisis . . . terminates in institutions" (292). To simply destroy institutions is not sufficient for a just revolt. We want to alter the relations between human beings in a way that allows for greater human flourishing. The values so asserted must be captured in some new institutions so that they can endure. These need not be parts of the state; they could be shared communal values and traditions, for example. But if revolt does not seek to establish an enduring response, it will not rectify the injustice that it addresses. This is a genuine restraint on revolt because it means that one must be thinking of the social consequences of one's action: Will it inspire others? Is it an action that asks for change in our institutions? And so on.

7. No institutions of violence.

"Authentic arts of rebellion will only consent to take up arms for institutions that limit violence, not for those which codify it" (1956, 292). Camus is concerned that the rebel should be explicitly opposed to the creation of institutions that will themselves perpetuate violence. As we noted, he does not claim that violence can always be avoided. Thus, when violence is used, this goal is essential. Often, violence is justified in ways that in turn can prepare the way for the establishment of enduring violence, including institutions of violence. If we describe violence as purifying, for example, we have to expect then that it will continue indefinitely. Ideological purity is a value that is never achieved, or at least can be continually pursued, so violence would presumably always be warranted. The goal of violence should always be to establish institutions that prevent violence.

The Soviets, Camus believed, used violent revolution to establish institutions, like the NKVD (predecessor to the KGB), that had as essential to their operation ongoing violence. Revolutionary violence thus perpetuated and fostered violence that ultimately killed millions. Revolt should explicitly seek to avoid the perpetuation of violence by opposing the establishment of such institutions. Consistent with this constraint, Camus believed that the state should not be allowed capital punishment. To make capital punishment legal is to willingly establish an institution of violence.

However, it must be admitted that we could have disputes over what constitutes an institution of violence. An army, for example, could presumably be considered an institution of violence—in as much as its function is to have, at the very least, a deterrence effect through developing and maintaining the capability for violence. Presumably, Camus would not object to a state having an army (as far as I know, he did not object to either France or the USSR having an army for deterrence). So what then are the distinguishing features of institutions of violence? It certainly does seem that groups like the Committee of Public Safety, which led the Terror of the French Revolution, or the NKVD, the terroristic secret police of the early USSR, are uniquely violent institutions. Furthermore, it would be dubious to claim that either had as their role the deterrence of violence. So one possibility might be to distinguish institutions that develop a capability for violence in terms of whether those institutions develop this capability as a deterrence. But although this seems a plausible criterion, we have the problem that the worst such institutions always insist that they are merely defensive. The NKVD and the Committee for Public Safety both would probably claim deterrence as their sole role. The very name of the group in charge of the French Terror proclaims such a subterfuge. So, at the very least, we again have a case where dispute might make following Camus's criterion challenging.

Perhaps the best way to clarify Camus's criterion would be to treat it as one that cannot stand alone. In this way, we can understand institutions of violence as institutions that are for violence and not just deterrence, and that also fail to respect the other principles of just revolt, such as an absolute respect for free expression or the respect of rights. The Committee on Public Safety or the NKVD, for example, did not tolerate criticism, nor constrain themselves within standard notions of human rights. But many nations have standing armies that, at least in principle, are not intended for use to suppress free speech and human rights. Obviously, even the best examples might have their own historical exceptions; at different times the French army was an institution of violence and torture, such as during the Algerian conflict—but then at such times we could apply Camus's criterion and say that the French army was acting as an institution of violence.

8. The rebel will not put loyalty to an institution or to an ideology above human solidarity.

> The revolutionary is simultaneously a rebel or he is not a revolutionary, but a policeman and a bureaucrat who turns against rebellion. But if he is a rebel, he ends by taking sides against the revolution. . . . Every revolutionary ends by becoming either an oppressor or a heretic. (1956, 249)

Along with the recognition of ignorance is the recognition that one's theory should not be held to be more valuable than a human being. One must constantly return to the facts of human beings, how they live and suffer, and the constraints that they face. Such commonsensical observations must always trump theory.

For this reason, the rebel is always an outsider. A revolt that leads to revolution and then to new institutions will sometimes result ultimately in some institutions that offend human nature and human solidarity. The rebel may have worked hard to put those institutions in place, but if he is true to the spirit of revolt, he will revolt against even these institutions if they offend justice. If his loyalties become to those institutions, then he is no longer a rebel. He is a member of a party, a state, a tribe. Camus could have added that, as a consequence, the rebel cannot rest (though he can give up being a rebel).

Here, the notion that the rebel is always an outsider can be related to Camus's objections to "formalism." Camus objects to formalism in art because he claims it removes art from its role to both engage with and criticize the world. He also objects to formalism in ethics: "Morality, when it is formal, devours" (1956, 124). I don't believe Camus's worry here is whether we study ethics using rigorous methods such as logic. Rather, his concern is that an ethical theory that is independent of everyday human existence and human needs will become tyrannical. That is, he objects to unrevisable institutions and laws. "Justice is a living thing," Camus reminds us (1956, 306). The rebel must always observe the lives of others. He must not be seduced into a kind of blindness that arises from giving oneself over completely to some theory of history or politics, or to some institutions. The rebel will thus always be prone to demanding revisions of the law, rather than encouraging simple obedience to the law. This is a consequence of fallibilism.

Note that this is also consistent with Camus's view that revolt is fundamentally a Western activity. His point is that in the West we no longer appeal to divine order to justify a political order. As a result, we can have the conception of the state as a set of institutions that can be perpetually revised and improved. This is in sharp contrast to views that the state should aim to both realize, and remain perpetually in, some kind of canonical ideal condition, previously prescribed in holy books. Revolt ends the moment one appeals to a final social order.

9. The rebel will not sacrifice the present, or a human span of time, for a goal very distant in time.

> "Obsession with the harvest and indifference to history," writes Rene Char admirably, "are the two extremities of my bow." If the duration of history is not synonymous with the duration of the harvest, then history, in effect, is no more than a fleeting and cruel shadow in which man has no more part. He who dedicates himself to this history dedicates himself to nothing and, in his turn, is nothing. But he who dedicates himself to the duration of his life, to the house he builds, to the dignity of mankind, dedicates himself to the earth and reaps from it the harvest that sows its seed and sustains the world again and again. (1956, 302)

Being focused on goals in the far future has a number of destructive effects, Camus believes. One problem is that this encourages egregious forms of consequentialism, in which we wrongly justify harm to current lives for some distant and dubious prospect. A second problem is that we lose focus on our own lives and our own role in the history of our own time. In the process we lose sight of the power of revolt: "it is those who know how to rebel, at the appropriate moment, against history who really advance its interests" (1956, 302). Thus, the rebel must attend to his time and place and reject appeals to some distant possible outcome.

Following constraints such as these nine, we can achieve revolt that is measured, and as a result some incremental but continual moral progress is possible. Camus is not a utopian. He has a tragic view of life, and this is essential to his political theory. A failure to recognize that injustice will always be with us can lead to disillusionment or, worse, extremism. But we cannot hope ever to arrive to a time without injustice and pain: "children still die unjustly even in a perfect society. Even by his greatest effort man can only propose to diminish arithmetically the sufferings of the world. But the injustice and the suffering of the world will remain and, no matter how limited they are, they will not cease to be an outrage" (1956, 303). Progress is possible; it will always be too slow; but the alternatives would be worse.

THE RESPONSE TO CAMUS'S ETHICS OF REVOLT

Much has been written about the public feud between Camus and Sartre. I do not want to assess the many claims made in the debate, both because my purview remains to develop an understanding of Camus's philosophy, focusing on his metaphysical claims and presuppositions, and because I do not believe it would be likely to change anyone's mind about the debate. Those familiar with the details are typically deeply invested in one side. However, and surprisingly, there is something to be said for another look, in light of the philosophical theories and claims that I have described in Camus's work. For, if my interpretation of Camus's work is correct, then the most remarkable thing about this famous public debate was that it never addressed the primary claims of *The Rebel*. Camus's metaphysical claims, which underlie his theory, are ignored.

The journal that Sartre founded, *Les temps moderne*, had not reviewed *The Rebel* when it was first published. Sartre did not like the book and apparently felt some discomfort at the prospect of stating this publicly. In the end it seemed necessary to respond in some way, and so Sartre assigned the review to a philosopher and writer who was very sympathetic to Sartre's thinking in all matters: Francis Jeanson.

Jeanson's review has been described by some as effective, but we must note that the review is full of ad hominem attacks and insults. There is very little engagement with the arguments and claims of *The Rebel*. This begins immediately: Jeanson starts the review with insinuating guilt by association. He observes that Camus's book has received positive reviews in some right-wing journals and newspapers, and writes that "it seems to me, were I in Camus' place, in spite of everything, I would be worried" (Sprintzen and van den Hoven 2004, 80). That is, Camus should be worried about the fact that the reactionaries like his book. This opening salvo sets the tone for the review, which only rises to making a few philosophical points in a long series of such attacks.

Jeanson's next claim about Camus is that there is "a certain incoherence in his thinking" (80), which makes it attractive to diverse reactionaries. He also attacks Camus's style, claiming it is too good. This leads to a claim that Camus is concerned only with abstractions—later in the essay

Jeanson will claim that Camus sees good as outside of history and evil as within history. Only deep in the review does Jeanson get to a proper discussion of some actual claims of *The Rebel*. Jeanson reads Camus as describing metaphysical rebellion as the source of historical rebellion. The important point here is that, whereas Camus sees his analysis of metaphysical rebellion as describing reoccurring tendencies in reasoning and justification that can influence revolts and revolutions, Jeanson instead reads Camus as rejecting historical and economic explanations in favor of metaphysical ones. This gets to the sole set of philosophical claims in the review, although Jeanson continually veers off the point. He attacks Camus's readings of Marx and Hegel as superficial or incorrect. But when he returns to his substantive point, we see that he interprets Camus as defending or proposing a defeatist inaction in the face of injustice. Sisyphus, from *The Myth of Sisyphus*, is a solitary figure learning to be happy with his sole task, and this is reimagined as Camus's image of the uncorrupted rebel, undertaking no genuine labor, and doing so happily.

Jeanson even stoops to psychoanalyzing Camus, proposing that this whole metaphysical project in *The Rebel* is a justification for Camus's own personal defeatism and retreat. This is followed by a taunting Hegelian analysis of Camus first as someone giving into the "law of the heart." This notion, introduced by Hegel, is that those who follow the law of the heart are led to self-righteously denounce the social order as failing to live up to the law. Jeanson then switches to Hegel's notion of the "beautiful soul," who withdraws from action to remain pure. Both are ad hominem attacks that seem to be there both to insult Camus and to demonstrate that Jeanson has read Hegel.

Sprinkled in this discussion is the dilemma that Jeanson, Sartre, and others will continually aim at Camus: either one is committed to revolution, or one is quietly acquiescing to (if not openly siding with) injustice—indeed, one is even acquiescing to some kind of denial of the right of men even to exist: "But after all, Camus, perhaps revolutions are also made, are *especially made*, by men, by simple men who try—as best they can and in solidarity—to gain the right to exist as men" (175). Camus's conditions of revolt are seen as too strict to ever allow action: "Perhaps the ideal conditions of a pure rebellion are not present when real men rebel effectively against real structures.... If this is the way it is, do you then think it better to abstain from acting?" (175).

This is what Jeanson and Sartre take to be the central issue: Does Camus's account of revolt make it impossible for there to be effective revolt? Does revolt, as Camus conceives it, fail to result in improvements? Is revolution alone the means we have to create a more just society? Or, if not the sole means, is it the best means? Jeanson claims Camus is captured in a dilemma between ineffective individualist efforts or a kind of solidarity that can only result in revolution: "either Camus urges a strictly individualistic kind of project or he must acknowledge that he's in the exact same position as the revolutionary, even the Stalinist, and that the only difference between them lies in the definition of the future that they project and in the means that they believe they have to employ in order to realize it" (100). Jeanson ignores the conclusion of *The Rebel*, in which Camus lays out tentative criteria for a just revolt. That is, the "means" is something Camus had addressed, and yet Jeanson treats this as trivial, as irrelevant to Camus's arguments. For Jeanson, the means will just follow from the revolutionary project. In sum: all that matters is which of the two sides of Jeanson's dilemma you are on.

Jeanson ridicules Camus's belief in a human nature as a nostalgia for transcendence. This term "transcendence" is used ambiguously throughout the debate, so that under one interpretation (meaning something like "not socially constructed") it does apply to Camus's claims, but used in a different sense (meaning something like "beyond history") it does not apply to Camus's claims. We can describe a consistent interpretation of Camus's theories that does not require some supernatural explanation, nor a telos for history or the universe. Such an interpretation could be consistent with contemporary naturalism. One could say: it is a historical accident that we evolved, but now that we have evolved there is a fact of the matter about what helps, and what hinders, human flourishing.[3] Note that such a claim would be "transcendent" in the first but not the second sense stated above. This would not be a complete account of ethics, of course, but it would address the question of whether a theory of human nature requires reference to supernatural or superhistorical facts or properties.

Jeanson also criticizes Camus for leaving no allowance for efficacy. But, as we have seen, we can instead read Camus as having a tragic view of political efficacy. If human beings are corrupted by the use of violence, then we should not praise its efficacy. If violence is sometimes necessary, that does not change that it is harmful not only to its victims but also to the perpetrators and their community. Jeanson seems to be insisting that we *absolve* the evil deeds done in the name of efficacy, because they were efficacious. But this is a move that Camus explicitly rejects.

Camus's response to the review, written as a long letter to *Les temps moderne*, was defensive and angry. He refused to address Jeanson but rather addressed Sartre as "the Editor." He attributed Jeanson's views to Sartre. It seems likely that Jeanson wrote the essay on his own, but there is some truth to Camus's claim; Jeanson held no views that differed in significant ways from Sartre's own. Camus devotes much of the article to addressing the many ad hominem arguments that Jeanson makes. These replies are reasonable, but they give Camus's response a tone of being aggrieved and defensive. The tone is unfortunate since it obscures that his reply includes some important points. A few are worth noting.

One important observation Camus makes is to draw attention to the false dilemma that plagued the thinking of those on the French left. He claims that Jeanson "can't help thinking that there is no precise border between the man of the Right and the critic of dogmatic Marxism. According to him, they overlap at least somewhere, and then a sinister confusion comes into play. Whoever is not a Marxist, be it frankly or ashamedly, is moving to the Right or is solidifying his position there" (Sprintzen and van den Hoven 2004, 109). Related to this point, Camus also observes that Jeanson is contemptuous of other leftist movements, such as the syndicalists, whom Camus endorses in *The Rebel* as offering an alternative model to Marxism. Jeanson is taking an ideological position in equating socialism and Marxism. Socialism predates Marx and Marxism, and there has always been a socialist tradition that is not Marxist. Camus is attacking what he calls authoritarian socialism or Caesarian socialism—exemplified by Stalinism. That Jeanson calls this search for alternatives a call for inaction reveals that, Camus claims, Jeanson equates all hopes of political progress with endorsement of Marxism and, in France, the French Communist Party.

Camus also observes that Jeanson reasons fallaciously when he concludes that, because Camus does not discuss economics in *The Rebel*, he is implicitly arguing that history is solely a product of metaphysical theories. *The Rebel*, Camus claims, is focused on something that other works on revolution have not described, but he does not deny that other factors play an essential role in causing revolutions.

Sartre wrote a reply to Camus. It is too long, and it is strangely rife with ad hominem arguments also. It assesses Camus as a person and has very little to say about his book. There is a long discussion of whether one must side with the oppressed, and presumably this matters because Sartre seems to be saying then that this requires some form of allegiance to violent revolution. I will note one philosophical claim made in the essay, which is relevant because it clearly shows how uncharitable Sartre was being, but it also shows that Sartre never recognizes that Camus has different metaphysical assumptions. Sartre wrote:

> You have such a mania for not going to the source. After all, you *know perfectly well* that a brake can only be applied to real forces in the world and that the physical action of an object is restrained by acting upon the factors which condition it. But freedom is not a force. It's not me who makes this so; it's inherent in its definition. It is or is not; but if it is it escapes the chain of causes and effect, being of another order. (Sprintzen and van den Hoven 2004, 145)

Sartre's point here is to attack Camus's use of phrases like "unbridled freedom" and "freedom with limits." Sartre is claiming, following Descartes, that free will is a binary property: either we have it or we do not. This is the conception of free will that I called "event freedom" in chapter 2. Sartre takes it to be the only definition of "freedom," but it is not. There is also agency freedom. (It is also noteworthy that in common usage there is nothing incoherent in talking about limits to freedom.) So Sartre is using the term "freedom" in a technical sense and claiming this technical sense is the only correct sense. But it is clear that Camus's use of such notions as "a limit on freedom" means something like deciding to obey norms that one is free not to obey. After all, Camus is calling for moral reform, not physical constraints. That Sartre's attack here is uncharitable is clear also from the fact that Simone de Beauvoir had already based her theory in *The Ethics of Ambiguity* on limits to freedom. Sartre did not criticize her view, even though it is actually explicitly inconsistent with his own. Because this attack on Camus goes straight to a profound metaphysical difference in their conception of the human being, I will discuss it at length below.

What was the revolutionary program that Sartre favored over the moderated revolt recommended by Camus? In his 1946 essay in *Les temps modernes* "Materialism and Revolution," Sartre lays out his vision for a revolutionary ethics. It is a polar opposite of the vision that Camus offered in *The Rebel*. "Thus, the revolutionary is not a man who demands rights, but rather a man who destroys the very idea of rights, which he regards as a product of force and custom. His humanism is not based on human dignity, but, on the contrary, denies man any particular dignity" (1955, 217). Violence is welcome as a means of political control; it need only be constrained when the class enemy to be killed would be useful:

> The declaration that "we too are men" is at the bottom of any revolution. And the revolutionary means by this that his oppressors are men. Certainly he will do violence to them, he will try to break their yoke, but if he must destroy some of their lives, he will always try to reduce his destruction to a minimum, because he needs technicians and experts. (217)

All a human can hope for is creating some new values as he "transcends" the values of his time since our current values are all just an oppressive invention of the bourgeoisie. Why should we believe the new values will be better? That is never explained. Might there not be some possibility, some small glimmer of hope, for a universal human ethic? A philosophy that offers human universal values and ends the violence? Perhaps, but "this philosophy is open, at first, to revolutionaries only" (238). Finally, "It is true that the Communist Party is the only revolutionary party" (238).[4]

This indicates the most important oversight of their debate. Camus has proposed that without a human nature there can be no values and there can be no successful ethical theory. This claim is never assessed by Jeanson and Sartre. Rather, they quickly dismiss it as a nostalgia for "transcendental" values.

Jeanson wrote a lengthy reply; it too is full of ad hominem attacks. And Camus wrote but did not publish a pithy final reply. What the debate reveals is that it was difficult for Camus to get his arguments treated seriously. For Jeanson or Sartre, it is simply obvious that revolution is sometimes the best response to some social harm, and it is simply obvious that human values are wholly chosen or created by human beings. Incrementalism is seen as a false front for quietism. The metaphysical assumptions of Camus, such as his changed views on the absurd, and his attempts to build an ethics from minimal presuppositions, were simply ignored. The debate did clarify what ultimately was most radical in Camus's philosophy, in the judgment of his peers: the idea that there is a human nature that results in enduring human values, and the idea that incremental progress is superior to revolution. Altogether, the exchange was a missed opportunity to actually engage with the most interesting ideas in *The Rebel*. Instead, Jeanson and Sartre treated it as an opportunity to assert their belief that revolution is an effective means for human progress. I leave it to the reader to assess whether the revolutions of the twentieth century were a success, and whether pursuit of incremental progress has proved a failure.

Although it is beyond my remit, I feel compelled to make one editorial observation. The most clear and egregious proof of personal animosity came from Beauvoir. Beauvoir wrote a novel, *The Mandarins*, published in 1954 and presumably written during this period. One of the two principal protagonists of the novel is Henri Perron, a character very obviously based on Camus. All critics recognized and openly declared that the character of Perron was meant to represent Camus, and Beauvoir never seriously denied it. (Every person in their circle of acquaintants has a very thinly disguised portrayal in the novel. For example, one of the characters was based on Beauvoir's lover Nelson Algren. Algren was annoyed that she portrayed him so directly in the novel, literally just lifting passages from her journal that were written during and about her time living with Algren.) In the novel, Perron has an affair with a very young and insipid Nazi sympathizer; then, to prevent this lover from being prosecuted for her sympathies and treasonous activities, Perron lies in a court of law, under oath, in order to get a particularly vile Nazi sympathizer out of prison. Beauvoir's motives in portraying Camus in this way cannot have been anything less than very personal and nearly hateful. It is hard to imagine a more craven insult than to portray Camus as a Nazi lover, willing to lie to protect other Nazi sympathizers. It is also distressing to note that the insult is made of a person who was active in the resistance, and the insult is made by a person at best inactive during the Nazi occupation.

By the time *The Mandarins* came out, Camus was done with publicly confronting Sartre or his friends. He merely noted in his journal on December 12, while in Rome, that a copy of a French newspaper had come to him, with a discussion of the novel, and "It appears that I am the hero. In fact, the author has taken a situation (the director of a newspaper originally from the Resistance) and all the rest is false: thoughts, feelings, and actions. Better: the questionable acts of Sartre's life are liberally heaped on my back. Garbage anyway. But not intentionally, just sort of as one breathes" (2010, 130–31). Obviously, at this point, the contempt was fierce and mutual.

In some of his writings at this time, Camus can appear self-pitying, or overly sensitive, when he assesses the lack of support or sympathy he received in Parisian intellectual circles. He would have been better served by not taking the whole debate personally, focusing on his theories, and ignoring the endless personal insults. But since reviews of *The Mandarins* failed to point out how craven the novel's portrayal of Camus was, it appears that Camus was not wrong to believe that by this time there existed a strong bias against him among some intellectuals. He had become unfashionable in Paris. Perhaps he still is.[5]

REVOLUTION BENEATH THE CEILING OF FREEDOM

As I noted above, it was clear from Sartre's attack that he never considers the different metaphysical presuppositions that Camus has about freedom and responsibility. For this reason, this is perhaps the most telling aspect of the difference between the conception of human beings held by Camus and by the existentialists. In this section, I want to draw attention to the importance of these different conceptions by contrasting Beauvoir's ethical theory and how she relates it to political action.

In chapter 2, I showed that there is a valid argument for Beauvoir's existentialist ethics. But Beauvoir needed the claim that freedom can be limited in order to defend the claim that the unveiling of being can come in degrees. In what sense can freedom be limited? Beauvoir does introduce a new term for freedom in *The Ethics of Ambiguity*: she distinguishes moral freedom (*liberté morale*) from natural freedom (*liberté naturelle*). The latter is the kind of bivalent property that Sartre, like Descartes before him, takes to be freedom. The former notion of moral freedom is, however, distinct from Sartre's own. Beauvoir needs some distinction like this, and some scholars of her work have recognized it as central to her ethical theory (e.g., Arp 2001). The importance of this moral freedom is that it can come in degrees. How should we understand this?

Let us call this the "limits of freedom claim": some persons are less free than others. One possible interpretation of this limits of freedom claim I will call the "libertarian interpretation." On the libertarian interpretation, people are less free to the degree that they are physically restrained or otherwise threatened with restraint or violence in order to discourage certain actions. A clear example here is slavery. Beauvoir repeatedly refers to slavery in *The Ethics of Ambiguity*, presumably for the unambiguous illustration that it provides.

Another possible reading of the limits of freedom claim we might call the "positive freedom" interpretation. This would be the combination of both the libertarian claim and also the claim that people are less free if they lack certain resources that will enable their projects. Thus, starving is a limit to freedom because it makes the individual less likely to achieve his purposes.

Sartre argued that even the slave was free, but he also recognized that facticity could include physical limitations on a human being. One could argue then that the libertarian and positive freedom readings are consistent with his version of existentialism. These interpretations have another advantage: it is practically possible in most situations to determine whether a person has had their freedom "reduced" in these senses. One can observe their physical conditions. And, more importantly, one could simply ask the individual. On the libertarian interpretation, we could determine if someone's freedom was restrained by asking them such questions as, "If this door were unlocked, would you leave this room?" And someone holding the positive freedom interpretation could ask, "What do you lack that would help you achieve your ends?" Each person would be able to testify to their goals and the limitations they encountered, and where those limitations were the product of human action, these would be the kind of actions that Beauvoir could counsel against.

But Beauvoir introduces and primarily makes use of a different interpretation. Call this the "ignorance and error interpretation" of the limits of freedom claim. She first introduces this interpretation when she describes the way of being in the world for a child. A child has a "ceiling" (*plafond*) on his freedom. The child can act out in various roles, knowing that he is not fully responsible because his freedom is limited by the adult world. This account of childhood is not obviously at odds with existentialism; perhaps children must develop into their full freedom. Beauvoir, however, extended the idea to some slaves:

> There are beings whose life slips by in an infantile world because, having been kept in a state of servitude and ignorance, they have no means of breaking the ceiling which is stretched over their heads. Like the child, they can exercise their freedom, but only within this universe which has been set up before them, without them. This is the case, for example, of slaves who have not raised themselves to the consciousness of their slavery. (1948, 37)

She goes on to claim that "The negro slave of the eighteenth century, the Mohammedan woman enclosed in a harem have no instrument, be it in thought or by astonishment or anger, which permits them to attack the civilization which oppresses them" (38).

The most striking example comes later in the book:

> Certainly the proletarian is no more naturally a moral man than another; he can flee from his freedom, dissipate it, vegetate without desire, and give himself up to an inhuman myth; and the trick of "enlightened" capitalism is to make him forget about his concern with genuine justifications, offering him, when he leaves the factory where a mechanical job absorbs his transcendence, diversions in which this transcendence ends by petering out: there you have the politics of the American employing class which catches the worker in the trap of sports, "gadgets," autos, and frigidaires. (87–88)

Thus, we see that the ignorance and error interpretation of the limits of freedom is explicitly aimed at describing how individuals can be less free, and not know that they are less free. This can happen even when the libertarian or positive freedom interpretations of the limits of freedom claim would fail to find any limit to freedom.

This ignorance and error interpretation has at least two independent flaws. First, if Beauvoir wants her theory to be consistent with Sartre's own, this interpretation fails this requirement. If people can be less free and not know that they are less free, then it is not reasonable to declare that they are "condemned to be free." One might argue that Sartre allows for this kind of limitation of freedom with his concept of bad faith. But the two cases are not analogous. Bad faith arises when one attempts to evade recognizing one's responsibility for one's actions. Thus, one can in good faith choose a life of sports, gadgets, autos, and frigidaires as long as one recognizes and accepts the implications of these choices. It is for this reason that Sartre rightly avoids ever suggesting that one can undo the bad faith of another; it is something that arises from how an individual relates to his choices, whatever those choices are. Beauvoir is instead arguing that some choices evade freedom intrinsically. They cannot be had in good faith. As a result, the person who is less free in this sense is also not responsible.

Recall the context of Sartre's follow-on response to *The Rebel*, where he mocks and excoriates Camus for calling for "limits" to freedom. Sartre's reading here was obstinately uncharitable. It is clear in *The Rebel* when Camus uses phrases like "limits to freedom" that he is referring to his belief that we should choose to act in obedience to certain norms. The ignorance and error interpretation instead is precisely the kind of limit on freedom that Sartre said was impossible.

The second problem is more grave. There is a fundamental epistemic problem: how can we determine which actions are less free, and when individuals are thus in need of the "liberation" that can only come from reeducation? What if an American autoworker thought that Sartre and Beauvoir were less free, because instead of making useful things, they wrote incomprehensible books? One might argue that an auto unveils more being than does Sartre's book *The Critique of Dialectical Method*. How do we decide contesting accusations of reduced freedom? Beauvoir offers no way out. On the libertarian or positive freedom interpretation, we could just ask the purportedly oppressed person for confirmation. On the ignorance and error interpretation, somehow people like Beauvoir decide who is less free, and over any objections they are then justified to take action to remedy the situation.

We have come far from the ideas of radical freedom and personal responsibility that are the guiding principles of existentialism. From the idea that we are all radically free and fully responsible for our actions, we have arrived at the idea that many of us are less free, we do not know we are less free, and without justification some other people are going to diagnose us as less free. How did Beauvoir end up here? I would contend that Beauvoir is representative of an error that is one of Camus's primary targets: a belief that progress (at least sometimes) requires revolution.

Beauvoir's theory of the limits of freedom serves a purpose opposed to the goals of Camus. She needed a claim that freedom can be limited, without the agent knowing they are less free, in order to consistently endorse the revolutionary politics that she shared with Sartre and Jeanson. If someone believes that revolution is often justified, even when the people it is supposed to help are opposed to the revolution, then we will need an additional claim that these people are "trapped" in false beliefs.

This provides then a clear contrast between their two theories. Camus argues in *The Rebel* that revolution has, at least in Europe, tended to be based on a belief in a grand telos for history, coupled with the belief that human beings are blank slates to be written on by history in pursuit of this telos. The revolutionaries must act on the belief that human beings are malleable, able to be remade into the ideal of their historical project (such as the ideal communist): "The triumphant revolution must prove by means of its police, its trials, and its excommunications that there is no such thing as human nature" (1956, 250). This leads to consequentialist justifications of the overthrow and replacement of institutions, and of ever more extreme violence and oppression of people who do not submit to the political project. Often, in these projects, the search for greater freedom becomes instead a search for greater power over others. That is, the search becomes a kind of nihilism, in the limited sense that nothing in the present matters, nothing now is above being sacrificed for the efficacy of the revolutionary project. Against revolution, Camus contrasts an incremental process driven by individuals when they recognize that some injustice harms their human nature or the human nature of others. Thus, Camus asserts that there is a human nature. As a result, there is a fact of the matter about what is better or worse for human beings, independent of any historical or political considerations. Revolt is not dedicated to some grand telos, and thus revolt is not justified on long-term consequentialist grounds. Consequentialist reasoning should only hold sway when the expected outcome is very plausible, has a short time horizon, and when those making the consequentialist argument are themselves taking on the necessary dangers the argument requires. When revolt goes too far, when it becomes lost in grand historical projects, then it becomes revolution and terror.

Beauvoir does not accept this analysis. Rather, injustice must sometimes be confronted by revolution. Some people—including the people the revolution is alleged to help—will oppose the revolution. We will thus require a theory of why they are wrong to do so. Beauvoir argues that injustice is primarily required because of oppression: "But today the fact is that there are men who can justify their life only by a negative action" (1948, 81). These unjust men believe they are benefiting from limiting the freedom of others. With this, Camus could perhaps agree. But Beauvoir goes further; she argues that some men can limit my access to the unveiling of being:

> My freedom, in order to fulfill itself, require that it emerge into an open future: it is other men who open the future to me, it is they who, setting up the world of tomorrow, define my future; but if, instead of allowing me to participate in this constructive movement, they oblige me to consume my transcendence in vain, if they keep me below the level which they have conquered and on the basis of which new conquests will be achieved, then they are cutting me off from the future, they are changing me into a thing. (1948, 82)

This is oppression. Oppression "divides the world into two clans." This is where Beauvoir needs the revolutionary interpretation of limits of freedom. For Sartre, we are all completely free, and we are each fully responsible for our choices. I can be a revolutionary, in Sartre's ethics, because I can choose to do so. No further justification is required, although if I want to be an authentic revolutionary I must also recognize my responsibility for my actions. But for Beauvoir's ethics, I should only be a revolutionary if I can show that it will lead to greater unveiling of being. Revolution requires widespread destruction of institutions and the development of new institutions through violence, and, in the revolutions of the twentieth century, those institutions made ongoing violence against dissent part of the state apparatus. But violence and destruction prima facie inhibit the freedom of others. Beauvoir thus needs an account of why revolution is required, presumably on consequentialist grounds. Beauvoir's answer is that, sometimes, some groups are oppressed and are unable to understand their oppression. Revolution, and the violence that constitutes revolution, is thus necessary to overthrow the institutions that maintain this ignorance.

How does such oppression arise? Beauvoir claims that in some cases, oppression is justified by the claim it is natural. "One of the ruses of oppression is to camouflage itself behind a natural situation since, after all, one cannot revolt against nature" (1948, 83). Slavery is her example of such a case: "The slave is submissive when one has succeeded in mystifying him in such a way that his situation does not seem to him to be imposed by men, but to be immediately given by nature, by the gods, by the powers against whom revolt has not meaning" (85).

There are many examples of slavery being justified by claims that the slaves were inferior and fit only for life as a slave. But Beauvoir is making the further additional claims that some slaves accepted this justification. This is an empirical claim; it is not obvious that slaves did typically believe such justifications. Beauvoir backs it up by referring to claims that some released slaves in the United States were "bewildered by a freedom which they didn't know what to do with and who cried for their former masters" (86). But this anecdote (stated without a source) does not constitute sufficient evidence for the claim. It could well be that most, if not all, slaves everywhere have generally always known that claims of their inferiority were simply justifications for their oppression.

Why does Beauvoir make this additional empirical claim? The reason becomes clear when we remember the context of her commitment to revolutionary politics. She wants to endorse the possibility of revolution. Contemporary revolutions were not against slavery but rather against capitalism. Beauvoir needs to expand her account if it is going to justify revolution in places like France and the United States. We see this when Beauvoir changed her account from describing slavery to describing workers in the United States. The majority of American workers did not want revolution. Beauvoir had traveled in the United States, and she could not help but recognize that many American workers actually did like their sports, gadgets, autos, and frigidaires. A revolutionary politics that calls for the overthrow of capitalism must thus explain why a revolution that acted against the explicit will of these workers would still count as increasing their freedom.

The problem here is an old one for Marxists: often the workers don't agree with the Marxist intelligentsia, an intelligentsia who believe that they know best what workers should believe. Engels lamented this in a letter to Marx on October 7, 1858:

the English proletariat is actually becoming more and more bourgeois, so that the ultimate aim of this most bourgeois of all nations would appear to be the possession, *alongside* the bourgeoisie, of a bourgeois aristocracy and a bourgeois proletariat. In the case of a nation which exploits the entire world this is, of course, justified to some extent. Only a couple of thoroughly bad years might help here, but after the discoveries of gold these are no longer so easy to engineer. (2010, 344)

The proletariat just won't believe what they should.[6]

Similarly, a commitment to revolutionary politics in the late 1940s and the 1950s required the belief that the intellectual knows the interests of the workers better than the workers—at least if the intellectual is aiming to justify the prospect of revolution in France or the United States. Beauvoir needs an addendum to her theory that can make this consistent with her ethics. She achieves this with the claim that sometimes people have limited freedom and are deceived about the limitations to their freedom. These people do not know that they are unable to fully or best unveil being. They must be reeducated, and the institutions that support their ignorance must be destroyed.

How are we going to determine when someone has limited freedom? Beauvoir offers no method or criteria to assist in this endeavor. The result is that revolutionary violence threatens to be arbitrary, and as a result to realize Camus and Popper's warning that in the end the only criterion will be efficacy, that "might makes right." Beauvoir appears to be aware of this difficulty in her account. In the closing sections of *The Ethics of Ambiguity*, in what perhaps is meant to be an application of a dialectical method, she considers a number of arguments that revolutionary violence appears unjustifiable. Each argument attempts to justify revolutionary violence, and in turn collapses into failure, leading her to make such claims as "Thus one finds himself in the presence of the paradox that no action can be generated for man without its being immediately generated against men" (1948, 99). These inconclusive arguments are more convincing than her conclusion, which is that revolutionary violence is justified on consequentialist grounds, when those committing the violence are aware of the uncertainties of their situation. Thus, even Stalinism is defensible:

> The opponent of the U.S.S.R. is making use of a fallacy when, emphasizing the part of criminal violence assumed by Stalinist politics, he neglects to confront it with the ends pursued. Doubtless, the purges, the deportations, the abuses of the occupation, and the police dictatorship surpass in importance the violences practiced by any other country. . . . [But] One can no more judge the means without the end which gives it its meaning than he can detach the end from the means which defines it. Lynching a negro or suppressing a hundred members of the opposition are two analogous acts. Lynching is an absolute evil; it represents the survival of an obsolete civilization, the perpetuation of a struggle of races which has to disappear; it is a fault without justification or excuse. Suppressing a hundred opponents is surely an outrage, but it may have meaning and a reason; it is a matter of maintaining a regime which brings to an immense mass of men a bettering of their lot. (145–46)

What are we to say to the person who insists that Stalinism and the USSR are an obsolete civilization? What criteria make it clear that Stalinism is not "absolute evil"? How are we to know if it is reasonable to believe that a communist state can actually exist and can be achieved through these means? Here again Beauvoir has no concern with epistemic difficulties. Beauvoir's theory—under the ignorance and error interpretation—is unable to confront these basic questions. Beauvoir was not a Stalinist, of course.[7] But like Sartre and others in her circle, she did not seem to ever consider that Marxism had allowed, and perhaps had inevitably generated, Stalin's tyranny. This is something Camus's account of revolution entails, and this essential point was never addressed in the criticisms of *The Rebel* by Jeanson, Sartre, or Beauvoir.

The problem is more general than how to evaluate Stalinism. The assumption that a utopian (or even just a better) outcome is likely, given certain acts of revolutionary violence, is central to any revolutionary project. Beauvoir evades the question of how we can evaluate such assumptions. I have claimed that Jeanson and Sartre did also. This was a central question of *The Rebel*, but for them this question was not deserving of consideration because they assume revolution is indeed sometimes necessary.[8]

The positive freedom interpretation of the limits of freedom claim would, however, allow for an existentialist ethics that would entail that people must identify their own potential for freedom; we cannot decide that for them. In this regard, it would be akin to libertarianism. Once someone has decided on how he or she can be more free, we would have the responsibility to help, and not hinder, their pursuit of that freedom. But this would not allow for an endorsement of revolutions of the kind that would reeducate American workers.

What this contrast between Beauvoir and Camus helps us see is that the critical rejection of Camus's work by Sartre and Beauvoir and Jeanson did not grapple with the fundamental differences between their theories. My theme in this book has been to argue that Camus made interesting metaphysical claims and assumptions that inform his ethical theory. But if this is right, then we can only evaluate his theory of revolt and revolution by also recognizing and evaluating these claims and assumptions. Camus's conception of human beings, human purposes, and human freedom are different from Sartre's or Beauvoir's. These are essential to his theory of revolt. If we criticize Camus by assuming blank-slatism and assuming that free will is event freedom, then we have simply begged the question.

In her later life, Beauvoir told one her biographers that *The Ethics of Ambiguity* was "a frivolous, insignificant thing, not worthy of attention" (Bair 1990, 321). And, in her memoir, she wrote that "Of all my books, it is the one that irritates me the most today" (1992b [1963], 67). Her reason is rather striking. She is not concerned with the implications of her theory but rather considers it too abstract, resulting in "a solution quite as hollow as the Kantian maxims," because "I was in error when I thought I could define a morality independent of social context" (67). Beauvoir thus does not reject any detail of her ethical theory in *The Ethics of Ambiguity*, so much as she rejects the whole approach. Ethics, she comes to believe, is not a matter for general theories but rather always must be confronted in its particulars.

The most vivid case of the question of revolution in Beauvoir's lifetime was the Algerian War. Camus held out for a long time the hope that some peaceful resolution to this conflict would be possible, and when this failed he became silent on the question of the Algerian conflict. In contrast, Beauvoir throughout the conflict supported the FLN revolutionaries opposing the French occupation. But her most explicit involvement concerned the particular case of a young woman, Djamila Boupacha, tortured by the French forces in Algeria. Beauvoir lent the force of her fame to helping to publicize the young woman's case, and she wrote the preface to the book that Djamila Boupacha's lawyer wrote, titled simply *Djamila Boupacha*.

This preface is remarkable for the scathing tone, but also the simplicity, of the writing. It begins: "A twenty-three-year-old Algerian woman and liaison agent for the FLN was imprisoned, tortured, raped with a bottle by French military men, and it's considered ordinary" (2012 [1962], 272). The remainder of the preface describes the kinds of corruption and complicity that had become common in the efforts to perpetrate torture and also to make its denial and erasure more easy, and the travails that Boupacha's lawyer confronted in defending her. But the preface begins and ends with an appeal to Beauvoir's fellow French citizens. She hopes that her litany of facts will have the power to convert reluctant readers:

> There exists only one choice for you who grieve so readily and so abundantly over past tragedies, like Anne Frank or the Warsaw ghetto. You can either take sides with the torturers of those who are suffering today and passively consent to the martyrdom they endure in your name . . . or you can refuse not only certain practices, but the end that authorizes and demands them. . . . You are being confronted with the truth from all directions; you can no longer continue to stammer, "We didn't know . . ." And, knowing, will you be able to feign ignorance or content yourselves with a few token laments? (2012, 281)

It is worth noting that consequentialist defenses are abandoned here. One could imagine a debate, using something like Beauvoir's early consequentialist theory, about whether the consequences of using torture to maintain French control of the Algerian colony would increase freedom for the maximum number of people. In contrast, one would expect a consequentialist argument about how ending torture would result in an increase of freedom for the maximum number of people. But Beauvoir's angry, moralizing tone makes it clear that she considers torture (at least when it is done by the French government) simply inexcusable. She nowhere addresses the implied consequentialist defense of the torturers, but rather considers her recounting of torture a revelation of an obvious wrong. She is correct to call this turn in her writing one from abstraction to particulars in at least this sense: theory is not discussed, and she considers it sufficient to refer to the actual facts of torture in order to refute its use.

Although Beauvoir remains sympathetic to revolutionary politics, and she never renounces consequentialist defenses of violence or revolution, it is clear that in the years following the publication of *The Ethics of Ambiguity*, there was a change in her concerns and method. She rejects "abstract" ethical theories and embraces a situationist ethics that, as she phrases it, puts things in their "context." In *The Second Sex* (2011 [1949]), we can see the beginnings of this turn. The phenomenological method is used to describe her own "lived experience," and also to make observations and claims about the experiences of other women. The reasoning is that unearthing these contexts will allow for the liberation of particular women from different cases of particular oppression (just as she assumes the description of torture should be sufficient to motivate action against torture). As a result, the epistemic problem in Beauvoir's existentialist ethics is not resolved in her later work. Rather, it became distant from her primary concerns, and her method of close phenomenological description is such that consequentialist defenses of certain kinds of actions does not arise.

I would argue that Beauvoir's earlier project is representative of defenses of revolution at the time of her writing. It rests on the assumptions of consequentialism, blank-slatism, and that revolution is sometimes necessary for moral progress. It is accompanied by the belief that (at least sometimes) revolution requires that a revolutionary vanguard develop certain beliefs about how to proceed and then act on these, and these beliefs must resist revision when there is opposition, including opposition from those supposedly liberated by the revolution (those who are "beneath the ceiling of freedom"). Camus offered instead an approach that seeks to limit consequentialist reasoning, asserts there is a human nature, and is incremental and revisable. As regards Beauvoir's later turn: it also is representative, and partly determinative, of later intellectual trends (which come after Camus's death). It became common for intellectuals, especially the postmodernists, to make strident condemnations of some social phenomena, while simultaneously avoiding and even denigrating ethical theory.

AN OVERSIGHT

We should make one final observation about Camus's theory of revolt. It has one obvious shortcoming, which he never addresses: he never considers the question of whether some reactions that appear to be like revolt might not be revolt. There will surely be human actions that are not based on the assertion of some human purpose that deserves our respect, but rather are based on the assertion of some human purpose that does not deserve our respect. Indeed, once people understand that calling their action "revolt" lends it moral authority, such false claims are sure to be common.

Consider the kind of false claims that have traditionally preceded pogroms. A group of individuals suffers a harm (for example, economic hardship), and they falsely accuse another group of having caused that hardship. They then seek redress. If we were to entertain the claims of the accusers, their activities might look like revolt. More importantly, what if they engage in a pogrom and call it a "revolt"? Or consider a group that insists they have suffered a harm to their traditions, when these traditions entail that another group must have a reduced social status. For example, a reactionary patriarchy that "revolts" against the liberation of women in their community. Or consider looters motivated by greed but who justify their looting as a kind of "revolt" against supposed economic injustice. And so on.

The first kind of case can perhaps be dismissed by the additional claim that a revolt that is based on some claim of harm must itself be accurate. In the case of the pogrom, the claim that one's problems were caused by the target group were (by supposition in my example) untrue. Thus, it is not unreasonable to add to Camus's restraints on revolt:

10. Any factual claims essential to the motives for a revolt must be true.

But the second kind of case is harder to handle, given the tools Camus has provided us. We will be presented with dueling ethical claims: the revolt of the oppressed women, and the revolt of the men who want to oppress them and who claim the liberation of the women is a kind of harm.

I hope the reader understands: I believe that, in my hypothetical example, the revolt of the women is justified, and the reactionary "revolt" of the men is not justified. But I am not certain how Camus's theory of revolt explains this asymmetry. If the men in this example articulate false theories ("Woman are incapable of managing themselves or managing personal freedom"), we can apply criterion 10 for just revolt. But if they appeal to something normative ("Our ancient traditions and norms forbid this behavior, and it would harm us and our culture to change these traditions and norms") then it will not be so obvious that the claim can be refuted like an empirical claim.

Some of these cases have historically been settled by proper recognition of generalization principles. For example, when the founders of the United States signed a document claiming "All men are created equal," they and many others went on to contradict this principle. They made specific exceptions, but when proper recognition of generalization is enforced, these contradictions of the principle are obvious.

But for other cases, where we don't have an obvious inherent failure of generalization like this, I can think of one suggestion: it could be that our theory of justice, as it has developed through past revolts, can act as a guide to help us see the difference between such cases. For example, over time revolt has led us to understand that human liberty should be universal among those old enough and capable enough to have autonomy. This obviously includes the women in my example. Thus, it may be that in many such cases, our current understanding of justice as developed through revolt can help us handle such cases. However, our theory of justice is itself evolving through revolt, and so some just revolts must contradict our current theory of revolt. Thus, it cannot be that any action in contradiction of our theory fails to be revolt. This need not be a catastrophic problem, however, given that we have assumed that there will be greater coherence among our purposes as realized in a more just social arrangement. That is, perhaps some "contradictions" will affect more of our theory than other "contradictions." The minor contradictions must be taken seriously as potential improvement; the large contradictions can be rejected. Stated then as a principle, we have

11. The motive for a revolt should be consistent with our emerging theory of justice, or it should give us sufficient reason to revise our theory of justice.

This principle has introduced something new into Camus's theory, a kind of coherentism through which we can reason together to consider when we should and should not revise our theory of justice, in light of the demand from some kind of action that seems like revolt. Camus's theory would need this addition, or something of equivalent power, to handle the kind of case that I have described.

Finally, this principle would entail the possibility that we will not see that some unjust "revolts" are unjust. This can happen if our emerging theory of justice has not evolved sufficiently to allow us to see this, or if our reasoning about justice is faulty. But surely the observation that we are not faultless reasoners is no demerit for this proposed eleventh principle.

SIX

The Fall and a New Paradox of Liberalism

A MISUNDERSTOOD MASTERPIECE

The Fall remains Camus's most enigmatic novel. In form, in tone, and in its philosophical implications, it is unlike his earlier novels, and unlike his unfinished novel *The First Man*. This is reflected in the scholarship on the novel, much of which has been fixated on identifying parallels to Camus's own life, or on the symbolic themes of the work. Both of these approaches lead us astray. The novel does include parallels to Camus's own life, but that is true of most novels by most novelists; their own lives can provide a rich source of material details. That does not make their novels disguised confessions. And although the symbolism of the novel is notably coherent and profound—most of it is Christian imagery and a cosmology echoing Dante's—this too is just a distraction if we do not identify the central theme that this symbolism expresses and augments. That this theme is often missed is peculiar given that the narrator of the novel, Jean-Baptiste Clamence, tells us explicitly at the beginning of the novel of his profession: he is a judge-penitent. He describes the purposes of his entire narrative as explaining what this is. Thus, the question "What is a judge-penitent?" is the unifying question of the novel. The unnamed interlocuter brings us back to the question repeatedly. Clamence insists that all his stories, all that he says, is part of his explanation. And what we discover when we focus on this concept is that Camus has described a new kind of paradox for liberalism, one that is consistent with but distinct from his concerns in *The Rebel*.

My purpose in this chapter is thus revisionary. I believe that *The Fall* has not been properly understood. It is not a confessional novel, and though full of Christian symbolism, it is not a Christian allegory. It is a novel that recognizes a new kind of political actor, and as such the novel is properly set alongside works like *Darkness at Noon* and *Demons* for warning of a potential danger before us. Camus's idea of the judge-penitent was an original and penetrating concept of a type of political strategy within liberalism. Camus combines a hypothesis from Alexis de Tocqueville with some observations about social criticism, to portray an unnoticed tendency in liberalism toward self-destruction. What he reveals in his portrait of a judge-penitent are new doubts and new concerns about his own culture. We can read *The Fall* as continuing the work of *The Rebel*, but in this case recognizing a new and insidious disease. This judge-penitent is an actual type, a way of being in the world, that reveals a problem that has only grown more acute for the liberal West.

INTERPRETING *THE FALL*

Many interpretations of *The Fall* have tended to downplay the role of the judge-penitent. This is particularly the case with those critics and many contemporaries who claimed that the novel is confessional. Other critical analyses include that it is partly confessional, mixing both Camus and Sartre in the character of Clamence (King 1962); is meant to portray the ambiguity of existence without god, where we cannot ever be innocent or have pure motives (Cruickshank 1960); portrays a man seeking to escape judgment without repenting (Walsh 1990);[1] is a warning that if we reflect on our lives like philosophers, and focus on justice instead of compassion, we will fail to care for human suffering (Sagi 2002); expresses a longing for something like a Christian world coupled with a belief that there is no Christ or redemption (Brockmann 1962), or at least a portrait of what the lack of God does to the character of modern man (Abel 1957); depicts a man who "has lost control over evil" and failed to stop or oppose evil (Kałuża 2020); portrays suppressed trauma caused by World War II (Davis 2011; Felman 1992); portrays Clamence as realizing he was motivated by self-righteousness (Girard 1964); is an ironic dialogue between the views of Camus and Sartre (Gifford 1978); is a revisioning of Dostoevsky's underground man (Trahan 1966);[2] portrays a perverse solidarity in universal guilt that acts as a kind of parody of the vision of solidarity in *The Rebel* (Sharpe 2015b); is a critical rejection of the absurd hero as portrayed in *The Plague* (Thody 1961); and so on. This enigmatic novel spurs an explosion of diverse interpretations. These interpretations are interesting and insightful, but most of them miss the importance of the idea of the judge-penitent.

Consider one reading: Robert Solomon argues *The Fall* is about pride. Clamence in Paris, before his fall, is (Solomon claims) what Aristotle called a *megalopsychos*, a great-souled man. His fall is one from proud success to failure. Solomon claims that Camus is describing himself as someone prone to guilt because he cannot do enough; "it is in this context that [Camus] invented the ultimately good and guilty 'judge-penitent,' Clamence" (2004, 52). And thus, "we should view Clamence in his Parisian incarnation, not as an example of false pride but as a striking example of a *megalopsychos*, a virtuous, contented, and rightfully proud person" (43). The real culprit of Clamence's fall is self-reflection. He begins to doubt his own motives and sees selfishness in his actions. Echoing Nietzsche, Solomon holds that the reflective individual is a resentful one, who judges and rejects the innocent *megalopsychos*. Clamence fell from a state of merited pride to resentful pride.[3]

But this reading is incorrect. Clamence in his earlier life was not good. Clamence's repeated failings reveal that his values were never genuine. As Clamence recounts episodes of his disillusionment, each such episode concerns his realization that his values are insincere. "For more than thirty years I had been in love exclusively with myself" (1984 [1956], 100) and "I, I, I is the refrain of my whole life, which could be heard in everything I said" (48). He particularly likes pretending, after someone dies, that he cared for them, when he in fact never did. The climax of the novel is his failure to save a drowning woman whom he passes one late night. After this incident, Clamence realizes, rightly, that this failure reveals his values were all display. He is only pretending to believe the things that he claims to believe; once tested under conditions where he must face a little danger, he fails. His "virtues" were not convictions constituting his character, but tactics intended to garner more praise. A woman is drowning and no one is there to see an act of heroism, so he won't act heroically. Thus, Clamence's pride is hollow: it is based on a lie. Once he realizes he has been faking his virtue—hence he is a "double," as he oft repeats—Clamence takes to scorning the virtues of others whom he fears are better than himself:

> I wanted to upset the game and above all to destroy that flattering reputation, the thought of which threw me into a rage. "A man like you . . ." people would say sweetly, and I would blanch. I didn't want their esteem because it wasn't general, and how could it be general, since I couldn't share it? Hence it was better to cover everything, judgment and esteem, with a cloak of ridicule. (1984, 93)

Clamence seeks to mock virtues that he lacks and wants to drag others down with mockery and ridicule of the virtues that they still hold dear.

Solomon dismisses the event of the drowning woman, the key action of the novel, by claiming that it doesn't matter whether the event really happened in the novel; reflection even on a hypothetical would make one doubt whether one would save the girl in such an event in the future. This makes Solomon's interpretation unfalsifiable. He might call this his point: as a logical matter, all reflection destroys the Aristotelian virtues. But such a move evades the fact that Clamence was not virtuous; a virtuous man would have tried to save the woman. Clamence realizes this, and realizes his virtues are false. It is not runaway self-reflection that undermines his life, but rather the realization of the truth. (We should note that Solomon's reading and many other readings make much of the title of the book, but little should be made of this: Camus's biographer reports that the title was suggested by a friend [Lottman 1997, 591–92]. Camus had considered various other titles before, such as *The Order of the Day* and *A Puritan of Our Time*.)

Is the novel best understood as a kind of Christian allegory, a portrait of what the Christian finds in a world where he has rejected God and rejected the prospect of redemption? The novel is full of Christian imagery, and some compelling analyses draw out these themes. However, the problem with reading *The Fall* as a Christian allegory is that Camus explicitly states in his notebooks (from circa August 13, 1957) that he sees Christianity as complicit in the corruption that infects his era and also Clamence:

> A comment about *The Fall* since they do not understand. Shaped by and ridiculing the modern attitude and this strange and salacious secular remorse of sin. Cf. Chesterton "The XIXth century (id the XXth) is full of Christian ideas gone mad."
> ... Nemesis. Profound complicity of Marxism and Christianity (to develop). This is why I am against both. (2010, 192)

The final note there refers to the project that Camus planned to complete next, on the theme of Nemesis as a goddess of balance, of *mesure*.

These remarks may strike some as strange since Camus did not choose to be openly critical of Christianity in his primary publications; his public persona is one of tolerance toward the religion. However, it is not hard to see his reasoning here. In *The Rebel*, Camus criticizes the revolutionary spirit in part for its commitment to a consequentialism coupled with a utopian vision that some future society is the highest, if not the only, value. The result is that any sacrifice now is justified for this future state. This, Camus claims, leads to an endorsement of efficacy as the primary criterion for evaluating action, and cruel violence quickly becomes the norm. Both Marxism and Christianity share the view that history has a purpose, and that our individual purposes should bend to that historical purpose. Thus, Camus considers that they may have some profound relationship. However, one should note, Christians do not (in general) have a consequentialist decision theory, and this makes a very substantial difference in their practical influence on political action and makes it unreasonable to lump Christians together with Marxists. Nonetheless, Camus sees Marxism and other revolutionary movements as "Christian ideas gone mad." This journal entry suggests he put the Christian imagery in *The Fall* to draw parallels between some Christian ideas (such as its special sympathy for the weak and for victims) with the judge-penitent.

Thus, we find that there is nothing like a consensus on how to interpret *The Fall*, and many interpretations are unconvincing. The book seems as enigmatic as its narrator. But what most of these accounts of *The Fall* lack is a convincing account of the central notion of the book: that of the judge-penitent. And yet the narrative of the novel makes explicit that this is the main theme of the text. In the first chapter of the novel, Clamence repeatedly describes himself as a judge-penitent. The second chapter begins: "What is a judge-penitent? Ah, I intrigued you with that business. I meant no harm by it, believe me, and I can explain myself more clearly. In a way, that even belongs to my official duties. But first I must set forth a certain number of facts that will help you to understand my story" (Camus 1984, 17). And later in the chapter we are shown that the interlocuter is asking again about this, and Clamence replies, "What? I'm getting to it, never fear; besides, I have never left it" (36). We are to understand that throughout their second conversation, the interlocutor is still curious about this role of the judge-penitent and asks about it, and that Clamence considers all he has been saying as part of his explanation of the judge-penitent. At the end of the fifth chapter, Clamence says, in response to the implicit question, "What is a judge-pentitent?": "Yes, yes, I'll tell you tomorrow what this noble profession consists of. You are leaving the day after tomorrow, so we are in a hurry" (118). This again reiterates that the purpose of his narrative is to explain what the judge-penitent is. And during their last day together, he tells his interlocutor, "With a clear conscience I can practice the difficult profession of judge-penitent, in which I have set myself up after so many blighted hopes and contradictions; and now it is time, since you are leaving, for me to tell you what it is" (130). Again, the task that he must be sure to complete with their remaining time is an explanation of the judge-penitent.

It is clear that the main theme of the novel is to illustrate and describe this role of the judge-penitent. And yet we do not have a clear analysis of what the judge-penitent is. A proper consideration of the philosophical import of the novel requires that we recognize and explain this judge-penitent role. What then is a judge-penitent?

THE JUDGE-PENITENT

Clamence ultimately describes the role of the judge-penitent in vivid terms. "You see in me, *très cher*, an enlightened advocate of slavery" (132). His solution to the burden of his own moral failure is that everyone must be revealed as a moral failure; he must pull down everyone. "In philosophy as in politics, I am for any theory that refuses to grant man innocence and for any practice that treats him as guilty" (131–32). But the full realization of this solution will occur in an indefinite future: "I'm well aware that slavery is not immediately realizable" (137). Until there is universal slavery, the role for Clamence—and, he suggests, the role for us—is to become a judge-penitent, who will speed this time of universal slavery, like the revolutionary who is trying to speed a revolution that Marx tells us is inevitable.

> I discovered that while waiting for the masters with their rods, we should, like Copernicus, reverse the reasoning to win out. Inasmuch as one couldn't condemn others without immediately judging oneself, one had to overwhelm oneself to have the right to judge others. Inasmuch as every judge some day ends up as a penitent, one had to travel the road in the opposite direction and practice the profession of penitent to be able to end up as a judge. (138)

From whence did this concept of the judge-penitent arise?

My proposal is that Camus's judge-penitent is the consequence of adopting two distinct principles and a strategy. The strategy is well voiced by Tocqueville, while the principles are ones that are commonly adopted in liberal societies.

Camus's journals are not always helpful in seeing the development of his thought, but during the period when he is formulating the ideas of *The Fall*, there are many revealing passages where he explores new concepts. These philosophical efforts are interspersed with brief descriptions of scenes and quotes that later appear in *The Fall*, confirming that he is working on the novel while struggling with these questions. During this period, he reads Tocqueville, perusing at least *Democracy in America*, *The Ancient Regime and the French Revolution*, and the *Correspondence* (see Camus 2010, 76). His observations in his notebooks include the following, from sometime in 1953: "These minds 'who seem to make the taste for servitude, a sort of ingredient of virtue.' Applies to Sartre and the progressives" (2010, 76). The passage he is citing is from volume 1 of *Democracy in America*, where Tocqueville claims that

> There is, in fact, a manly and lawful passion for equality that incites men to want all to be strong and esteemed. This passion tends to elevate the small to the rank of the great; but one also encounters a depraved taste for equality in the human heart that brings the weak to want to draw the strong to their level and that reduces men to preferring equality in servitude to inequality in freedom. (2000 [1835], 52)

Tocqueville's claim is that there are—or, more ominously, there could arise—substantial numbers of people in a democratic society who prioritize equality over liberty, and who believe it is permissible to seek equality through pulling everyone to a reduced (but equal) condition, using methods that attack liberty. Camus's accusation that this is true of Sartre and the progressives arises from his observation that Sartre is reluctant to criticize Stalin's Soviet Union, favoring the project for universal equality that Stalin's USSR (supposedly) represents over any concerns for liberty that it tramples.[4]

We can generalize the mechanism that such a belief embodies: it is the idea that we should seek equality by pulling down those of higher social status, rather than by improving the social status of those with low social status. Let us call this the "negative-sum strategy":

We should strive for equality by reducing the status of those of higher social status.

In a positive-sum game, competition can lead to all participants being better off, or at least it can result in a net gain for the whole.[5] In a zero-sum game, someone must lose so another can gain, but the net gain for the whole is zero. But in a negative-sum game, one can raise his *relative* utility (in Clamence's case, this utility is power and social standing) by reducing the utility of others; the result is a net harm for the whole, but some may end up comparably ahead, or at least less far below, their objects of envy.[6]

We should observe that those who adopt the negative-sum strategy are not necessarily devoted to the idea of equality. They can instead be motivated entirely by *ressentiment*. Jean-Baptiste Clamence is such a man. He repeatedly states that he wants to dominate. He fantasizes about heights because he can imagine himself a ruler looking down on other human beings as if they were little insects. He imagines his best place would be standing atop Etna. He says he likes islands because they are easier to dominate. And yet Clamence is living not in Sicily but in Amsterdam, one of the lowest cities of the continent of Europe. He rules over no one. He holds to the negative-sum strategy because he resents the success of others, not because he has a commitment to equality. Here we see again his "double" nature.

There can be other motives. It could be that one seeks a negative-sum strategy simply to increase one's relative status and one is not capable of doing so in any other way or cannot conceive of another way to do so. Furthermore, often the negative-sum strategy is a way for elites to distinguish themselves from others of their group: they express contempt for their own kind and for their nation or community as a way to assert their relative superiority. Camus made a comment about this in his journals in 1947: "Pecherin, a Russian émigré of the nineteenth century, who became a monk abroad and exclaimed: 'What a delight to hate one's native land and to long for its collapse.' The intelligentsia and the *totalitarian* interpretation of the world" (1978, 176). Interestingly, even at this early date, Camus associates this attitude with totalitarian ideology.[7]

Tocqueville also seems to identify a similar case of the negative-sum strategy. In *The Ancient Regime and the French Revolution*, Tocqueville argues that the aristocracy began denouncing each other at the same time that they undertook genuine efforts to improve the lot of the peasants. Thus, for example, the king and parliament of Toulouse disagreed publicly in 1792, but "On one point, it will be noted, both parties concurred: on giving the public to understand that their superiors were to blame for the evils that befell them" (1955 [1856], 182). But, as they did this, they also made evident their complete disdain for those peasants. "But what seems stranger still is that alongside demonstrations of their sympathy with the lower classes [the aristocrats] sometimes gave publicity to expressions of contempt" (184–85). This seems to have been a case of negative competition: each noble was claiming to be more just than the others, by way of denouncing the other aristocrats. And, like Clamence, they have contempt for the supposed subject of their sympathy; Tocqueville tells us that "For though they had learned to sympathize with their 'inferiors' they still despised them" (185). One assembly referred to the peasants as "uncouth yokels, boors with no respect for law and order, no sense of discipline" (185).

Other scholars have observed and articulated the negative-sum strategy. In *Demons*, a novel that Camus loved and which he adapted for the stage, the infamous character of Shigalyov describes his personal political manifesto as a sprawling text that reasons that 90 percent of the population should be enslaved: "Starting from unlimited freedom, I conclude with unlimited despotism. I will add, however, that apart from my solution of the social formula, there can be no other" (1995 [1872], 402). Although Shigalyov is a minor figure in the novel, Camus includes him and this passage in his own stage adaptation of the novel. Camus also devotes a short section of *The Rebel* to a discussion of Shigalyov (1956, 173–76).

Two additional observations will give us the judge-penitent. Both observations are of phenomena that are products of mores that some hold in liberal civilization: a sense of justice and self-criticism that asks us to give special consideration to those less fortunate than ourselves.

First, we all intuitively understand and recognize from liberal culture the impulse to side with the victim because he is a victim. Call this the "underdog principle":

It is virtuous to defend or support a person who is oppressed or of low social status, solely because he is oppressed or of low social status.

Presumably there are relative underdogs, such that the underdog principle invites us to defend and support those of lower social status in each context over those of higher social status in that context. If this is correct, then the underdog principle asks for a kind of ordering of all social relations such that it endorses a kind of inverted hierarchy. Furthermore, it is clear that the underdog principle is applied by way of an ideology. For example, for the Marxist, the proletarian communist is the underdog—but someone such as a poor worker who also happens to be right-wing will often not count as an underdog. Or, to consider another example, we saw that metaphysical revolutionaries tend to celebrate crime and criminals (see chapter 3). For those who have such an ideology, the victims of crime are often not seen as underdogs but rather as emblems of the status quo.

Clamence may be such a man since, although he claims "widows and orphans" were his primary kind of client, every specific example he gives of a former client is a criminal, and at the time of his monologue he is making his meager living by giving legal advice to criminals.

Thus Clamence says, "I had a specialty: noble cases. Widows and orphans, as the saying goes—I don't know why, because there are improper widows and ferocious orphans. Yet it was enough for me to sniff the slightest scent of victim on a defendant for me to swing into action" (Camus 1984, 17). This is a remarkable passage because it describes the sentiment but also recognizes the problem for such a principle: there really is no reason to believe the underdog is deserving of special moral consideration simply because he is the underdog. Although it may be considered a virtue to give special consideration to the demands of those less fortunate than ourselves, there is no reason to believe their demands will be more justified than the demands of others, or that they are more virtuous than others.[8] As Clamence observes, there can be evil underdogs. We might add that there can be virtuous successful people.

The judge-penitent uses the underdog principle in two ways. First, and primarily, one can get a kind of social status from proclaiming adherence to the underdog principle. We saw this in Tocqueville's example of the self-denouncing nobles; it can be a way to signal superiority to the other members of the group to which you belong. One can express adherence to the underdog principle by way of making a judgement consistent with the underdog principle that denounces one's own group. This sets one apart as ethically superior to the other members of your group by both demonstrating loyalty to the ideology that underlies the underdog principle and also demonstrating that one values that ideology more than one values solidarity with one's group. Furthermore, given that the underdog principle is often ideological, it may matter more if one expresses agreement with this ideology than whether one applies the principle with any particular objectivity and fidelity. Second, there is a possibility that the judge-penitent can denounce himself so thoroughly that he becomes the underdog and thereby wins a kind of status. There is, after all, something paradoxical about the underdog principle: If it were followed absolutely, then those on the bottom of a social hierarchy would end up on the top of that social hierarchy. What then if we applied the underdog principle again to this new result?

Sartre adopted the underdog principle. His primary defense of his refusal to criticize communism, and to do no more than offer tepid rejections of Stalinism, is his indignant sense that those who opposed communism were bullies attacking those weaker than themselves: "An anti-communist is a dog," he angrily cried. He explicitly reasons that his position as anti-anti-communist is justified because the communists declare themselves representatives of those of low social status. Furthermore, his unspecified ethics always included a belief that we should be striving for a socialist revolution. "Ethics *today* must be revolutionary socialist ethics" (1992, 13). Without ever defending such a value theory, he adopts just the position that Camus had repeatedly criticized: taking the hypothetical socialist revolution as an obvious good and combining this with a consequentialist decision theory. Given this position, Sartre is abasing himself and elevating the underdog when he claims that "It is obvious that [the revolutionary] is to be found only among the oppressed" (1955 [1946], 209). But he signals his superiority to other intellectuals of his class by the vigor of his denunciation of his class.

Some go beyond the underdog principle and adopt the view that those of low social status have special epistemic authority. Call this the "standpoint principle":

Individuals who are oppressed or of low social status have authority when they make judgments about any matters related to their oppression or low social status.

Sometimes the epistemic warrant is extended further, including a claim that the oppressed have special insight on other matters, or even all matters. Sartre articulates this latter view when he says that if there is a universal ethical truth then only the oppressed can know it: "the meaning of this philosophy is open, at first, to revolutionaries only, that is to men in the *situation of the oppressed persons*, and it has need of them in order to become manifest in the world" (1955, 238).

What then is the judge-penitent? It is someone who believes and acts on these principles and strategy. From the underdog principle, there is an incentive to denounce one's peers as a sign of allegiance to the principle and to the associated ideology, and there is even an incentive to claim to be oppressed or otherwise to be a person of low social status in order to be favored by others who may also hold to the underdog principle. From the standpoint principle, one wants to be perceived as oppressed or of low social status in order to be empowered to judge others. Combined, these can result in the desire to be perceived as oppressed or of low social status so that one may use one's special epistemic warrant as the weapon to act on the negative-sum strategy: one is committed to achieving greater relative status by judging and debasing others.[9]

This negative-sum strategy has a powerful group dynamic also: if adopted by many, it creates a rush toward judgment and self-abasement, in a potential acceleration of negative-sum competition. "Deprived of their natural curb, the judges, loosed at random, are racing through their job. Hence we have to try to go faster than they, don't we?" (Camus 1984, 117). This is a danger to everyone, but—as Clamence explains—the trick is (1) "to go faster," which presumably means to be first to debase yourself and do so with the most vigor, and (2) to adeptly seize on the standpoint principle:

> I stand before all humanity recapitulating my shames without losing sight of the effect I am producing, and saying: "I was the lowest of the low." Then imperceptibly I pass from the "I" to the "we." When I get to "This is what we are," the trick has been played and I can tell them off. I am like them, to be sure; we are in the soup together. However, I have a superiority in that I know it and this gives me the right to speak. . . . The more I accuse myself, the more I have the right to judge you. (140)

One is reminded of those communist party meetings where no one wants to be the last to start clapping, or the first to stop clapping, for the great leader.

Clamence is an ersatz Socrates. Socrates claims he does not know, and this makes him the wisest man in Athens. Clamence instead claims he is the lowest of the low, and this empowers him to be the most judgmental man in Amsterdam.

As well as I have been able to determine, Camus's first use in writing of the term "judge-penitent" appears in his journals on December 14, 1954. He writes: "Existentialism. When they accuse themselves one can be sure that it is always to crush others. Judge-penitents" (2010, 131).[10] This is of course after the infamous falling out with Sartre and Beauvoir, which was initiated by their publication in *Les temps moderne* of Francis Jeanson's contemptuous review of *The Rebel*. Why denounce Sartre and Beauvoir and Jeanson as judge-penitents? Given now that we understand what the term means, it is possible to show that Sartre's attack on Camus stoops at least once to the judge-penitent strategy. Near the beginning of his infamous public reply to Camus, Sartre writes: "You may have been poor, but you are no longer poor. You are a bourgeois, like Jeanson and me" (Sprintzen and van den Hoven 2004, 134). For a supporter of the communists, this is a terrible admission: the bourgeoisie are unable to be true members of the revolutionary project. They are corrupted by their class interests. Marxist epistemology (which is precisely the Marxist version of the standpoint principle and is in fact the ancestor of the standpoint principle) tells us that only the worker (albeit when the worker is a communist) can correctly diagnose the political and economic situation in a way to allow for revolution. This makes the proletariat the most important potential political force, and Sartre believed the communist party was the only political entity that could rally this force. As we already noted, his justification also includes his "anti-anti-communism," which he sees as siding with the underdog. But Sartre was also sympathetic to Marx's philosophy and went as far as to claim it is the most fundamental philosophy. To the Marxist, and especially the communist, to be a bourgeois is the worst possible class. It means one's material conditions instilled into you all the wrong ideological predispositions. Thus, Sartre begins his attack on Camus by demeaning himself: he puts himself into the lowest possible position for the Marxist—albeit while claiming that Camus is also in this same situation—before his attack.

Consider Sartre's essays in *Les temps moderne* in 1952 and 1954, collected as *The Communists and Peace*. These essays are shrill to the point of monotony and, as is typical of the genre, include exaggerated predictions of a dismal future for the working class if the communists do not succeed. But the relevant point here is that Sartre attacks the bourgeoisie as a kind of way of being in the world, for whom politics is a luxury activity that changes nothing and which can even include endorsing (ineffectually) leftist causes. "But for the worker, politics cannot be a luxury activity: it is his sole defense and his only means of integrating himself into a community"

(1968b, 124). Thus, the bourgeois unreflectively lives and perpetuates his oppressive worldview, even if he claims to be a leftist radical, but the communist must earn his freedom:

> To be a bourgeois is not difficult; it is enough to pick the right parents;[11] afterwards one lets nature take its course. On the other hand, nothing is less easy than to be a proletarian: one asserts oneself only by a thankless and difficult action, by going beyond fatigue and hunger, by dying to be reborn. In order for action to be possible at any moment, *praxis* must exist within the masses themselves as a call, an example and also, very simply, as a sort of *figuration* of what can be done. In short, there is needed an organization which is the pure and simple incarnation of *praxis*. (127–28)

This organization is of course the communist party. But what about the freedom of the individual? Doesn't the communist party undermine and attack liberty? Well, of course, such talk of freedom is a bourgeois ruse: "*True* bourgeois freedom, positive freedom, is a power of man over man" (122). Freedom for the worker comes only through the party:

> [The worker's] freedom, which is simply his power to transcend the given situation—in short, to act—manifests itself then within this given reality which is the organization; he forms his opinions on the problems which the Party submits to him and does so within the context of the principles which the Party gives to him. In short, he doesn't judge the Party in the name of a policy whose principles are engraved in his unconscious, produced by his spontaneous reaction or by the contradictions of bourgeois society. Trained, molded, raised above himself by the Party, his freedom is only the power to transcend each particular situation by acts, within the very body of the organization and towards the common goal. In a word, the Party is his freedom. (130–31)

Yes, even when it oppresses you, the communist party is freedom.

Where does this place Sartre? His political writings are a good example of the judge-penitent strategy, since of course Sartre never stayed silent.

He claimed to speak for the workers and the communists, and he denounced and attacked critics of communism—critics such as Camus. He denounces his class and takes this denunciation as a mantle of virtue to justify his denunciation of those intellectuals who would criticize the communists (and who would dare to criticize Sartre). The arguments are secondary; it is enough to denounce oneself and to judge.

Early in the 1950s Camus writes in his journals: "T.M. polemic—Knavery. Their sole excuse is in this terrible era. Finally, something in them aspires to servitude. They dreamt of going there by some noble pathway, full of thoughts. But there is no royal path to servitude. There is cheating, insult, denunciation of the brother. After that, the sound of the thirty deniers" (2010, 51). Here again he is explicit: he sees in the defense of communism by Sartre and his colleagues an endorsement of servitude. They are adopting the negative-sum strategy, seeking equality through slavery. They are, as Clamence phrased it, "waiting for the masters with their rods." Furthermore, in an unusually candid interview that appeared in the *New York Times* shortly after the publication of *The Fall*, Camus said:

> My character [Clamence] is a build-up. There are touches drawn from different sources. From the existentialists comes the mania for self-accusation, so that they can accuse others more easily. That has always seemed to me an extra dirty little trick. It's what shocks me the most in these gentlemen's activities. This passion for accusation always ends by a defense of the servitude which is the direct issue of existentialism. (Aury 1957, 36)

But Sartre exemplified the judge-penitent strategy even more aggressively after Camus's death. We turn to this next.

SARTRE AS AEGISTHUS

Sartre frequently endorsed violence as a tool of politics. But in at least one text—his 1961 preface to Franz Fanon's *The Wretched of the Earth*—he also adopted the view that violence can be therapeutic. Fanon's book is a call for violence against colonizers, not only as a strategy for expelling them but as a kind of necessary therapy for the colonized. Fanon claims "decolonization is always a violent event" (2004, 1) and "decolonization reeks of red-hot cannonballs and bloody knives" (3). This violence liberates the mind of the colonized, while also transforming them: "At the individual level, violence is a cleansing force. It rids the colonized of their inferiority complex, of their passive and despairing attitude. It emboldens them, and restores their self-confidence" (51). After the colonists are killed, Fanon claims, then the colonized will live in peaceful harmony together because violence will have formed a bond between them.

In his preface, Sartre wholeheartedly endorses Fanon's call for revolutionary violence as a therapy, but he also explicitly adopts the judge-penitent strategy. He describes the Europeans as a unique evil in the world, as if they alone had invented colonization and war: "Not so long ago the Earth numbered 2 billion inhabitants, i.e. 500 million men and 1.5 billion 'natives'" (2004a, xliii). Europe's values are a false cover for its greed and colonial ambition, and these are leading to its decline: "Europe is doomed" (xlviii). Sartre is a European of course, and he is denouncing himself as he is denouncing his peers, but he gets his moral outrage and authority from being the one most aggressively denouncing the Europeans, including himself. He is the judge-penitent. He celebrates and calls for the violence that will end colonialism but also that will end the colonial culture of Europe. This violence is necessary since "no indulgence can erase the marks of violence: violence alone can eliminate them" (lv). There is no reflection on his part—nor on Fanon's part—on how this logic entails that all violence should spawn a perpetual cycle of revenge. Rather, they focus on the immediate therapeutic benefit. Sartre writes, "killing a European is killing two birds with one stone, eliminating in one go oppressor and oppressed: leaving one man dead and the other man free" (lv). Sartre sounds wistful when he recognizes that the Europeans won't get their just desert: "Slowly but surely it is our turn to head down the road to 'native' status. But in order to become genuine 'natives' our territory would have to be occupied by the formerly colonized and we would have to be starving to death" (lxi).

The most notable feature of this text, so clearly adopting the judge-penitent strategy, is that it is baldly contradictory of Sartre's philosophical theory. According to Sartre's existentialist philosophy, each human being is wholly responsible for his actions, but not for anything else. The idea that someone can inherit guilt, or that someone should feel shame for what his ancestors did or what others in his culture did, contradicts Sartre's theory.

We have already noted that Sartre's philosophy posits all human relations as fundamentally antagonistic. Shame arises from this antagonism:

> Shame . . . is only the original feeling of having my being *outside*, committed within another being and, as such, without any defense, illuminated by the absolute light that emanates from a pure subject: it is the consciousness of being irremediably what I always was, "suspended," i.e., in the mode of "not-yet" or "already-more-than." Pure shame is not the feeling of being this or that reprehensible object but, in general, of being *an object*, i.e. of recognizing myself in that degraded, dependent, and frozen being that I am for the Other. (2021, 392 [328])

Essential to Sartre's ontology is the claim that we, the for-itself, have no positive properties (other than some very abstract metaphysical properties, such as being free). We are pure freedom, and to believe we have any positive properties, to believe we are objects, is bad faith. Thus, shame is a kind of bad faith, albeit one that is primordial and very hard to avoid. The other sees me as an object, and I fall into shame when I see myself as an object also. Guilt is a degenerate version of this and is itself a form of bad faith. The guilty person concludes he has some positive property that adheres to him because of his past actions; his past action made him into a kind of thing (the guilty thing: a killer, a thief, a colonizer, etc.). This also can provide a kind of excuse for hiding from one's freedom: in believing that one is guilty, one falsely believes one is less free, and thus avoids the anguish of taking responsibility for this freedom. This is why Sartre could write in *Anti-Semite and Jew* that

> If one is going to reproach little children for the sins of their grandfathers, one must first of all have a very primitive conception of what constitutes responsibility. Furthermore one must form his conception on the basis of what the grandparents have done. One must believe that what their elders did the young are capable of doing. One must convince himself that Jewish character is inherited. (1965 [1946], 16)

Sartre has adopted this "primitive conception" by the time he is writing his introduction to Fanon's screed.

Sartre makes use of the existentialist ideal of individual responsibility in his first play, *The Flies*. This retelling of Aeschylus's play *The Libation Bearers* portrays an Argos where the citizens wallow in guilt and shame over their supposed complicity in the death of Agamemnon. Their guilt and shame are bad faith: they cannot inherit guilt from their ancestors, nor are they really objects (in this case, murderers or things complicit in murder) because of the past actions of others. But they have escaped their responsibility and their freedom by jealously fostering their own guilt and shame. Each year they have a festival of the dead where they wallow in a frenzy of shame and guilt, falsely believing that the spirits of the dead rise and abuse them. It is an orgy of self-flagellation and bad faith, and it is the primary tool that their tyrant Aegisthus uses to rule over them.

But an even greater villain in the play is the god Zeus. Zeus exists solely on the penitence of human beings; he is powerless to affect those who know they are free, and so his sole motive is to keep human beings in guilt and shame. He tells Aegisthus to kill Orestes, because Orestes is free. Zeus admits his own need:

> It's because you are atoning for [killing Agamemnon] that it served my ends. I like crimes that *pay*. I like yours because it was a clumsy, boorish murder, a crime that did not know itself, a crime in the antique mode, more like a cataclysm than an act of man. Not for one moment did you defy me. You struck in a frenzy of fear and rage. And then, when your frenzy had died down, you looked back on the deed with loathing and disowned it. Yet what a profit I have made on it! For one dead man, twenty thousand living men wallowing in patience. Yes, it was a good bargain I struck that day. (1989, 99–100)

Zeus thrives on the bad faith of the Argives, who feel collective shame, and see themselves as collectively guilty, for the death of Agamemnon.

Sartre has explicitly contradicted himself. With his denunciations of Europe and Europeans, with his theme of racial shame and racial guilt, Sartre has adopted the role of his own Aegisthus, if not Zeus. He transformed himself into one of those raving penitents that he portrayed at the festival of the dead. It is an astonishing example of ideology overcoming reason, and also an illustration of how the judge-penitent strategy is an enormously powerful temptation in liberal society.[12]

THE SECOND NEW PARADOX OF FREEDOM

Thus, the central theme of *The Fall* is a portrait of judge-penitence as a way of life. Does this make the novel merely an interesting character study of one kind of strange type? I think not. There are two senses in which this portrait is of profound import. First, Camus has identified a new paradox of freedom (one to be set beside the Paradox of Freedom as an End-in-Itself, which we described in chapter 3). Recall that we adopted the idea of a paradox of freedom from Popper. Popper was concerned that our need for criticism and open discussion opens the door for some to advocate the destruction of our open society and the oppression of criticism and open discussion. Popper's explanation of the paradox does not require that he provide empirical evidence that there are people in the liberal society who proselytize for intolerance; he need not use a random sample to show that they are a significant portion of the population and so on. Rather, he is warning about a structural flaw in liberalism, one that can and has been exploited, and one of which we need to be aware if we are to prevent the harms that can result from intolerance. Similarly, with the concept of the judge-penitent, Camus is describing a structural flaw in liberal society when some people adopt certain beliefs. The judge-penitent is a threat to liberal society, just as the intolerant are. Both would destroy liberal society if they were given sufficient power. We can call this the Paradox of the Judge-Penitent.

Second, Jean-Baptiste Clamence is not unique. Because many people in contemporary liberal societies endorse the underdog principle, and some of those people endorse the standpoint principle, these together create a perpetual temptation to adopt the negative-sum strategy and become a judge-penitent. In the same way that *Demons* described the impotence of Russian liberals faced with a violent revolutionary youth (a danger that within a few decades came to flower in the Russian Revolution and the rule by the Shigalyovs that followed), *The Fall* describes our own vulnerability to the judge-penitents. The threat is not idle: if large numbers of people adopt the strategy of the judge-penitent, a spiral of destructive negative-sum competition would result.

I note that a fellow scholar has pointed out to me that he met judge-penitents in a communist country where he has studied. These individuals were devoted to the communist ideology, and they used claims of being oppressed to attempt to gain political influence. This observation is unsurprising because the underdog principle is one shared by Marxists, at least when the underdog is deemed a proletarian; and, as noted, the standpoint principle is a generalization of Marxist epistemology. This observation is important because it illustrates that the judge-penitent is a threat in many kinds of society. However, I think it is worth identifying the appeal of the judge-penitent strategy as a paradox that is acute for liberalism because liberal societies are meant to encourage sympathy for the underdog and self-criticism *in order to* correct errors. The judge-penitent presents us with the paradoxical case where this error-correction mechanism actually causes the problem. Criticism and sympathy—usually virtues—run amok and create a pernicious kind of political actor. Thus, there may be judge-penitents in nonliberal societies, but they are most explicitly a paradox in liberal societies.

THE ARISTOCRAT

Let us review. Throughout his work, Camus was concerned with the question: How shall we best live, if the universe and history are absurd? He first suggests, in *The Myth of Sisyphus*, and develops at length in *The Rebel* the idea that moderate revolt is the correct response to this absurdity. Revolt for Camus is the assertion of, and the attempt to foster and preserve, our fragile human purposes in an indifferent universe—even when we are aware that this revolt is doomed to fail. But revolt is always dangerous, because if it becomes immoderate, it leads to revolution, which includes always justifications for murder and cruelty, and the destruction of innate human purposes. With this theory, *The Rebel* gives us a novel political philosophy based on the surprising claim that our response to the absurd drives much of contemporary history. But, as we have seen, in his last completed novel, Camus explores the new concept of the judge-penitent.

The judge-penitent is a person who wants to dominate others, just as does the immoderate rebel. However, the judge-penitent is different from the other revolutionaries Camus describes in *The Rebel*, in that he has a strategy to gather power by at first demeaning himself and then claiming moral authority from his own abasement. What then is the correct response to the judge-penitent? Is it moderate revolt?

One might attack the judge-penitents by arguing against the underdog principle. After all, it seems ultimately a foolish inference to assume victims have a kind of virtue in light of their victimhood. As we saw, Jean-Baptiste Clamence let slip recognition of this fact when he reports that "there are abusive widows and vicious orphans." One could also reject the standpoint principle and deny that the oppressed have priority in judgments against others. Although the standpoint principle has many defenders, it lacks any compelling justification since there is no reason oppression should filter inferior theories as an epistemic method must. And, of course, one could attack the negative-sum strategy because it results in an overall net loss. A society in which a negative-sum strategy dominates must soon destroy itself.

Camus takes a position inconsistent with the underdog principle, the standpoint principle, and the negative-sum strategy, but he does this not by offering a political strategy but by describing a class of personal virtues. At the same time that he was writing *The Fall*, Camus returns repeatedly in his notebooks to the idea that responsible citizenship requires a kind of commitment to duty that he calls "aristocratic." These thoughts are informed by Tocqueville and, arguably, Nietzsche, and in these remarks Camus seems to be striving for a conception of the opposite of the judge-penitent. His first mention is, "No matter what it claims, the century is in search of an aristocracy. But it does not realize that for this it must renounce the goal it so proudly assigns itself: well-being. There is no aristocracy without sacrifice. An aristocrat is, first, one who gives without receiving, one who *obligates* oneself. The Ancient Regime is dead for having forgotten this" (2010, 9). Here, the reference to the "Ancient Regime" suggests that Camus was already dipping into Tocqueville.

This is something relatively new in his thinking. In using the term "aristocrat" around this time, Camus seems to be indulging in anachronism, because in his time as in ours, the term had come to mean oligopoly where the positions of rule were inherited. But the term originally meant rule by the best (*aristos*)—by those with *arete*, excellence. It is this sense that Camus intends. In a lecture given in 1951, Camus evokes this ancient sense of "aristocrat" in the context of discussing the situation in Spain. He observes that Franco's minister of the interior, Suñer, had called for an aristocracy. In response, he says,

> I have nothing against aristocracy. On the contrary, I think the problem European civilization faces is to create new elites, its own having been dishonored. But Suñer's aristocracy is too much like Hitler's lords. It is the aristocracy of a gang, the royalty of crime, the cruel lordship of mediocrity. For my part, I know only two kinds of aristocracy: those of intelligence and work. (2022, 103)

Camus is imagining a kind of democratic aristocracy: a condition where each member—or at least many members—of the demos seek responsibilities and strive to meet those responsibilities with excellence. This is made more clear when he claims in his journals: "The only source of aristocracy is the people. Between the two there's nothing. This nothing, which for 150 years has been the bourgeoisie, tries to give shape to the world and obtains nil, a chaos that survives only because of its past roots" (2010, 92). Here Camus is voicing a criticism of the bourgeoisie that was common to both the left and the right in his time, and articulated by philosophers from Nietzsche to such contemporaries as Leo Strauss: that the bourgeoisie had prioritized comfort and expressed freedom through consumption, resulting in a lack of strength, direction, or virtue. Thus he rejects the bourgeoisie as unable to provide this kind of aristocracy. But "the people" is vague. Fortunately, he struggles with this in another entry:

> Necessity of an aristocracy. In the present, one can imagine only two of them: the one of intelligence and the one of work. But intelligence alone is not an aristocracy. Nor work (the examples, in both cases, are obvious). Aristocracy is not primarily the enjoyment of certain rights, but primarily the acceptance of certain duties that alone legitimize the rights. The aristocracy is asserting itself and at the same time stepping aside. To leave oneself (the definition of duty), intelligence cannot move toward privileges. Some take part of intelligence, others

are the opposite of intelligence. And duty consists neither of asserting oneself nor of suppressing oneself but of making sure one serves what one claims. Thus, intelligence can move only toward the work that is its duty and its limit. Work, for its part, cannot move toward stultification, unconscious or conscious (generalized humiliation of intelligence), which is either itself or its opposite (see above). Thus, work can only move toward intelligence. Finally, in the present, the aristocracies of work and intelligence are not possible until they recognize one another and begin to walk toward the other in order to one day establish a single superior image of man. (2010, 91–92)

Furthermore, Camus reflects that every stable society must be based on such an aristocracy: "Every society is based on aristocracy, because this one, the true one, is demanding with regard to itself, and without this demand every society would die" (2010, 118). Earlier in his journals, apparently in 1952, he also equates aristocracy with practical ethics as he considers the idea of writing a text: "Title: Short Treatise of Practical Morality—or (to provoke) of Everyday Aristocracy" (51).

In an unusually personal passage about his marriage, Camus ends with an image that makes this search for an aristocracy a personal problem: "This world wiggles quite a bit because, like a cut worm, it has lost its head. It searches for its aristocrats" (2010, 132). How does this notion of aristocracy fit with Camus's theory of revolt as developed in *The Rebel*? Fortunately, Camus is clear when he reflects on this. "The oppressed has no real duty because he has no rights. Rights only return to him with rebellion. But as soon as he acquires rights, duty falls on him without delay. Thus rebellion, source of rights, is by the same token mother of duties. These are the origins of the aristocracy. And its history" (2010, 172). Thus, through revolt we learn about human nature and acquire rights and liberty. But in *The Rebel* we learn that revolt can spin out of control, leading to violence and cruelty, and then to severe diminishment of liberty and severe abuses of human ends. With this concept of an aristocracy, we get a different but consistent analysis—an analysis from the perspective of the individual and his own particular duties. From the perspective of the individual, the rights acquired from revolt also bring duties. To neglect or to deny these duties is to revolt without *mesure*. But when we recognize these duties, we will recognize limits that we ought to respect on liberty and our own personal desires. In a renunciation of the judge-penitent strategy, he observes that "He who neglects his duty loses his rights and becomes the oppressor even if he speaks in the name of the oppressed" (2010, 172).

Note that this means only the aristocrat, freed through revolt, understands and respects his duties. This is inconsistent with the standpoint principle. The oppressed have no special epistemic authority; instead, they have the right and duty to reject their own oppression, but otherwise they have "no real duty." Furthermore, to *want* to be a victim would be to want to shed your duties. Thus, the aristocrat as Camus conceives him cannot adopt that perversion of the underdog principle that leads one to want to be an underdog in order to get the sympathy of others and, via the standpoint principle, the "right" to judge others. Jean-Baptiste Clamence is the opposite of this aristocrat.

Arguably, Camus has come to a position that was widely held in Western philosophy from the time of Plato and Aristotle to such thinkers as Tocqueville. This is the view that human beings have a host of inherit purposes, but that some of these (such as the appetites and desires) need to be restrained by strength of character and by institutions. If we do not restrain these dangerous purposes, we are not free individuals (in the sense of agency freedom) but are rather slaves to our desires and passions. People must be trained to do this. Some are perhaps not capable of taking this training. And, unfortunately, those who lack this kind of internal restraint strive to become tyrants; they strive to exercise their passions over others. Thus, both individual freedom and the avoidance of tyranny require the kind of training for character that Camus is here calling—as would have Plato or Aristotle—aristocratic. Someone like Tocqueville stresses that it is a host of social institutions that fosters this training of character. Thus, arguably Camus has come to a position that would have been recognizable to many philosophers, including the ancient Greeks. He presumably would not be surprised by this observation, given his repeated statements that it is the wisdom of the Mediterranean (which reached its pinnacle in the "boundless genius of the Greeks") to which he always appeals and to which he insists we must return.

There is, upon reflection, little that is surprising here, other than Camus's sudden and provocative use of the term "aristocrat." In *The Rebel*, he calls for an ethic where we seek to make our civilization more just through revolt against injustice, but also he recognizes that this revolt is in continual danger of accelerating into revolution and then tyranny. As we have seen, the solution that he calls for is a series of limitations on revolt, such as an absolute adherence to free speech, rejection of any attempt to build enduring institutions of violence such as secret police, and requirements that those who call for violence should be responsible for the violence. Such strictures he summarizes as having *mesure*, measure or balance. And this *mesure* is the assertion of constraints on oneself. We can call these constraints "duties," and the result is what Camus is now calling "aristocracy."

But there is an important shift in emphasis. Camus is stressing an element of "excellence" in this aristocracy. This excellence includes that the aristocrats are demanding of themselves and self-consciously striving with discipline. They are creators who have a kind of strength of character that Camus sees as missing from his world. This idea is nascent in the journals, and we cannot know what role it was going to play in Camus's planned next work in philosophy, *Nemesis*. But we can note that these new aristocrats are the opposite of the judge-penitent. They do not seek to demean themselves so that they can be victims. They do not value victimhood over excellence; as noted above, to want to be a victim would contradict the idea that they want to carry their responsibilities. And these aristocrats cannot endorse the standpoint principle, since the rights that create our duties arise from a shared human nature. Furthermore, since the oppressed lack the relevant duties, it would be a non sequitur to suppose they could have expertise about those duties. Finally, where the judge-penitent seeks to avoid competition and rather wants to pull down what is above him in any hierarchy, the aristocrat strives to create, even recognizing that creation will lead to some inequalities.

Camus did not make explicit use of these ideas about aristocracy in *The Fall*. And though the terminology would have been shocking to his fellow intellectuals in Paris in his time, his use of the term "aristocrat" is not wholly irregular. One of Camus's favorite adjectives was "noble," and he used it repeatedly in his personal and political writings. But when we look at his explanation of what "aristocracy" meant to him in this context, it is consistent with both *The Rebel* and the new paradox for liberalism that he illustrates in *The Fall*. The aristocrat has two critical features: first, he is self-controlled, understanding that self-control is required to maintain a good life and a just society. This is captured also in the observation that freedom includes responsibilities. Perhaps this is one of the features of Nemesis that he imagined: there is a kind of natural balance between liberty and responsibility, where the increase in one means a direct increase in the other. Second, the aristocrat is a creator. Only self-control and responsible action allow the artist to create new works, the engineer to build new infrastructure, the politician to build new institutions, or the worker to craft new things. This means that the effect of the aristocrat is to add to society, to create. The solution to the Paradox of the Judge-Penitent is to endorse and foster a liberal, self-ruling aristocrat.

But this solution is not described in *The Fall*. Instead, by putting us into the position of Clamence's interlocutor, Camus set a trap. Clamence appeals to fundamental values of liberalism—the virtue of self-criticism, the desire to help those less fortunate—and bends these toward his goal of domination. We follow Clamence into his labyrinth of reasoning, until, in the center of Amsterdam, we are confronted with a choice: will we also become judge-penitents?

NOTES

Introduction

1. In the hopes that it will help with comprehension, I have sometimes inserted in square brackets the date of original publication (or, in the case of a talk, the date of the talk). I have done this even when referring to an essay within a collection, aiming to give the date of the essay precedence over the date of the first publication of the collection. I do not do this when the sentence involved identifies the initial date, and I don't do it when repeatedly citing a work.

2. The term "metaphysics" and its cognates have diverse uses, some of them intentionally disparaging. But I understand metaphysics to be that part of philosophy concerned with questions about the fundamental character of reality, such as: What is a purpose? Does God exist? Do we have free will? Every use of the term "metaphysics" or its cognates in this book will be meant in this sense.

3. I should note that it is not just critics of Camus who claim he is not a philosopher. In their sympathetic discussion of the importance of Camus's criticism of Marxism, Guérin, and Wood state that "Camus himself was not a philosopher but a writer with deep moral convictions who lucidly denounced political terrorism, whether it originated from the Right or the Left" (1980, 363).

4. I am thinking of such passages as "The quantum theory, relativity, the uncertainty of interrelationships, define a world that has no definable reality except on the scale of average greatness, which is our own" (1956 [1951], 294–95) and "Being can only prove itself in development, and development is nothing without being. The world is not in a condition of pure stability; but it is only movement. It is both movement and stability. The historical dialectic, for example, is not in continuous pursuit of an unknown value" (1956, 296).

5. But the word derives from the Latin *amare*, to love. And thus, ironically, given the claim that he is an amateur in these endeavors, one can say that Camus is a lover of wisdom—that is, a philosopher.

6. For example, I find many of Camus's statements about the bourgeoisie an embarrassingly unreflective adoption of the attitudes of intellectuals in his time— e.g., "There is a bourgeois, individualist Europe, the one that thinks about its refrigerators and its gourmet restaurants, which says: 'I don't vote, myself.' That is bourgeois Europe, it is true. That Europe doesn't want to live" (2022 [1955], 149).

ONE The Absurd

1. For an extensive discussion, see Pölzler (2018).

2. Some scholars have put this experience of the absurd at the center of their accounts. David Carroll (2007) argues that for Camus the feeling of the experience of the absurd signifies facts about the absurd that cannot be captured in theory.

3. I understand epistemic fallibilism to be the view that, for any of one's theories or beliefs, it is possible that the theory or belief can be revised and improved, or replaced with a better theory or belief. (This is not to deny that there may be necessary truths; rather, it is to deny that there is any effective procedure to sort the necessary from the contingent truths and from the falsehoods.) More generally, one could be fallibilist about some domain, such that we could say that fallibilism about X is the theory that it is always possible that one's theories or beliefs about X could be improved.

4. All emphasis in quotations appears in the original source, unless I note otherwise.

5. Cruickshank (1960, 45n) quotes Sartre as saying: "Camus's philosophy is a philosophy of the absurd. For him the absurd arises from the relation between man and the world, between man's rational demands and the world's irrationality." I have been unable to find the original source of this quote.

6. Camus does recommend a certain form of skepticism as a personal virtue, but this is a different matter. In *The Rebel* he is concerned that we should not use our political theories to justify violence and argues that we should be skeptical about their accuracy. A valuable discussion of this is to be found in Sharpe (2015a). But this skepticism is actually derivable from the notion of teleological absurdity, since what concerned Camus was that the prophecies of Marx or Hegel were used as consequentialist justifications for violence. Here again, Camus is rejecting some kinds of teleological explanations and not causal explanations.

7. "Nihilism" is a term that is at least as ambiguous as "absurd." Usually it merely names the teleological absurd. The term comes from a Russian social move-

ment in which young people rejected their society's mores but offered little replacement of their own. But others have redefined and used the term in diverse ways; e.g., Nietzsche in *The Will to Power* writes, "The philosophical nihilist is convinced that all that happens is meaningless and in vain; and that there ought not to be anything meaningless and in vain" (1968 [1887/1888], sec. 36).

8. Edmund Husserl founded a school of philosophy called phenomenology. The phenomenological method included attempting to analyze one's own experiences while suspending any judgments about whether those experiences accurately represented something else.

9. Although, for a criticism of this view, see Marletto (2021).

10. This may rule out reductive theories of teleofunctions, such as we see in Millikan (1989), if such theories allow for the potential replacement of the teleofunctional explanation. This may not be the case for systematic accounts of teleology like that in DeLancey (2006), since such an account could allow for irreducible teleofunctional explanations.

11. Realism about *x* is the view that there can be evidence-transcendent truths about *x*. Intuitively, it asserts that the world is independent of our knowledge about it. Anti-realism denies this.

12. I am glossing over an important point here. Someone could argue that history has a purpose because humans have common purposes and humans strive to shape history such that human beings increasingly respect and foster those purposes. Presumably, Camus means something like this when he writes, "if the unity of the world cannot come from on high, man must construct it on his own level, in history" (1956, 206–87). But this would be a purpose that is wholly explained by human purposes. My target in this case (because it is Camus's target) is the kind of explanation you have in Hegal and Marx, a kind that Popper called "historicism" (Popper 2002). For such explanations, history has a telos, and that telos is not reducible to individual human purposes but rather is explained by striving and combating social factors (circulating ideas for Hegel, economic production for Marx). As a rough rule of thumb, Hegel and Marx will explain human purposes in terms of history, instead of explaining history in terms of human purposes.

13. When I refer to "existentialists," I mean at least Heidegger, Sartre, and Beauvoir. Camus was not an existentialist. I say this because I assume existentialism includes commitment to the phenomenological method, foundationalism about purpose (which I explain below), and a strong version of blank-slatism. Camus does not share any of those three commitments.

14. This is a little bit too simple. Presumably there are ways that acting on one purpose could serve another fundamental purpose, but that are inferior to other possible actions. What's at stake in such cases is probably a matter of coherence: the foundationalist will propose several fundamental purposes, and a purpose that

serves one of these should not also contradict (i.e., inhibit the realization of) any of those other fundamental purposes. I don't believe anything in my discussions in this book will turn on such subtleties, so I gloss over them here.

15. More than a decade after its publication, Camus would tell an interviewer that "When I analyzed the feeling of the Absurd in *The Myth of Sisyphus*, I was looking for a method and not a doctrine. I was practicing methodical doubt. I was trying to make a '*tabula rasa*,' on the basis of which it would then be possible to construct something" (1970 [1951], 356).

16. "Dasein" is Heidegger's technical term for the kind of being that human beings are.

17. This will require recognition that we have purposes concerning other purposes (which one might call "metapurposes"). An example of a purpose that concerns a purpose could be this: agent A's purpose to be good includes a commitment to the purpose to be charitable. A can then value charity as both a purpose of A and also as a means to partly achieve another purpose of A.

18. For an insightful discussion of the role of Don Juan—"the Sisyphus of love"—in Camus's thinking and work, see Gay-Crosier (1968).

19. For a discussion of the relation of *Caligula* to other themes in Camus, and also for a review of the changes in the play, see Kałuża 2015.

20. See also Camus (2004, 205).

TWO Suicide and Murder

1. He expressed a similar view in his journals late in 1946: "Relation of the absurd to revolt. If the final decision is to reject suicide in order to maintain the confrontation, this amounts to implicitly admitting life as the only factual value, the one that allows the confrontation, that *is* the confrontation, 'the value without which nothing.' Whence it is clear that to obey that absolute value, whoever rejects suicide likewise rejects murder" (1978, 149).

2. It is not essential to Camus's point that absurd suicide be a common occurrence, or even that it had ever occurred. I did try to investigate whether there was any evidence that some suicides are absurd suicides, but I could not determine from my own limited review of the psychological literature whether there was any evidence on this question. It is of interest that Viktor Frankl claimed that "what happens if one's groping for a meaning has been in vain? This may well result in a fatal condition." He does not identify suicide but rather illegal drug use as this fatal consequence: "I think of those youngsters who, on a worldwide scale, refer to themselves as the 'no future' generation. To be sure, it is not just a cigarette to which they resort: it is drugs" (2006 [1959], 139). He also argues that those he knew in Nazi concentration camps who had no purpose to their life were the most likely to die.

3. Here is another interesting contrast with the work of Frankl. Frankl argues that human beings have a "will to meaning," an essential and intrinsic drive to find and pursue a purpose. As far as I can tell, Frankl never considered the question of whether a purpose is sufficient or justified, and so we cannot determine if this intrinsic purpose to have a purpose is sufficient and justified in his own view.

4. I use the term "contradict" loosely here. Of course contradictory values (You should do A; it is not the case that you should do A) would be a problem. But there is also the issue that some values could be, strictly speaking, not logically contradictory but still be in a kind of conflict, such that satisfying one leads to the inhibition of the other.

5. All of the existentialists at some point denied that they were existentialists. Recall that my necessary criteria for existentialism, as I understand it, were given in chapter 1, note 13. If we add the right genealogy—a descent from Nietzsche and Kierkegaard—these are sufficient conditions. Heidegger is the first to satisfy those criteria. Nothing substantial in my arguments turns on this, but it does mean that I take Sartre, Beauvoir, and Heidegger as "existentialists" regardless of their protestations, and it means also that Camus is not an "existentialist."

6. See Sartre and Sicard (1979).

7. Of course, this did not prevent Sartre from making strident ethical demands. His reasoning in doing so seems to have been that which we see shared by many Marxists and then by many postmodernists: an assumption, not defended nor even explicitly stated, that one should side with the underdog because he is the underdog and oppose the "powerful" because they are "powerful." For Camus's views on a similar strategy, see chapter 6.

8. Closely related to this question of completeness is the question, must every ethical problem have an available solution? It is at least logically possible that there could be ethical problems for which there is no available solution. By "available solution," I mean a solution that we are able to accomplish. This is a poignant question regarding Camus's ultimate silence on the question of Algerian independence. He sought some kind of peaceful solution to the conflict. When this appeared impossible, he fell silent. Some of his contemporaries treated this silence with contempt. But one could argue it was wisdom; perhaps there was no available solution in this case that would achieve the kind of peaceful outcome most people would argue we should have wanted.

9. I am using "weak" here in a merely formal sense: a theory can be too weak to prove some result, such that additional axioms must be added to the theory in order for it to be able to prove that result. "Weak" is thus a relative judgment—relative to the thing one wants to prove. In this case, we want to prove that we can distinguish some choices from others such that we can say, "Do this and don't do that." Sartre's theory is too weak to do this. This is an issue of logic.

10. Here "serious" is a technical term for Beauvoir. It refers to the person who denies the ambiguity of human existence and thus falsely believes his own values are objective and settled. Thus, "the serious mind" is making a mistake in this passage.

11. This error is not uncommon. Often the moral realism versus moral antirealism debate is framed still in such terms. But what we want of our moral theory is stable and consistent judgments, and this does not require a measure or criterion that is external to nature or even external to human beings. This should be clear when one considers utilitarianism; there is general agreement that it is a realist theory, but the criterion for moral judgments refers to the mental states of individuals.

12. In *The Ethics of Ambiguity*, Beauvoir does write that "I have tried to show in 'Pyrrhus and Cineas' that every man needs the freedom of other men and, in a sense, always wants it, even though he may be a tyrant. . . . Only the freedom of others keeps each one of us from hardening into the absurdity of facticity" (1948, 71). However, she does not develop the idea of others taking on one's projects in *The Ethics of Ambiguity*. Her implicit claim thus seems to be that these two justifications are consistent. That seems plausible, but it is not the case that her account in *The Ethics of Ambiguity* makes significant use of any of the presuppositions or conclusions of "Pyrrhus and Cineas."

13. I have throughout used Frechtman's translation of *The Ethics of Ambiguity*, but I have translated "dévoilement" as "unveiling" instead of as "disclosing."

14. There is a significant problem. Beauvoir has allowed that freedom can come in degrees. Freedom and the unveiling of being are the same, and we seek more unveiling of being. She then concludes that we have an interest in all people being free. But it would have been valuable to have an explicit argument for this universal claim. We have not been told why greater unveiling of being might not be had for some people by their oppressing some other people. (Beauvoir comes close to asserting that an elite may best know what is going to reveal freedom; also, she allows for consequentialist considerations by that elite. Hence it is possible that the oppression by Stalinism might reveal more being, in the long run. See chapter 5.) There are two issues here. One might be self-interested and find that one can increase the unveiling of being for oneself by oppressing others, even if this results in a net reduction in the unveiling of being. Or one might argue that there is overall net more unveiling of being by oppressing some group. This latter is analogous to the problems that arise for utilitarianism when someone proposes that there could be a society with greater overall utility by means of mistreating (e.g., enslaving) a minority. Similarly, could there be a society where by mistreating some people there is greater overall unveiling of being? Note a contrast here with classical liberalism. When Mill defines classical liberalism, his formulation calls for both maximum

liberty but also has built into it a constraint on harm to others: "the sole end for which mankind are warranted, individually or collectively, in interfering with the liberty of action of any of their number, is self-protection. That the only purpose for which power can be rightfully exercised over any member of a civilized community, against his will, is to prevent harm to others" (2015 [1859], 12–13). This holds even if one judges that he can help another by enforcing some benefit on him: "The only freedom which deserves the name, is that of pursuing our own good in our own way, so long as we do not attempt to deprive others of theirs, or impede their efforts to obtain it. Each is the proper guardian of his own health, whether bodily, or mental and spiritual. Mankind are greater gainers by suffering each other to live as seems good to themselves, than by compelling each to live as seems good to the rest" (2015, 15). (Note: In this book, I use the term "liberalism" and its cognates to refer only to this conception here described succinctly by Mill.) Mill is introducing a new ethical principle here; this is not a direct consequence of his utilitarianism. This might seem pedantic, but there are important consequences. If Beauvoir does not have a compelling argument for why greater freedom for everyone always results in more unveiling of being for everyone, then her theory would have to be emended with something like Mill's harm principle, as described above, to achieve her stated outcome.

15. The terminology here is my own, though it is similar to much of the terminology used in the free will debate literature. I believe event freedom and agency freedom are not compatible notions, but there are some scholars who combine them (e.g., "The libertarian insists that a man is only responsible or free if sometimes he could do otherwise than he does do. It must at least sometimes be genuinely up to him what he chooses or decides to do" [Wiggins 1998, 270]). I am articulating a problem I see underlying the debates and disagreements between the existentialists and Camus. But I believe that Camus had some inkling of this worry when he frequently refers to creativity in his writings. He sometimes presents creativity as a solution to social and existential problems. Creativity is free action, guided by a purpose, that finds a new solution to realizing that purpose; the person is the source of the solution, but the solution is determined by the telos of the creative act. This may be a good example of what I am calling agency freedom.

16. The tight relationship between blank-slatism and economic determinism was sometimes expressed by communist party communications that reference a future, improved human (e.g., East Germany's "Ten Commandments for the New Socialist Man").

17. In *Anarchism or Socialism?*, Stalin argues that "In social life . . . first the external conditions change, and then the thoughts of men, their habits, customs, and their world outlook change accordingly. That is why Marx says: 'It is not the consciousness of men that determines their existence, but, on the contrary, their social existence determines their consciousness'" (1953 [1906], 23).

18. The term "transcendent" and its cognates plays an obfuscatory role in these debates. Sometimes it is used simply to mean something like being true independent of historical conditions. Thus, if we understand "historical conditions" not to include evolution but rather to refer to something like social and economic events of (relatively) recent time, then one could call Camus's claims about human nature a belief in "transcendent" features of human being. But there is a motte and bailey often played with the term "transcendent," where its meaning shifts to something like Beauvoir's dismissive "written in heaven." This ambiguity underlies many uncharitable attacks on Camus by his contemporaries; see chapter 5.

19. This view that there can be nothing "behind" our observations, no patterns in nature that are "behind" events and which can be discovered, is shared by both Sartre and Beauvoir. Sartre makes the following claim in *Being and Nothingness*: "An electric current has no secret other side; it is nothing but the collection of physicochemical actions (electrolytic processes, the incandescence of a carbon filament, the movement of the galvanometer's needle, etc.) that manifests it. None of these actions is sufficient to reveal it. But it does not point to anything *behind* it; each action points to itself and to the total series" (2021, 2 [11]). Such a view, sometimes called "phenomenalism," is hard to square with any sense that science is producing true theories or that it is making progress; a consequence of phenomenalism is typically anti-realism, the view that our scientific theories are not describing entities independent of us.

20. Thanks to Esther Gabriel for this observation.

THREE Metaphysical Revolt

1. The development of Camus's concept of revolution, and his use of the term, is complex. He used the term favorably in writings before the end of the war, but also it is clear that at such times he associated revolution with a kind of moral transformation and not with anything like one finds predicted in a theory like Marxism. For a review of this development, see Lévi-Valensi and Guérin (1991).

2. There is an interesting variation on this reasoning in Dostoevsky's *Notes from Underground*. The narrator is insulted by limitations on his freedom, which arise both from nature and from social convention. And so he claims that others, reasoning in this same way, will act destructively in order to assert their will and autonomy: "man, whoever he might be, has always and everywhere liked to act as he wants, and not at all as reason and profit dictate" (2021, 25–26). Sometimes, this will include acting against convention, solely to assert that one is not controlled by those conventions. "'Well, gentlemen, why don't we reduce all this reasonableness to dust with one good kick, for the sole purpose of sending all these logarithms to

the devil and living once more according to our own stupid will'" (25). There is a noticeable difference, however: where the metaphysical revolutionary that Camus imagines seems motivated by a wild ambition, the underground man of Dostoevsky seems motivated entirely by a kind of spite—spite against nature and social convention, emerging from a kind of impotence.

3. "Highest" here means the purpose such that every other purpose is either justified by that purpose or must be subordinate to that purpose.

4. This translation is from the Lillian Goldman Law Library Avalon Project, https://avalon.law.yale.edu/18th_century/rightsof.asp.

5. Raymond Aron noted a similar motivation among intellectual leftists: "To the intellectual who turns to politics for the sake of diversion, or for a cause to believe in or a theme for speculation, reform is boring and revolution exciting. The one is prosaic, the other poetic, one is the concern of mere functionaries, the other that of people risen up against their exploiters. Revolution provides a welcome break with the everyday course of events and encourages the belief that all things are possible" (1962, 43).

FOUR Historical Revolt

1. There are substantial differences also; I don't mean to suggest that these thinkers agreed in most ways or considered the others as their allies. Voegelin, for example, had contempt for Popper (though great respect for Camus).

2. Again, Kopelev: "For I was convinced that I was accomplishing the great and necessary transformation of the countryside; that in the days to come the people who lived there would be better off for it; that their distress and suffering were a result of their own ignorance or the machinations of the class enemy; that those who sent me—and I myself—knew better than the peasants how they should live, what they should sow and when they should plow" (1977, 12).

3. To my surprise, Popper does not offer two criticisms of utopianism that I would consider both essential and consistent with Popper's philosophy. First, he does not discuss the fact that utopians produce a list of features for their utopia, and they assume that these can be realized together. Thus, Marx imagines such things as a classless society, a society where people feel no urges to free ride, where workers are not alienated from their work, where labor specialization will disappear, and where the state will disappear. Whether any one of these things can be realized is questionable. But whether this combination of things is possible is far more unlikely. It is as if one imagines a fantasy animal: One can imagine the hippogriff, but could such a thing evolve? Could it survive with its bizarre combination of features? It surely could not fly. Second, the utopians remain certain that they and other

people will prefer the things they imagine. But, until we try it, we won't know what it's like—to pick one example—to live in a society with enforced equality; we may discover that the fantasy that it would be delightful is very wrong indeed. This second point is related to the unfortunate method of argument used by utopians but also by many other ideologues, in which they compare some real system (such as our economies today) to what they imagine their utopia will be like. This is a worthless method.

FIVE Just Revolt

1. Relevant coverage of one such effort is "Cheney Pushes Senators for Exemption to CIA Torture Ban," *USA Today*, November 4, 2005.

2. My analogy here is partly inapt. Camus believed that torture was never justified and also it was never necessary. He states this clearly in his preface to *The Algerian Reports*, observing that in addition to being an unacceptable immorality, it is ineffectual and earns one ever more enemies.

3. This may be a kind of metaphysical fact, if we mean by "metaphysical fact" a fact more general than the kind described in a current physical theory. For example, it might be that the kind of things living organisms are will always have certain features that determine what is beneficial and what is harmful to them; such a fact might be true of a range of different possible worlds (when philosophers say "world" in this way, they mean a complete but different possible way the world could be). As a result, this might be a metaphysical fact, and if that is all we mean by "transcendence," then this would be a transcendent fact. But it would be no more mysterious than other metaphysical claims, such as when theoretical physicists speculate about what our universe would be like if some physical fact were different.

4. I am avoiding the question of when, and to what degree, Sartre was a Marxist. This is not an unimportant issue, especially in this context, but there is much contention about it and it is not essential to the point I make here: Sartre did support revolution as a means, regardless of his credentials as a Marxist, and he sees Camus's rejection of revolution as a form of naive quietism. But Sartre felt, at least at some periods, that the French Communist Party (the PCF) alone could bring about socialism. By the end of the decade, Sartre would write: "We agree with Garaudy when he writes: 'Marxism forms today the system of coordinates which alone permits it to situate and to define a thought in any domain whatsoever—from political economy to physics, from history to ethics'" (1968a [1960], 31). And also: "To be still more explicit, we support unreservedly that formulation in *Capital* by which Marx means to define his 'materialism': 'The mode of production of mate-

rial life generally dominates the development of social, political, and intellectual life'" (33–34). Sartre's deep desire was to position himself as a thinker helping to foster revolution. For a time, at least, it is clear that Beauvoir felt similarly.

5. It is interesting that the "New Philosophers," who arose in the 1970s and were notable for their criticisms of Marxism, seemed largely to ignore Camus and take Solzhenitsyn as their inspiration. For a discussion, see Guérin and Wood (1980).

6. In *The Rebel*, Camus makes a similar observation about Lenin: "He roundly declares, from 1902 on, that the workers will never elaborate an independent ideology by themselves. He denies the spontaneity of the masses. Socialist doctrine supposes a scientific basis that only the intellectuals can give it. When he says that all distinctions between worker and intellectuals must be effaced, what he really means is that it is possible not to be proletarian and know better than the proletariat what its interests are. He then congratulates Lassalle for having carried on a tenacious struggle against the spontaneity of the masses. 'Theory,' he says, 'should subordinate spontaneity.' In plain language, that means that revolution needs leaders and theorist" (1956, 225).

7. Beauvoir did seem to think, with Sartre and others, that there needed to be some kind of balancing between Stalin's regime and the influence of the United States. Among some, such concerns came close to equating Stalinism and the United States as somehow morally equal opposites. Sartre's letter to Camus captures this nicely: "The Iron Curtain is only a mirror, where each half of the world reflects the other. Each turn of the screw here corresponds to a twist *there*, and, finally, both here and there, we are both the screwers and the screwed" (Sprintzen and van den Hoven 2004, 143). One is reminded by Raymond Aron's observation that the Americans are just too hard to forgive for being needed (1962, 222).

8. It is interesting to note that Beauvoir and her generation of revolutionary thinkers did not question that violence would always be the most effective means of substantial political change. As we have seen, Camus seemed to believe this might be true in many cases. And yet the empirical evidence gathered since their era suggests that, at the very least, we have reason to doubt many cases where it seems necessary. Chenoweth and Stephan (2011) make a convincing argument that the most successful political struggles in recent decades have been nonviolent, even in cases where they confronted extremely violent opponents. My point here is merely that the assumption that certain kinds of violence are necessary for political change is an empirical assumption, one that many political thinkers at Beauvoir's time treat as obviously true. The evidence of history should remind us that these beliefs were dubious, as were consequentialist arguments that depended on grand prophecies about the efficacy of violence.

SIX   *The Fall* and a New Paradox of Liberalism

1. Walsh's interpretation of *The Fall* is the one to which my own is closest. Walsh identifies the judge-penitent as the key to the book and observes that Clamence "realizes that he can escape the only judgment left, the judgment of human beings, by regaining his superiority over them. But this cannot be done by surpassing them in virtue, since he has none. It can only be successful if he exceeds their condemnation through self-condemnation" (145–46). What I do below is offer a genealogy for this strategy.

2. Trahan's case is very compelling. There are deep similarities between the novels, including even in their form.

3. Solomon makes no mention of Dostoevsky's *Notes from Underground*, but this is one of the explicit themes of that novel. The narrator tells us that "I am convinced that not only too much consciousness but even any consciousness at all is a sickness" (2021, 7). The narrator blames his own inability to accomplish anything as a result of his intelligence and self-consciousness, for "it is even impossible for an intelligent man seriously to become anything, and only fools become something" (5). But the narrator of *Notes from Underground* is most definitely not a *megalopsychos*. He's a spiteful, diminished human being. Camus's Clamence is much more like the narrator of *Notes from Underground* than he is like the fallen hero Solomon proposes.

4. Camus also lists in his journals a quotation that I cannot find in the *Ancient Regime* but which captures the form of degenerate motivation that he is identifying via Tocqueville's work: "They seemed to love freedom; it turns out they only hated the master" (2010, 77).

5. Camus reflected in his journals that creation was a powerful kind of positive-sum task: "Creation. The more it gives, the more it receives—Giving generously to grow richer" (2010, 28). Earlier in his journals it is clear he saw negative polemics as the antithesis of this creation. He exhorts himself: "Never attack anybody, especially not in writing. The time of criticism and polemics is over—Creation" (22). Later, on October 26, 1956, he wrote: "The opposite of reaction is not revolution, but creation. The world is in an unending state of reaction and thus unendingly in danger of revolution. What defines progress, if it is such, is that without compromise, creators of all kinds triumph over the mind, over reaction, and over inactivity without revolution being necessary" (111).

6. Crime and corruption are the purest examples of negative-sum competition. The criminal gets better off relative to before the crime (if successful) but we are all worse off as a result. The corrupt politician gets a little better off but the entire state suffers. In both cases, everyone would be substantially better off without

the crime or corruption, but this is irrelevant to the motive of the criminal, who is seeking only relative improvement of his own status. It is of interest that all the metaphysical revolutionaries glorified crime, and the underdog principle, another essential element of the judge-penitent strategy, is often taken to include sympathy for criminals as a kind of underdog.

7. In 1948 in his journals Camus speculates that communism offers aspiring but unsuccessful writers status through the negative-sum strategy: "Recruiting. Most would-be writers go toward Communism. It's the one position that allows them to look down on artists. From this point of view, it's the party of thwarted vocations. Heavy recruiting, you may imagine" (1978, 215).

8. An interesting anecdote from Camus's journals about his visit to South America shows him reflecting on the natural inclination in himself to adopt the underdog principle. He visits a dance hall, and at first he is surprised that the black patrons do not dance differently than do the few white patrons. "Except for the color of their skin, nothing distinguishes this dance hall from a thousand others throughout the world. Speaking of this, I notice that I have to conquer in myself a reverse prejudice. I like blacks *a priori*, and I'm tempted to see in them qualities that they don't really have. I want these people to be beautiful, but if I imagine them with white skin, I find a rather pretty collection of clerks and dyspeptic employees" (1987 [1949], 93).

9. Judgment and judging are the key themes of the novel. By my count, words including the root "judge" occur 86 times in the short novel. "Judge" appears 27 times, "judgment" 26 times, "judges" 18 times, "judged" 8 times, "judging" 5 times, and "judgements" twice. It is one of the most common words of the book. There is no comparable substantial word that appears as often.

10. In that entry from his journals where Camus first uses the term "judge-penitent," he makes two other observations. One concerns acting, but the other could be meant to be part of his denunciation of the "existentialists." He writes: "With Luke true treason begins, causing the disappearance of Jesus's desperate cries" (2010, 131). This passage is intriguing because Camus uses this idea in *The Fall*. He puts a similar phrase into the mouth of Clamence. Clamence claims that Jesus was plagued by guilt because of the slaughter of the innocents. This guilt overwhelms Jesus, and he seeks death in order to escape it. "Knowing what he knew, familiar with everything about man—ah, who would have believed that crime consists less in making others die than in not dying oneself!—brought face to face day and night with his innocent crime, he found it too hard for him to hold on and continue. It was better to have done with it, not to defend himself, to die, in order not to be the only one to live, and to go elsewhere where perhaps he would be upheld. He was not upheld, he complained, and as a last straw, he was censored. Yes, it was the third evangelist, I believe, who first suppressed his complaint" (1984, 113).

I struggle to interpret the intent behind these passages, but I have a hypothesis. This passage is a kind of ultimate gambit for the judge-penitent: he judges even Jesus. But what is the betrayal here by Luke? Interestingly, this too is "double"—it is open to two interpretations. From Clamence's perspective: Clamence revels in the idea that the pleas of Jesus are proof that Jesus had limitations. Jesus (according to Clamence) meant to escape his guilt by dying and ascending. But he doubts his ascension and complains to his father. He is revealed as human, as no better than Clamence. This is "censored" by Luke, who hides Jesus's intimate appeal to his divine father. Thus, the judge-penitent sees Jesus as just another judge-penitent; Clamence announces that "he [Jesus] was not superhuman, you can take my word for it" (114). But from Camus's perspective: Jesus asserts his divinity when he demands God recognize him as son. Jesus is saying his suffering is unjust, inappropriate, unexpected, too long. It is not a good thing. It is not something that is the reason for his ability to judge. He is judge because of his perfection, not because of his suffering. Luke's omission offers implicit support for the view that Jesus can judge because he suffered, not because he is divine; it lowers Jesus, so that one might dare to claim his authority is merely a product—a la the standpoint principle—of his suffering alone.

11. This passage is ironic, given Sartre's accusation that Camus is bourgeois. Camus was raised in poverty by a deaf widow. He was not, like Sartre, born with the right parents.

12. Sartre's introduction to *The Wretched of the Earth* is particularly apropos since the text is primarily concerned with Algeria. Sartre calls for siding with the revolution in Algeria and endorses the violence of the revolution. It was of course Camus, himself born in Algeria, who had dreamed of another possible path, in which Algeria found some way to become a nation where those of more recent European descent could live in peace with those whose descent had older roots in the region. Perhaps Camus had been naive to dream this was possible, but history conclusively proved Fanon and Sartre wrong. The violence of the Algerian revolution continued unabated for decades after they had defeated the French colonists. Violence did not transform the revolutionaries into brothers. It merely continued between factions within their nation. Tens of thousands died in these internal struggles.

WORKS CITED

Abel, Lionel. 1957. "Man without Grace." *Commentary*, May.
Arendt, Hannah. 1985. *The Origins of Totalitarianism*. New York: Harcourt, Brace, Jovanovich.
Aristotle. 2000. *Nicomachean Ethics*. Translated by Roger Crisp. Cambridge: Cambridge University Press.
Aron, Raymond. 1962. *The Opium of the Intellectuals*. Translated by Terence Kilmartin. New York: W. W. Norton.
Arp, Kristana. 2001. *The Bonds of Freedom*. New York: Open Court.
Aury, Dominique. 1957. "Talk with Albert Camus." *New York Times Book Review*, February 24.
Bair, Dierdre. 1990. *Simone de Beauvoir: A Biography*. New York: Simon & Schuster.
Beauvoir, Simone de. 1948. *The Ethics of Ambiguity*. Translated by Bernard Frechtman. Secaucus, NJ: Citadel Press.
———. 1992a. *All Men Are Mortal*. Translated by Leonard Friedman. New York: W. W. Norton.
———. 1992b. *Force of Circumstances*. Translated by Richard Howard. New York: Paragon House.
———. 2004. "Pyrrhus and Cineas." Translated by Marybeth Timmerman. In *Philosophical Writings*, edited by Margaret A. Simons, 89–147. Urbana: University of Illinois Press.
———. 2011. *The Second Sex*. Translated by Constance Borde and Sheila Malovany-Chevallier. New York: Vintage.
———. 2012. "Preface to *Djamila Boupacha*." In *Political Writings*, edited by Margaret Simons and Marybeth Timmerman, 272–82. Urbana: University of Illinois Press.

Breton, Andre. 1975. *Manifestoes of Surrealism*. Translated by Richard Seaver and Helen Lane. Ann Arbor: University of Michigan Press.

Brockmann, Charles. 1962. "Metamorphoses of Hell: The Spiritual Quandary of 'La Chute.'" *French Review* 35 (4): 361–68.

Camus, Albert. 1956. *The Rebel*. Translated by Anthony Bower. New York: Vintage Books.

———. 1958. *Albert Camus: Caligula and Three Other Plays*. Translated by Stuart Gilbert. New York: Vintage.

———. 1970. *Lyrical and Critical Essays*. Translated by Ellen Conroy Kennedy. Edited by Philip Thody. New York: Vintage.

———. 1978. *Notebooks 1942–1951*. New York: Harcourt, Brace, Jovanovich.

———. 1984. *The Fall*. Translated by Justin O'Brien. New York: Knopf.

———. 1987. *American Journals*. Translated by Hugh Levick. New York: Paragon House.

———. 1991a. *The Myth of Sisyphus*. Translated by Justin O'Brien. New York: Vintage.

———. 1991b. *The Plague*. Translated by Stuart Gilbert. New York: Vintage.

———. 1995. *Resistance, Rebellion, and Death*. Translated by Justin O'Brien. New York: Vintage.

———. 2004. "In Defense of *The Rebel*." In Sprintzen and van den Hoven (2004), 205–21.

———. 2010. *Notebooks, 1951–1959*. Translated by Ryan Bloom. Chicago: Ivan R. Dee.

———. 2022. *Speaking Out: Lectures and Speeches, 1937–1958*. Translated by Quinton Hoare. New York: Vintage International.

Carroll, David. 2007. "Rethinking the Absurd: *Le Mythe de Sisyphe*." In *The Cambridge Companion to Camus*, edited by Edward Hughes, 53–66. Cambridge: Cambridge University Press.

Chenoweth, Erica, and Maria J. Stephan. 2011. *Why Civil Resistance Works: The Strategic Logic of Nonviolent Conflict*. New York: Columbia University Press.

Cruickshank, John. 1960. *Albert Camus and the Literature of Revolt*. New York: Oxford University Press.

Davis, Colin. 2011. "What Happened? Camus's 'La Chute', Shoshana Felman and the Witnessing of Trauma." *French Forum* 36 (1): 37–53.

DeLancey, Craig. 2006. "Ontology and Teleofunctions: A Defense and Revision of the Systematic Account of Teleological Explanation." *Synthese* 150 (1): 69–98.

———. 2021. "Camus's Absurd and the Argument against Suicide." *Philosophia* 49 (5): 1953–71.

———. 2022. "Explanation and the Unreasonable Silence of the World." In *Coming Back to the Absurd: Albert Camus's The Myth of Sisyphus 80 Years On*, edited by Peter Francev and Maciej Kałuża, 176–201. Leiden: Brill.
Descartes, René. 1985. *Principles of Philosophy*. In *The Philosophical Writings of Descartes*, vol. 1, translated by John Cottingham, Robert Stoothoff, and Dugald Murdoch. Cambridge: Cambridge University Press.
Dostoevsky, Fyodor. 1995. *Demons*. Translated by Richard Pevear and Larissa Volokhonsky. New York: Vintage Classics.
———. 2021. *Notes from Underground*. Translated by Richard Pevear and Larissa Volokhonsky. New York: Vintage Classics.
Engels, Friedrich. 2010. "Letter to Karl Marx, 7 October 1858." In *Marx and Engels, Collected Works*, vol. 40, *Letters 1856–1859*. London: Lawrence & Wishart.
Fanon, Frantz. 2004. *The Wretched of the Earth*. Translated by Richard Philcox. New York: Grove Press.
Felman, Shoshana. 1992. "Camus' *The Fall*, or the Betrayal of the Witness." In *Testimony: Crises of Witnessing in Literature, Psychoanalysis, and History*, by Shoshana Felman and Dori Laub, 165–203. New York: Routledge.
Foley, John. 2008. *Albert Camus: From the Absurd to Revolt*. New York: Routledge.
Frankl, Victor E. 2006. *Man's Search for Meaning*. Boston: Beacon Press.
Gay-Crosier, R. 1968. "Camus et le Donjuanisme." *French Review* 41 (6): 818–30.
Gifford, P. 1978. "Socrates in Amsterdam." *Modern Language Review* 73 (3): 499–512.
Girard, René. 1964. "Camus's Stranger Retried." *Proceedings of the Modern Language Association* 79 (5): 519–33.
Guérin, Jeanyves, and Diane S. Wood. 1980. "Albert Camus: The First of the New Philosophers." *World Literature Today* 54 (3): 363–67.
Heidegger, Martin. 1962. *Being and Time*. Translated by John Macquarrie and Edward Robinson. Oxford: Blackwell.
———. 1995. *The Fundamental Concepts of Metaphysics: World, Finitude, Solitude*. Translated by William McNeill and Nicholas Walker. Bloomington: Indiana University Press.
Jeanson, Francis. 1980. *Sartre and the Problem of Morality*. Translated by Robert V. Stone. Bloomington: Indiana University Press.
Judt, Tony. 2008. *The Burden of Responsibility: Blum, Camus, Aron and the French Twentieth Century*. Chicago: University of Chicago Press.
Kałuża, Maciej. 2015. "Caligula and the Letters to a German Friend—Deliberations regarding the Actions of Camus's Characters in Regard to the Ethics of Absurdity and the Concept of Metaphysical Rebellion." *Journal of Camus Studies* 2015:65–86.

———. 2020. "The Woman Had to Fall? Jean-Baptiste Clamence and the Literary Infection by Evil." *Acta Universitatis Lodziensis* 59 (4): 81–99.
King, Adele. 1962. "Structure and Meaning in *La Chute*." *Proceedings of the Modern Language Association* 77 (5): 660–67.
Kopelev, Lev. 1977. *No Jail for Thought*. London: Secker & Warburg.
Lenin, V. I. 1965. *Lenin's Collected Works* 4th English ed. Vol. 31. Translated by Julius Katzer. Moscow: Progress Publishers.
Lévi-Valensi Jacqueline, and Jeanyves Guérin. 1991. "Camus et l'idée de Révolution." *Cahiers de Fontenay* 63–64:221–41.
Lottman, Herbert. 1997. *Albert Camus: A Biography*. Corte Madera, CA: Gingko Press.
Mao Tse-tung. 1967. *Selected Works of Mao Tse-tung*. Vol. 3. Elmsford, NY: Pergamon Press.
Marletto, Chiara. 2021. *The Science of Can and Can't*. New York: Viking.
Meillassoux, Quentin. 2010. *After Finitude: An Essay on the Necessity of Contingency*. Translated by Ray Brassier. London: Continuum.
Mill, John Stuart. 2015. *On Liberty, Utilitarianism, and Other Essays*. Edited by Mark Philp and Frederick Rosen. Oxford: Oxford World Classics.
Millikan, Ruth. 1989. "Biosemantics." *Journal of Philosophy* 86 (6): 281–97.
Milosz, Czeslaw. 1990. *The Captive Mind*. Translated by Jane Zielenko. New York: Vintage International.
Nagel, Thomas. 1971. "The Absurd." *Journal of Philosophy* 68 (20): 716–27.
Nietzsche, Friedrich. 1968. *The Will to Power*. Translated by Walter Kaufman and R. J. Hollingdale. New York: Vintage.
———. 1997. *Untimely Meditations*. Edited by Daniel Breazeale. Translated by R. J. Hollingdale. Cambridge: Cambridge University Press.
Orwell, George. 1958. *The Road to Wigan Pier*. New York: Harcourt.
———. 1968. *The Collected Essays, Journalism and Letters*. Vol. 2, *My Country Right or Left. (1940–1943)*. Edited by Sonia Orwell and Ian Angus. Boston: Nonpareil Books.
Plato. 1961. *The Collected Dialogues*. Edited by Edith Hamilton and Huntington Cairns. Bollingen Series 71.1. Princeton, NJ: Princeton University Press.
Pölzler, Thomas. 2018. "Camus' Feeling of the Absurd." *Journal of Value Inquiry* 52: 477–90.
Popper, Karl. 1963. *The Open Society and Its Enemies*. Vol. 1. New York: Harper Torchbooks.
———. 1967. *The Open Society and Its Enemies*. Vol. 2. New York: Harper Torchbooks.
———. 2002. *The Poverty of Historicism*. New York: Routledge.

Sagi, Avi. 2002. *Albert Camus and the Philosophy of the Absurd*. Translated by Batya Stein. Value Inquiry Book Series. New York: Rodopi.
Sartre, Jean-Paul. 1955. *Literary and Philosophical Essays*. Translated by Annette Michelson. New York: Criterion Books.
———. 1963. *Saint Genet*. Translated by Bernard Frechtman. New York: Braziller.
———. 1965. *Anti-Semite and Jew*. Translated by George J. Becker. New York: Schocken Books.
———. 1968a. *Search for a Method*. Translated by Hazel Barnes. New York: Vintage Books.
———. 1968b. *The Communists and Peace*. Translated by Martha Fletcher. New York: George Braziller.
———. 1989. *No Exit and Three Other Plays*. New York: Vintage International.
———. 1992. *Notebook for an Ethics*. Translated by David Pellauer. Chicago: Chicago University Press.
———. 2004a. Preface to *The Wretched of the Earth*. In Fanon (2004).
———. 2004b. *Critique of Dialectical Reason*. Vol. 1, *Theory of Practical Ensembles*. Translated by Alan Sheridan-Smith. New York: Verso Books.
———. 2007. *Existentialism Is a Humanism*. Translated by Carol Macomber. New Haven, CT: Yale University Press.
———. 2013. "*The Stranger* Explained." In *We Have Only This Life to Live: The Selected Essays of Jean-Paul Sartre 1939–1975*, edited by Ronald Aronson and Adrian van den Hoven, 26–43. New York: New York Review Books.
———. 2021. *Being and Nothingness*. Translated by Sarah Richmond. New York: Washington Square Press.
Sartre, Jean-Paul, and Michel Sicard. 1979. "Entretien. L'écriture et la publication." *Obliques* 15.
Scott, Nathan. 1969. *Albert Camus*. New York: Hilary House.
Sharpe, Matthew. 2015a. "On a Neglected Argument in French Philosophy: Sceptical Humanism in Montaigne, Voltaire and Camus." *Critical Horizons* 16 (1): 1–26.
———. 2015b. *Camus, Philosophe: To Return to Our Beginnings*. Boston: Brill.
Solomon, Robert. 2004. "Pathologies of Pride in Camus's *The Fall*." *Philosophy and Literature* 28 (1): 41–59.
Sprintzen, David A., and Adrian van den Hoven, eds. and trans. 2004. *Sartre and Camus: A Historic Confrontation*. Amherst, NY: Humanity Books.
Stalin, Joseph. 1953. *Anarchism or Socialism?* New York: International Publishers.
Thody, Philip. 1961. *Albert Camus*. New York: Macmillan.
Tocqueville, Alexis de. 1955. *The Old Regime and the French Revolution*. Translated by Stuart Gilbert. New York: Doubleday.

———. 2000. *Democracy in America*. Translated by Harvey C. Mansfield and Delba Winthrop. Chicago: University of Chicago Press.

Trahan, Elizabeth. 1966. "Clamence vs. Dostoevsky." *Comparative Literature* 18 (4): 337–50.

Voegelin, Eric. 1952. *The New Science of Politics: An Introduction*. Chicago: University of Chicago Press.

Walsh, David. 1990. *After Ideology*. San Francisco: Harper.

Wiggins, David. 1998. *Needs, Values, Truth*. 3rd ed. Oxford: Oxford University Press.

Willhoite, Fred H. 1968. *Beyond Nihilism: Albert Camus's Contribution to Political Thought*. Baton Rouge: Louisiana State University Press.

Wollheim, Richard. 1953. "The Political Philosophy of Existentialism." *Cambridge Journal* 7 (1): 3–19.

INDEX

A
Abel, Lionel, 175
absurd
 defined, 9–26
 experience, 11–12
 as paradox, 19–20
 teleological, 10–12, 26–38
 tension, 12–13
 t-epistemic, 17–26
 as unintelligibility, 14–15
accomplishment hypothesis, 86
agency freedom, 77, 82–83, 85, 156, 207n15
Algerian conflict, 149, 168, 169, 205n8, 214n12
Algren, Nelson, 158
All Men Are Mortal, 71, 87, 89
Ancient Regime and the French Revolution, The, 180, 182, 195, 212n4
Angst, 11–12, 33, 35, 39
Anti-Semite and Jew, 191
Arendt, Hannah, 122
aristocracy, 139, 194–200
Aristotle, 28–33, 37, 55–56, 84, 85, 86–87, 176, 198

Aron, Raymond, 122, 209n5, 211n7
Arp, Kristana, 159
Aury, Dominique, 189

B
Bair, Dierdre, 4, 168
Beauvoir, Simone de, 4, 43, 63–90, 156, 158, 159–70
Being and Nothingness, 34, 66, 87, 208n19
Being and Time, 23, 39, 64–65, 72–73
Breton, Andre, 110
Brockmann, Charles, 175

C
Caligula, 10, 45, 85, 204n19
Carroll, David, 10, 202n2
Chenoweth, Erica, 211n8
closed society, 100–101, 130, 131, 135
consequentialism, 127–30
correlationism, 23, 73
crime, celebration of, 108–9, 116, 183, 212n6
Critique of Dialectical Reason, 68–69

221

Cruickshank, John, 15, 175, 202n5 (chap. 1)

D
Dasein, 204n16
Davis, Colin, 176
Darkness at Noon, 175
Democracy in America, 180
Demons, 175, 183, 193
Descartes, René, 29, 44
   argument from doubt, 49–50, 52, 60, 62, 156, 159
Djamila Boupacha, 169
Don Juan, 10, 36, 44, 146, 204n18
Dostoevsky, Fyodor, 87, 107, 114, 208n2, 212n3

E
Engels, Friedrich, 165–66
ethics, minimal theory, 63–64
Ethics of Ambiguity, The, 64, 69–76, 97, 156, 159–69, 206nn12–14
event freedom, 69, 76–78, 82–83, 156, 168, 207
"Existentialism is a Humanism," 29, 67–68

F
Fall, The, 174–200, 212n1
fallibilism
   epistemic, 140, 202n3
   about purpose, 14
   and revolt, 140–41
foundationalism about purpose, 28–30, 103, 124
Fanon, Frantz, 189–90, 192, 214n12
Felman, Shoshana, 176
Flies, The, 192–93
Foley, John, 15

for-itself, 34, 55, 65–66, 78, 191
Frankl, Victor, 204n2, 205n3
free will
   agency freedom, 77
   event freedom, 76–78, 156
   limits to, 83

G
Gabriel, Esther, 208n20
Gay-Crosier, R., 204n18
General Will, 123, 124
Gifford, P., 176
Girard, René, 176
Guérin, Jeanyves, 201n3, 208n1, 211n5

H
harm principle, 115–16, 206n14
Hegel, Georg Wilhelm Friedrich, 125–26
Heidegger, Martin, 12, 23, 54–55, 72–73
   and ethics, 64–65
historicism, 131–32, 135, 140, 203n12
Hitler, Adolf, 116–19, 196
human nature, 10, 37, 55, 58, 59, 60–63, 77–84, 90–92, 95, 97, 98, 137, 138, 150, 154, 157–58, 163, 170, 197, 199
Husserl, Edmund, 18, 203n8

I
internalism, about motivation, 57–59
irony, 42

J
Jeanson, Francis, 66, 82
   critique of *The Rebel*, 152–55

journalism, 4
Just, The, 144, 146–47

K
Kałuża, Maciej, 176, 204n19
Kant, Immanuel, 67, 69, 74, 146, 168
Kierkegaard, Søren, 13, 205n5
King, Adele, 175
Kopelev, Lev, 128–29, 209n2

L
Lenin, V. I., 211n6
Les temps moderne, 152, 187, 189
"Letters to a German Friend," 45–46, 48, 50
Lévi-Valensi, Jacqueline, 208n1
liberalism, 112–16, 137, 143, 174–75, 193–94, 200, 206n14
Lottman, Herbert, 177

M
Mandarins, The, 158–59
Mao Tse-tung, 80, 81
Marletto, Chiara, 203n9
Marx, Karl, 25, 80–81, 103, 122, 123, 126, 131–34
Marxism, 25, 80–81, 91, 97, 110–11, 126–30, 143, 155, 165–67, 178, 183, 187, 194, 201n3, 202n6 (chap. 1), 203n12, 205n7, 207n17, 208n1, 209n3 (chap. 4), 210n4, 211n5
Mediterranean, 37, 103, 198
Meillassoux, Quentin, 23
Mill, John Stuart, 115–16, 118, 137, 142, 206n14
Millikan, Ruth, 203n10
Milosz, Czeslaw, 122, 134

Myth of Sisyphus, The, 9, 10–38, 41, 44, 45, 48, 54, 163, 194, 204n15

N
Nagel, Thomas, 38–43
negation, 52–53
 as absurd, 50
negative-sum strategy, 61, 181–83, 186, 189, 193, 194, 195, 212n6, 213n7
Nicomachean Ethics, 28
Nietzsche, Friedrich, 29, 36–37, 40, 61, 103, 106, 110–11, 115, 195, 196, 202n7, 205n5
nihilism, 52, 202n7
Notebooks for an Ethics, 65, 67, 127
Notes from Underground, 208n2, 212n3

O
open society, 100–101, 130–34, 193
Open Society and Its Enemies, The, 7, 122, 133, 134
Orwell, George, 116–19, 143

P
paradox of freedom, new, 112–15, 193–94
Plague, The, 10, 14, 40, 41, 102, 120, 176
Plato, 112–14, 130, 131, 141, 198
Pölzler, Thomas, 202n1
Popper, Karl, 112, 122–23, 130–34, 209n3 (chap. 4)
 and paradox of tolerance 112–13
pour-soi. *See* for-itself
progress
 impossibility of, 88
 metaphysical revolt as cause, 119–20

purpose, justified and sufficient, defined, 32
"Pyrrhus and Cineas," 69–72, 206n12

R
ressentiment, 61
revolt hypothesis, 96
revolution, defined, 98–99

S
Sade, Marquis de, 104, 106–8
Sagi, Avi, 175
Sartre, Jean-Paul, 12, 15, 29, 30, 34, 35, 55, 63–69, 72, 77–79, 83, 87, 125, 152–59, 175, 176, 180–81, 185, 187–93, 202n5 (chap. 1), 203n13, 208n19, 210n4, 214nn11–12
and ethics, 65–69, 76, 127
Scheler, Max, 61
science, 14–19, 21, 22, 26, 58, 89, 133–34, 208n19
Scott, Nathan, 15
Second Sex, The, 64, 170
Sharpe, Matthew, 176, 202n6 (chap. 1)
Shigalyov, 183
Sicard, Michel, 205n6
Solomon, Robert, 176–77
Stalin, Joseph, 59, 81, 118, 207n17
Stalinism, 81, 97, 118, 155, 167, 181, 185, 206, 211n7
Stephan, Maria J., 211n8
Stranger, The, 10, 15

suicide, 10, 12, 13, 35, 37, 41
argument against, 11, 48–57
philosophical, 18, 25

T
teleofunctions, 21–26
teleological absurd. *See* absurd
t-epistemic absurd. *See* absurd
Thody, Philip, 176
Tocqueville, Alexis de, 180–84, 195, 198, 212n4
Trahan, Elizabeth, 176, 212n2

U
United States, 211n7
unity, 15–16
unveiling of Being, 72, 74

V
value, 10–11, 29, 34, 37–38, 44, 46, 50–51, 55, 63–100, 105–6, 125–26, 137, 147, 157–58, 176, 178, 185
Voegelin, Eric, 122, 209n1

W
Walsh, David, 175, 212n1
Wiggins, David, 207n15
will to power, 105, 110, 114
Will to Power, The, 29, 110, 202n7
Willhoite, Fred H., 15
Wollheim, Richard, 15
Wood, Diane S., 201n3, 211n5
Wretched of the Earth, The, 189, 214n12

CRAIG DELANCEY is professor of philosophy and chair of the department of philosophy at the State University of New York at Oswego. He has published books and papers on metaphysics and logic. His most recent book is *Consciousness as Complex Event: Towards a New Physicalism*.

www.ingramcontent.com/pod-product-compliance
Lightning Source LLC
Chambersburg PA
CBHW050138240426
43673CB00043B/1712